The Peruvian Mining Industry

Series in Political Economy and Economic Development in Latin America

Series Editor
Andrew Zimbalist
Smith College

† *Rural Women and State Policy: Feminist Perspectives on Latin American Agricultural Development,* edited by Carmen Diana Deere and Magdalena León

The International Monetary Fund and Latin America: Economic Stabilization and Class Conflict, Manuel Pastor, Jr.

Cuban Political Economy: Controversies in Cubanology, edited by Andrew Zimbalist

Struggle Against Dependence: Nontraditional Export Growth in Central America and the Caribbean, edited by Eva Paus

The Peruvian Mining Industry: Growth, Stagnation, and Crisis, Elizabeth Dore

† Available in hardcover and paperback.

The Peruvian Mining Industry
Growth, Stagnation, and Crisis

Elizabeth Dore

Westview Press
Boulder & London

Series in Political Economy and Economic Development in Latin America

This Westview softcover edition is printed on acid-free paper and bound in softcovers that carry the highest rating of the National Association of State Textbook Administrators, in consultation with the Association of American Publishers and the Book Manufacturers' Institute.

Copyright © 1988 by Westview Press, Inc.

Published in 1988 in the United States of America by Westview Press, Inc., 5500 Central Avenue, Boulder, Colorado 80301, and in the United Kingdom by Westview Press, Inc., 13 Brunswick Centre, London WC1N 1AF, England

Library of Congress Cataloging-in-Publication Data
Dore, Elizabeth.
   The Peruvian mining industry.
   (Series in political economy and economic development in
Latin America)
   Bibliography: p.
   Includes index.
   1. Mineral industries—Peru. I. Title.
HD9506.P42D67 1988   338.2′0985   85-8802
ISBN 0-8133-7061-2

Printed and bound in the United States of America

The paper used in this publication meets the requirements of the American National Standard for Permanence of Paper for Printed Library Materials Z39.48-1984.

10   9   8   7   6   5   4   3   2   1

FOR JOHNNY

The Miners

photo by Fran Antmann

Workers' Portrait at Mine Entrance

photo by Sebastian Rodríguez

TABLE OF CONTENTS

LIST OF PHOTOGRAPHS AND MAPS

LIST OF TABLES

LIST OF FIGURES

LIST OF APPENDIXES

ACKNOWLEDGMENTS

As a graduate student I decided to study one of the key sectors of the Peruvian economy and was drawn to the mining industry. My inclination to do so was strengthened when Josh DeWind, a friend and fellow student, returned from several years in Peru where he studied the history of the Cerro de Pasco Corporation. He convinced me that scholars of Peru had as many questions as answers about the industry. His enthusiasm was contagious and several months later I was in the central highlands of Peru visiting the mines, the first phase of my research. At that time the framework, explicit and implicit, for my study was dependency theory. Soon, however, through discussions with John Weeks, I became critical of the methods and conclusions of dependency. As I began to question assumptions about the relationship between the mining industry in Peru and the international metals market my research took on a different focus.

Many people in the United States, Great Britain, and Peru have contributed to this study. Throughout the years Margaret Crahan encouraged me and gave me invaluable academic and practical advice. My professors in graduate school, Herbert Klein and Karen Spalding, both guided my study of Latin American history and supported my own research inclinations. Herbert Klein's enthusiasm drew me to study at Columbia. Karen Spalding's research sparked my interest in the history of Peru and encouraged me to broaden my approach to the study of history. I was fortunate that Marcello Carmagnani was a visiting professor at Columbia just prior to my departure for Peru. Our theoretical discussions about how and why to study history inspired me. I am indebted to Anwar Shaikh who made invaluable comments on my dissertation. Equally important to my development as a historian were my colleagues in graduate school. Discussion and reflection with Brooke Larson and Steven Volk helped to form my understanding of Latin America.

I am grateful to many people in Peru who welcomed me into the circle of Peruvianists. Many thanks to Heraclio Bonilla both for his continual encouragement of my interest in Peruvian history and for arranging my affiliation with the Departamento de Economía of the Pontificia Universidad Católica del Perú. My discussions and friendships with many faculty members and students at La Católica contributed not only to my knowledge of Peruvian history, but to my understanding of the Velasco period, when I began the research for this book. Among the many scholars to whom I owe thanks Francisco Verdera, Baltazar Caravedo, José María Caballero, Jenny Romero, Javier Iguíñiz, Roelfien Haak, and Denis Sulmont stand out.

I am grateful to Aníbal Quijano, who shared his insights into Peruvian politics and society and his analysis of contemporary events; and to my good friends, Luis and Ana María Rodríguez Pastor, who were always interested in my research and who generously offered to search out documentation that I needed while preparing the manuscript. Many thanks to Manuel Cisneros Orna and Hernán Peralta Bouroncle of the Instituto para el Desarrollo de la Pesca y la Minería for their recent encouragement and support. When I arrived in Lima to begin my research Geoffrey Bertram was just completing his own study of Peruvian mining. His enthusiasm about my rather hazy plans gave me confidence and his knowledge of the libraries and archives helped to get me started on my research.

Special thanks go to Víctor Villanueva. The many hours that we spent in his study discussing Peruvian history and politics were a major contribution to this study. In Lima, while conducting the research for this book, William Bollinger, John Weeks, and I sought to develop a theoretical framework for understanding Peruvian history in the twentieth century. Our discussions and joint work were critical to my analysis of the Peruvian mining industry. More recently Florencia E. Mallon's work on Peruvian mining influenced my own. In light of her analysis I reinterpreted some of my original conclusions.

The research for this book would not have been possible without financial support from a number of institutions. I am grateful to Columbia University, the Social Science Research Council, and the Middlebury College Faculty Professional Development Fund for generous support. My thanks to Robert Churchill for drawing the maps. The preparation of the manuscript was done with skill and care by Douglas S. Yoon and Joshua T. Gould. Terri Crowl helped me to assemble the bibliography, and Helen Reiff, my copyeditor, made numerous crucial suggestions and changes.

My thanks to Matthew and Rachel Dore-Weeks for their interest in, support of, and patience with my work on this book. Finally, but most importantly, I thank my husband, John Weeks. He both asked piercing questions that forced me to rethink my analyses and conclusions, and was generous in his praise of my work: a rare and wonderful combination.

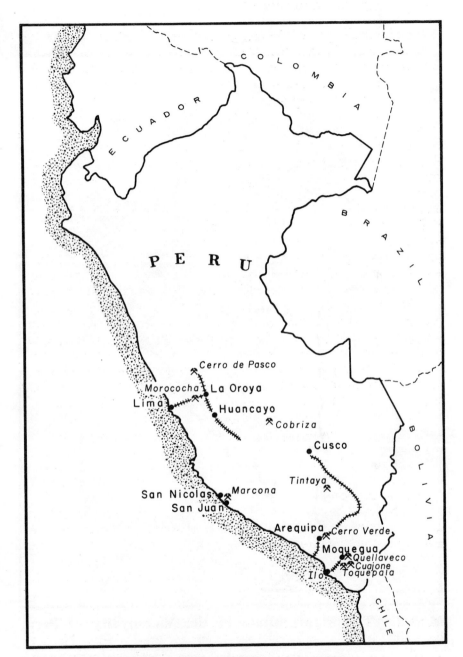

Map 1. The Major Mines in Peru, c. 1970
Cartographic Laboratory, Middlebury College

Map 2. The Major Mines in the Viceroyalty of Peru, c. 1700

Cartographic Laboratory, Middlebury College

INTRODUCTION

Mining in the Context of Underdevelopment

From the colonial period to the present the mining industry has been one of the most important and dynamic sectors of the Peruvian economy. For over four hundred years the expansion and contraction of the industry has had major repercussions throughout Peruvian society.[1] The labor requirements of the mining industry shaped the characteristics and size of the work force first in the Viceroyalty and later in the Republic of Peru. The large population concentrations in the mining centers have influenced patterns of internal trade.

Without question Peru's international relations always reflected the importance of mining. For three hundred years the Spanish crown's avarice for precious metals mined in the Viceroyalty of Peru conditioned the economic and political relationship between the colony and the crown.[2] In the nineteenth century British interest in developing Peru's mineral potential played a major role in the economic and political relations between Britain and Peru. In the twentieth century the mining industry has been dominated by large foreign companies, principally North American firms. This had considerable influence on the nature and policies of the Peruvian state. Finally, Peru's external sector reflects the performance of the industry, since metals are Peru's leading export. Fluctuations in mining production affect the balance of payments, the fiscal deficit, and the foreign debt.

The purpose of this book is to analyze patterns of growth, stagnation, and crisis in the Peruvian mining industry in this century. This involves an analysis of the historical roots of Peruvian mining, an interpretation of the transformation of production relations in the regions surrounding the mines, an examination of the secular and cyclical trends in mining production, and an investigation of why the Peruvian mining industry expanded in some periods and contracted in others.[3] The study concludes with an analysis of nationalizations in the industry in the 1970s, and of their effect on the industry in the 1980s.

There are many studies of the Peruvian mining industry. Most of this literature is presented explicitly in the context of dependency theory. The majority of authors who analyze the development of Peruvian mining in the nineteenth and twentieth centuries devote their attention to how external factors conditioned the expansion of the industry. In particular they analyze the manner in which foreign capital and the world market for metals influenced the sector. These studies examine such issues as the foreign ownership of the industry, the extent to which foreign firms "extracted surplus" from Peru, and the effect of world market prices and the international demand for metals on mining production in Peru. Within this theoretical framework the long-term problems of the industry generally are ascribed to the behavior of foreign firms. And cyclical changes in the level of output are interpreted as responding to fluctuations in world market prices and international demand, as well as to the tariff policies of the advanced industrial countries.[4] A number of studies of the Peruvian mining industry endeavor to demonstrate that the Cerro de Pasco Corporation, along with other large foreign firms, extracted an economic surplus from Peru. Authors of these studies argue that surplus extraction contributed to the underdevelopment rather than to the development of the country.[5]

It is hardly surprising that authors seeking case studies to prove the validity of dependency theory have studied the history of the Cerro de Pasco Corporation.[6] For decades this North American company owned the richest mines in Peru, monopolized the smelting and refining of minerals, held shares in many of the smaller mining companies, controlled every metal processing and metallurgy company in Peru, and simultaneously was the largest landowner in the country.[7] It is no wonder that dependency theory dominated the Peruvian mining literature of the 1960s and 1970s. In the field of development studies dependency theory became "the new orthodoxy,"[8] and despite a decade of criticism and debate it retains its hegemony. The authors who applied dependency theory to explain the dynamics of the Peruvian mining industry made extremely valuable contributions to our understanding of this sector. Without these studies our knowledge of the history of Peruvian mining would be rudimentary indeed.

However, the framework of dependency tended to lead scholars to concentrate on external variables, such as the behavior of foreign firms and the world market, at the expense of a range of factors internal to the Peruvian economy and society that affected the development of mining in Peru. In particular, dependency theorists frequently paid little attention to the social structures that characterized the mining regions, the nature of the labor force, and the production process involved in mining and processing the ores. Their approach reflected a belief that economic growth in underdeveloped countries is determined by relations of dependence with the advanced capitalist countries.

The theoretical assumptions that underlie this study are quite different from those of dependency theory.[9] The conclusions of this study suggest that barriers to economic growth in developing countries arise primarily from the class structure of society and the nature of the production processes, rather than from trade, profit repatriation, or political and economic dependence. In this perspective production relations and forms of property ownership are the primary factors that condition the pace of technical change, the possibilities of increasing productivity, and the expansion of production. This suggests that the nature of the labor force and how it develops, the form of ownership of resources and machinery, the characteristics of the labor process, and the impact of struggles between workers and owners, taken together, condition how production is organized. Therefore, within this framework the characteristics of the social relations of production are the primary determinants of the process of economic development.

This is not to imply that the direct foreign investment in the developing countries that originates in the advanced industrial countries has no impact on the economies of the underdeveloped countries. On the contrary, this export of capital is a major element in shaping the structure of the economies and production relations in underdeveloped countries. However, this study concludes that it is not direct foreign investment as such that limits economic growth.

Several recent studies of Peruvian mining also reject dependency theory, explicitly or implicitly. These analyze the formation of the labor force, the development of the internal market, the structure of production, and the relationship between North American companies, local firms, and the state.[10] While the focuses of these studies differ from that of this book, many of their conclusions are complementary.

In addition to the large literature that deals directly with mining, there are numerous books that describe how the mining industry affected the social structures in the regions surrounding the mines and visa versa.[11]   These studies analyze the processes of social differentiation, migration, and the development of capitalism on *haciendas* and in peasant communities. With its examination of the formation and characteristics of a wage labor force in the mining regions this literature makes important contributions to an understanding of the development of the mining industry.

The long-standing debates over the validity of dependency theory and the causes of underdevelopment were influential in the selection both of the topic of this study and the manner in which particular issues are addressed.[12]   Therefore, these debates are analyzed in Chapter One. To evaluate the extent to which external factors conditioned the expansion of the Peruvian mining industry, this study proceeds to an investigation of the correlation between periods or years of growth, stagnation, and crisis of the mining sector in Peru and fluctuations in world demand and market prices. World market prices and world demand are considered "external" factors because, for the most part, they are determined outside of the Peruvian society and economy and conditions in Peru have little effect on them. Historically mining companies in Peru attempted to expand production in periods of favorable prices or rising demand. However, frequently they were unable to take advantage of favorable market conditions. I argue that the possibility for growth in mining production was determined by the interaction of a complex of technical, social, and financial factors. The particular nature of the mineral reserves, the available means of production, and the characteristics of the labor force and of the labor process all conditioned the level of output in Peru.

In general whether mining companies are able to expand production at any particular moment depends upon some constraints that are largely of a technical nature, such as the quality and location of the ore. Similarly financial factors affect the level of output since increasing the scale of production frequently requires additional investments that may depend upon access to capital markets and the availability of credit. In addition, the ability to increase output may be constrained by the nature of the labor force and by contractual and customary agreements between mineowners and mine workers. For instance, the possibility of increasing productivity may depend upon the extent to which companies can reorganize the production process to facilitate the introduction of new techniques. Likewise, expanding production may be limited by the supply of labor or by industrial disputes. Finally, the level of wages, along with other determinants of the costs of production, conditions profitability and may restrain the expansion of mining.

This study evaluates the degree to which the performance of the Peruvian mining industry was affected by "external factors," or conditions of supply and demand in the world metals market. This is accomplished by comparing the trend of output in the Peruvian industry with the trends of world prices and of the demand for metals. These comparisons, using relatively simple statistical techniques, indicate that there is no statistically significant relationship between the pattern of change in Peruvian mining and the dynamic of the world metals market.

Following the analysis of the impact of external factors on the Peruvian mining industry, I present an assessment of the nature of some internal constraints which may have prevented mining companies in Peru from responding to price incentives and increased demand for their products. The theoretical framework for this study posits that barriers to economic growth are rooted in the nature of the social relations of production and in the class structure of societies. This hypothesis implies that an analysis of the formation of classes in the mining sector, in the regions surrounding the mines and in the society at large will contribute to an understanding of the dynamics of the Peruvian mining industry. One aspect of these class relations—the nature and characteristics of the labor force in the mines and processing plants—is the focus of this study. This book presents an analysis of a set of inter-related factors that reflect the development of the working class in the mining industry. These are the size and composition of the labor force, the level of wages, worker militancy, and changes in productivity. The objective of the study is to assess the manner and extent to which these factors affected the development of mining in Peru. These variables alone provide only limited insights into the nature of the labor force in the mines and the complexities of how relations of production conditioned economic growth in the mining industry. This analysis becomes meaningful when examined in the context of a broader understanding of the process of social transformation in the mining regions as well as in Peruvian society as a whole.

The factors that are examined in depth were selected because they are useful indicators of the nature of the labor force in the mining industry. In particular, they are suggestive of the manner in which characteristics of the work force may constrain the expansion of production. One of the factors analyzed in detail in this study is productivity, or the average volume of output per worker for each working day.[13] Productivity is a critical indicator of the ability to expand the level of production because increasing productivity necessitates the reorganization of the labor process and the introduction of technical changes. This process is fundamental to the long term expansion and competitiveness of the mining industry, for it is technical change that enables companies to increase output and lower costs of production, in particular labor costs, and thereby increase their profit margin.[14]

A second factor examined in detail is the level of wages in the industry. The payment of wages involves two different processes. In the exchange between capital and labor, capitalists purchase labor power, and as such the wage represents labor costs to the companies. The real cost of employing workers, measured by the ratio of the money wage to the price of the products that workers produce (metals in this case), will be called "the wage cost to capital." For workers, wages are the medium whereby they obtain the products that are necessary for survival and wages reflect the standard of living of the working class. However, during most of the period covered in this study the products that represent the standard of living of miners are acquired through non-wage as well as wage relationships. Therefore, the ratio of money wages to the prices of commodities that workers consume will be called "price-deflated wages" instead of the more common "real wages." There is no necessity for movements in the wage cost to capital to parallel changes in the standard of living of the working class. Indeed, the dominant tendency as capitalism develops is for the wage cost to capital to decline given the standard of living.[15] This study examines how each of these aspects of the wage affected the growth of the mining industry. Finally this study examines the size and composition of the labor force in the mining sector. This analysis contributes to an understanding of the availability of labor in different periods, as well as of the changing divisions within the work force between manual and skilled workers.

In this book productivity, wages, and the size and composition of the labor force are considered "internal" factors. They are "internal" in the sense that they reflect conditions that are generated within the Peruvian economy and society in general, and the social and technical changes within the mining sector in particular. This is not to suggest that the determinants of internal and external factors are entirely separate, nor that conditions that influence one set of factors have no effect on the other. Certainly this is not the case. The distinction is made for heuristic purposes to facilitate an analysis of the determinants of economic growth.

A brief comment on the data base is necessary. The objective of this book is to understand how and why the Peruvian mining industry changed over a long period—the causes of growth, stagnation, and crisis. Therefore, first it was necessary to establish the patterns of secular and cyclical change. This involved constructing consistent time series data for the volume and value of production in the Peruvian mining industry throughout the twentieth century, since this had not been done previously. Then, in order to analyze the relationship between the Peruvian industry and the world metals market, it was necessary to construct comparable time series data for world market prices and world-wide production levels. Similarly, to analyze changes in productivity and in the size and composition of the labor force over a period of seventy years (1905-1975), I constructed consistent time series that are comparable to the production data. Because of the nature of the available data it was not possible to construct a consistent time series for wages before 1945. Therefore, although wages are considered from the 1920s, the detailed analysis of wages covers the thirty years from 1945 to 1975. Because one of the contributions of this book is its presentation and analysis of time series data covering more than seventy-five years, in Appendix A I discuss the sources for the data, the construction of the time series, and the statistical methods I use.

However, statistical data alone reveal little about social relations in the mining industry or the characteristics of the labor force. To interpret statistical data correctly they must be analyzed within a broader historical background. In this study analyses of the process of transformation of the class structure within the mining regions, in Peruvian society at large, and of technical change in the mining industry facilitate an interpretation of the statistical information. The analysis of the broader historical framework is drawn largely from a number of excellent secondary sources.[16]

The theoretical argument of the book is presented in the context of a chronological analysis of the development of the Peruvian mining industry. Chapter One is an analysis of the limitations of dependency theory and a presentation of the theoretical assumptions which underlie this study. The comparison of the mining sector in Peru with world demand and prices is presented in Chapter Two. Using a variety of relatively simple statistical techniques I analyze whether the Peruvian mining industry is a reflection of the world industry, and to what extent the performance of the Peruvian industry is determined by the dynamic of the world metals market. This analysis clearly indicates that the pattern of growth in the Peruvian mining industry is largely unrelated to trends in world market prices and international demand.

Chapter Three is an analysis of the transformation of highland society and the historical roots of industrial mining from the colonial period through the nineteenth century. The period from the beginning of the twentieth century through the depression of the 1930s is analyzed in Chapter Four. These years were characterized by the consolidation of foreign control of the industry and the predominance of a labor system based on debt-peonage. Constraints on raising labor productivity emerged in the nineteen-forties and underlined the need for a fundamental reorganization of the industry. The restructuring of capital from undergound to open-pit mining in the nineteen-fifties and sixties and changes in the labor process are the themes of Chapter Five. These transformations facilitated the expansion of the mining sector which was based on rising productivity. However, the proletarianization of the workers in the industry was accompanied by rising wages which affected profitability. By the nineteen-seventies the re-emergence of barriers to increasing productivity combined with rising wages triggered a crisis in the industry.

Chapter Six focuses on the crisis of the mining industry in the 1970s and the nationalization of two large North American firms. In order to understand the essence of the nationalizations I analyze the nature of the Peruvian state during the government of President Juan Velasco Alvarado (1968-1975), a period known as the "Peruvian Revolution." The chapter concludes with an analysis of the industry in the 1980s and of the effects of the indebtedness that was a legacy of President Velasco's ambitious development strategy for the mining sector.

CHAPTER ONE

The Barriers to Capitalist Expansion in Underdeveloped Countries

Within the unorthodox development literature there are two broad approaches to understanding the causes of underdevelopment.[1] One school of thought maintains that inequality in levels of development among countries is caused primarily by inequities in international exchange. This framework has become known as dependency theory. While it may appear that authors within this school have quite different positions, they all subscribe to one fundamental tenet: that underdevelopment is caused by the extraction of a surplus product from backward countries.[2] Differences within the dependency literature focus on the mechanism of surplus extraction. Many writers who use the framework of dependency theory argue that underdeveloped countries lose access to their "surplus" through unequal terms of trade.[3] Other theorists of dependency specify that the inequality of the exchange relationship is caused by wage differentials between high and low income countries. Another current within the dependency literature focuses on profit remittances as the form of surplus extraction. Notwithstanding the variety of explanations of how surplus is extracted from underdeveloped countries, all dependency theorists maintain that underdevelopment is caused by international exchange.

The second approach to analyzing underdevelopment locates the barriers to economic development in the particular nature of traditional social relations of production and in the class structures that characterize underdeveloped countries.[4] Authors who hold this position analyze the process of the historical transformation of a country in order to understand how precapitalist social relations of production restrain economic growth. Scholars in this tradition examine the forms of access to land, labor, and tools. This allows them to analyze how the nature of these particular structures constrain the reorganization of the labor process and the introduction of technical improvements, which condition economic development. This second theoretical position is concerned with understanding why and how class relations change; specifically how capitalist relations of production develop. Integral to this framework is an analysis of the precise forms of the export of capital from the advanced capitalist countries to the backward countries, and of how the export of capital affects the transformation of class relations in underdeveloped countries.[5]

This chapter presents a critique of dependency theory. It focuses on those authors who have made important contributions to the development of the theory. The chapter concludes with a theoretical discussion of the barriers to economic development that emerge from the nature of precapitalist social relations of production. Particular attention is given to those obstacles to growth that have been critical to the development of the Peruvian mining industry: the nature of the labor force, the role of wages, and productivity.

Surplus Extraction as the Cause of Underdevelopment

By far the most prevalent explanation of the causes of inequality in the level of development among countries is that surplus is extracted from backward countries and is appropriated and subsequently used in the advanced countries.[6] To analyze this view, emphasis here will be on the work of Paul Baran and Andre Gunder Frank, because of their clarity of exposition and consistent use of this explanatory thesis. It may be argued that these writers are out-of-date. I disagree. To this day the arguments of Baran and Frank are very influential, and their views are accepted by many scholars and policymakers concerned with understanding the causes of underdevelopment.

In the work of Baran and Frank the appropriation of the surplus product has a twofold consequence. The backward country is impoverished because it loses access to "its" surplus, and the advanced country is enriched by appropriating this surplus product.[7] Inherent in this position is the argument that the surplus product extracted from the backward countries is crucial to the expansion of capital, and therefore to the maintenance of the capitalist system in the advanced countries. Baran argues that the surplus generated in underdeveloped countries is appropriated by the capitalist classes of the advanced countries, and is a major source of their profits.[8]

All dependency writers agree with Baran that this extraction-appropriation process is fundamental to the survival of capitalism in the advanced countries. However, some scholars who share this general perspective offer a different explanation of how the surplus extracted from developing countries is used in the advanced countries. For instance, Ruy Mauro Marini argues that the extracted surplus is appropriated by the working class in the imperialist countries. As such, the appropriation of surplus generated in underdeveloped countries serves to greatly weaken, if not eliminate, the class struggle in the advanced countries.[9]

Although within the dependency literature there is no consensus on which classes in the advanced capitalist countries are the direct beneficiaries of the surplus product that is extracted from underdeveloped countries, on a more fundamental issue there is total accord. Dependency theorists all agree that growth in the advanced industrial countries in large part is generated by the surplus that is extracted from the Third World, rather than by the exploitation of the working classes in the advanced countries.

According to the arguments of Frank and Baran exploitation is a relationship between countries, not between classes. This analysis suggests that under capitalism, exploitation occurs in the process of exchange, not in the process of production. Given this formulation, it follows consistently that to understand the causes of underdevelopment there is no need to analyze relations in production, nor the nature of the production process. Within this argument production itself becomes irrelevant to the analysis of underdevelopment, as all of the critical relations are located in exchange. Therefore, faithful to the logic of their position, Baran and Frank devote little attention to the production process in their explanation of the barriers to economic growth.

The next step in the logical progression of the surplus extraction thesis is that the essence of capitalism is trade. If exchange relations are primary, and exploitation occurs in exchange, then trade becomes the defining characteristic of capitalism. The extension of this argument is that, where there is exchange there is capitalism and it is through trade that capitalism expands. While this view is implicit in the writings of Baran, it has become a theoretical tenet of the arguments of many of his leading followers such as Frank, Paul Sweezy, and Immanuel Wallerstein.[10]

Notwithstanding its popularity, the dependency argument is fundamentally flawed. Exploitation is a relationship between classes, not between countries. Under capitalism exploitation occurs in the process of production, not in exchange. Above all, the essence of capitalism is the particular form in which labor power and the means of production are united in the production process. The essence of capitalism is not the exchange of products.

Equating capitalism with exchange demonstrates a misunderstanding of the nature of capitalism, for capitalism is not merely exchange. Exchange itself is compatible with many different modes of production.[11]   Capitalism is unique in that the reproduction of society occurs through exchange, and thus requires the general circulation of products as commodities. In capitalism the direct producers have been separated from the means of production. Therefore, they are compelled to exchange their capacity to work, their labor power, in order to purchase the products they need for survival. The same process that "frees" the direct producers from the land, tools, and animals, also sets free these same means of production to be exchanged against capital. Therefore, the essence of capitalism is not the existence of exchange, but the fact that exchange has become so widespread that not only are labor power and the means of production exchanged, but they must be exchanged before they can be united in the production process.

Under capitalism, exploitation is the appropriation by the capitalist class of the surplus labor time of the working class. In capitalist relations exploitation occurs in the process of production, and is concealed by the wage. While it appears that workers are paid for the total number of hours they work, they are not. In essence the wage reflects the value of labor power, or the cost of the commodities that workers normally consume. However, in capitalist economies only a portion of the working day under capitalism must be devoted to the production of the value of these commodities, the means of subsistence. For the remainder of the working day the working class labors for free for the capitalist class. This unpaid labor is the source of profits under capitalism.

The formulation of Baran and Frank, focusing as it does on the movement of a surplus product among countries and on exchange relations, overlooks the specific nature of both capitalist and precapitalist modes of production. Their method does not call for an analysis of the circuit of capital; of the particular dynamics of how a surplus product is produced and appropriated. Moreover, it does not address the fundamental issue of how social relations of production affect the development of the forces of production, and condition economic growth.[12] This leads Baran, Frank, and others who adopt this method, to lose sight of the historical specificity of the capitalist mode of production.

If the extraction of a surplus product from one country and its appropriation by another country is the cause of underdevelopment, if capitalism is trade, and if the particular characteristics of the social relations of production are ignored, then capitalism itself becomes irrelevant to the analysis. Capitalism becomes an unnecessary fifth wheel in a discussion of only polemical significance. If the analysis of the causes of underdevelopment fails to consider the nature of the social relations of production and its influence upon the development of the forces of production, we are left with little explanation of economic stagnation other than the plunder of one geographical region by another. In other words, the theory of underdevelopment constructed by Baran and Frank is not unique to the capitalist epoch. The domination and looting of one area for the enrichment of a class of expropriators in another geographical area has been a characteristic of virtually all historical periods.

The logical and inevitable conclusion from Baran's and Frank's arguments is that the nature of class relations and the particular dynamics of capitalism have little to do with underdevelopment in the world today. If their theory is correct, the causes of differences in economic growth among countries have varied little throughout history. However, this is not the case. The uneven development of the productive forces among countries is primarily caused by fundamental differences in the nature of social relations of production. Each unique form of social relations embodies particular barriers to the expansion of production. While it is advisable to exercise caution when generalizing about precapitalist social relations, these forms tend to be characterized by a relative inflexibility in the production process. Under precapitalist social relations laborers gain access to the means of production through a great variety of relationships which are not primarily economic; but overtly social, political, and religious. These relations tend to restrain the reorganization of the production process, the introduction of technical change, and the expansion of production.

Capitalism is progressive in that it tends to break down these particular constraints. Under capitalism social relations appear to be purely economic in character. Money becomes a claim on wealth in general, and laborers and the means of production are united only through the advance of capital. In consequence, capitalists have considerable flexibility and can reorganize the production process in order to increase productivity and profits. Most important, capitalists are compelled to reorganize the production process, increase productivity, and raise profits; or they are eliminated in the competitive struggle among capitals. It is this process of competition that ensures the expansion of production under capitalism. An understanding of these fundamental differences between capitalist and precapitalist societies, and an analysis of how particular social relations of production condition economic growth, is the starting point of an analysis of the causes of the development and the underdevelopment of specific countries.

However, Baran, Frank, and dependency theorists in general, do not take into consideration the particular nature of modes of production, be they precapitalist or capitalist, in analyzing the causes of economic development. In their theories the characteristics of the social relations of production are of scant significance, and development of the forces of production is determined by exchange relations; in particular by exchange among countries.

Surplus Extraction via Monopoly Capital

Although the theory of underdevelopment of Baran and Frank rests upon the extraction of surplus products from backward countries and appropriation by the developed countries, they devote little attention to how this transfer is effected. Their writings do not incorporate a conceptualization or an investigation of the mechanisms of surplus extraction. The reader is left to infer what these processes might be. Nevertheless, the theory of monopoly capital, closely akin to dependency theory, provides an explicit formulation of the mechanisms of surplus extraction through profit remittances and monopoly.[13] The theory of monopoly capital is predicated on the assumption that companies based in advanced capitalist countries that invest in backward countries subsequently repatriate a large part of their profits. Therefore, the theory postulates that profit repatriation becomes a barrier to the accumulation of capital in underdeveloped countries and results in economic stagnation.

There is a logical inconsistency in this argument as it is generally presented.[14] Most, if not all, dependency theorists maintain that the rate of profit is higher in underdeveloped countries as a result of some form of super-exploitation. Furthermore, they argue that it is this higher rate of profit that attracts investments from developed countries. If this is true, it would be reasonable to expect a high rate of reinvestment in backward countries as companies take advantage of higher profit rates; not a net outflow of capital. In order to argue that there is a continual extraction of surplus via profit remittances, the theory must incorporate an explanation of why companies do not continue to pursue high profit rates, and instead repatriate their earnings. The concept of monopoly capital endeavors to provide this theoretical justification.

The theory of monopoly capital is based on the hypothesis that the essential laws of motion of capitalism are fundamentally altered with monopoly capital. Most important competition is eliminated. Therefore, there is no necessity for technical change nor drive to increase productivity. The theory of monopoly capital posits the negation of the entire process that involves the continual development of the productive forces under capitalism.[15] This theory is implicit in the argument that surplus extraction is the cause of underdevelopment and, as such, is an essential element in the logic of dependency. Within the framework of dependency theory foreign companies investing in underdeveloped countries are monopolistic. They enter backward countries, destroy local competitors, and then protect their markets. By eliminating competition these firms are able to secure their markets without the necessity of investing either in technical improvements or in expanding production. Therefore, as there is no pressure for accumulation and further development of these hapless branches of production is stifled. Furthermore, since their monopoly position removes the compulsion to invest, these foreign companies remit their profits—extract the surplus.[16]

Finally, according to the theory of monopoly capital cum dependency, these foreign firms are able to reap large profits through monopoly pricing. In the logical extension of this argument, the rate of profit and the level of total profits is without limit since price is indeterminate. Prices are no longer directly related to the value of the product, but are set arbitrarily by all-powerful monopolies. By virtue of their monopoly power, these firms prevent other companies from investing in this particular branch of production in the underdeveloped country, and from taking advantage of the high profit rates. In dependency theory it is this process that blocks the development of the productive forces and results in "dependent" or "distorted" capitalism.

This, however, is an erroneous view of monopoly. For it equates competition exclusively with the number of firms in a single product market. Moreover, it perceives competition under capitalism as restricted to the struggle over market shares. In reality this is but one aspect of capitalist competition. Capitalism is characterized by many forms of competition: between capital and labor over the conditions of exploitation, among capitalists over labor power, and by competition among capitalists throughout the economy to take advantage of high rates of profit in different branches of industry. This last form of competition implies the movement of capital from one productive sector to another. This process tends to equalize the rate of profit throughout an economy and promotes generalized economic growth.

Competition is inherent in capitalism. Rather than being eliminated, competition intensifies as capitalism develops. In the early stage of capitalism, the period of manufacture, the primitive development of credit institutions is a barrier to the movement of capital among productive sectors. In this stage competition primarily is confined within separate branches of production. However, as capitalism develops these obstacles to the movement of capital are overcome. In advanced capitalism competition is no longer constrained within separate industries. In the contemporary era while capitalism continues to be characterized by the competition of companies within one branch of industry to conquer the market, the movement of capitals from one branch of industry to another is foremost in the competitive struggle among firms. Driven by the need to increase profits, capitals invade sectors of the economy characterized by higher rates of profit.[17]

Without the conceptual foundations of the theory of monopoly capital, the mechanism of perpetual profit remittances as the form of surplus extraction and as the cause of underdevelopment becomes highly problematical. Competition in all stages of capitalism necessitates reinvestment, technical change, and the expansion of production. Monopoly has contributed to underdevelopment. It is this reality that advocates of the theory of monopoly capital observe and attempt to explain. However, the phenomena they have observed are primarily monopolies associated with merchant capital. These extensions of feudal monopolies retarded economic growth in an earlier period.

By the early 1970s mounting criticism of dependency theory, in particular of the writings of Baran and Frank, led authors committed to the fundamental tenets of the theory to search for more rigorous analyses of the mechanisms of surplus extraction. Because dependency theory is conceptualized within the Marxist tradition, advocates of the theory particularly responded to the critique of dependency from a Marxist perspective. As a consequence, there appeared an influential literature whose explicit object is to locate surplus extraction within a Marxist framework. Some of the leading theorists in this tradition are discussed below.

Surplus Extraction Submerged in Underconsumptionism

The thesis that the development of capitalism is limited by the size of the capitalist market is called underconsumptionism. It takes this name because the essential argument is that the expansion of capitalism is blocked because total consumption in a capitalist economy is below the level of total production. This results in the impossibility of selling all of the commodities produced; or, more precisely, in the inability of realizing all of the value produced and embodied in the commodities. Underconsumptionism as a current in Marxist theory is as old as the theory itself. While there are such venerable proponents of underconsumptionism as Luxemburg,[18] there are even more compelling criticisms by Lenin[19] and Bukharin.[20]

Although it may appear that there is little similarity between the works of Baran and Frank, and the writings of Marini, in fact there is an underlying unity. For Marini, underconsumptionism provides the vehicle for "surplus extraction": the extraction of surplus value from the backward country which is realized, or valorized, in the advanced capitalist country. Nevertheless, Marini takes an important step forward compared to Baran and Frank by pointing out that the analysis of capitalism must be based in the sphere of production.[21] However, he argues, this applies to capitalism "at the center," and since "peripheral" or "dependent" capitalism is conditioned primarily by circulation, Marini reasons that phenomena in exchange become primary in an analysis of "dependent capitalism."

The problem with this formulation of the issue is that it assumes *a priori* what needs to be proven analytically. If it is the case that the sphere of circulation is primary in Third World countries, then it would be correct to center the analysis of underdevelopment in exchange and distribution. But the existence of a world market and foreign capital that plays an important role in the economies of underdeveloped countries does not imply that the analysis of the causes of backwardness should deal principally with conditions of exchange.   It simply establishes that the analysis of underdevelopment must at some point incorporate world market relations and the export of capital. It does not signify that these are best analyzed by proceeding from exchange rather than from the process of production.

After developing his analytical framework, Marini contrasts the function of distribution in developed and underdeveloped countries, treating distribution in the limited sense of the distribution between wages and profits.[22] He argues that in underdeveloped capitalist countries the role of the working class is only to produce, and the product of its labor is exported. Since the product is exported, there is no need for this working class to serve as consumers (to realize surplus value) and its wages can be forced down without limit. The value of commodities exported from "dependent" capitalist countries is realized in Marini's schema by the consumption of the working class in developed capitalist countries. This requires wages in the advanced capitalist countries to be high; so high as to realize the surplus value produced in the backward countries, as well as the surplus value produced in the advanced countries.

Marini points out that his analysis implies that the antagonism between labor and capital in developed countries is overcome since both classes share a common interest in keeping wages high.[23] In this schema, for capitalists in the advanced countries high wages are the vehicle through which surplus value produced in the Third World is realized. For workers in these same countries, the material and value form of their high living standard is produced by the working classes of the Third World. Thus, according to Marini's analysis, workers are super-exploited in the dependent country, and there is no mechanism for their wages to rise since they are not needed for the realization of value. Since wages do not rise, the internal market does not expand, and accumulation in the dependent country (*acumulación dependentista*) is retarded or "deformed."

Here we are presented with a wage theory in which wages in both underdeveloped and developed capitalist countries are determined independently of production, of the productivity of labor, and of the value of labor power. In Marini's theory wages are determined by the need to realize value produced at "home" and "abroad." Additionally, according to Marini, wage levels are equated to living standards. While one might argue that this is a valid wage theory, one should not ascribe it to Marx, and call for its acceptance on that authority. Marini's wage theory negates the Marxian postulate that the use value and the exchange value of the wage are two distinct concepts. The use value of the wage is the basket of goods that workers can purchase; while the exchange value of the wage reflects the value of labor power, or the time required to produce the commodities that workers habitually consume.

Marini's theory of surplus extraction is based on his theory of wages. In Marini's formulation the appropriation of surplus value occurs through the consumption by workers and capitalists in the advanced countries of consumer commodities produced in the dependent economies. For Marini, development is implicitly defined in terms of living standards rather than in terms of the development of the productive forces. Furthermore, in this theory the living standards of the working classes in both developed and underdeveloped countries are determined independently of the development of the productive forces.

Actually Marini has gone beyond Baran in his emphasis on surplus extraction. Baran, to an extent, sees the appropriated surplus being used productively, as a source of accumulation in the advanced capitalist countries. Marini treats the appropriated surplus purely as a consumption fund for the advanced capitalist society as a whole. Without the dependent economies the standard of living in the developed capitalist economies would fall drastically and the rate of profit would collapse. According to this theory the commodities exported from the periphery are both the source of high consumption (in their material form) and embody the surplus value of the capitalist class in the advanced country (in their value form).

There are serious problems with this formulation of the underconsumptionist thesis, not the least of which is, how is it possible for workers in the advanced capitalist countries to be paid sufficiently to realize surplus value, yet not eliminate profit? Profit is the form that unpaid labor time assumes under capitalism. Therefore, if workers consume the material form of surplus value, then previously they must have been paid its value equivalent. By introducing two countries into the analysis, and embedding surplus extraction in underconsumptionism, this problem is only obfuscated, not resolved. Marini's formulation of the underconsumptionist argument implies the elimination of profits from production in the advanced capitalist countries.

While it is beyond the scope of this book to present a detailed critique of underconsumptionism, there are convincing arguments that there is no inherent barrier to the realization of surplus value under capitalism.[24] Briefly, most of the value produced in a capitalist economy is embodied not in the commodities that workers, or even capitalists, consume; but in machinery, raw materials, and other inputs that are productively consumed in the production process. Therefore, the realization of value primarily depends upon the advance of capital to purchase the means of production, not upon the personal consumption of either workers or capitalists.[25]

Surplus Extraction in the Form of Unequal Exchange

Perhaps the most influential forms assumed by the surplus extraction thesis are the theories of Aghiri Emmanuel and Samir Amin. Emmanuel, in his book *Unequal Exchange*, endeavors to determine the conditions establishing the exchange ratios of commodities in international trade.[26] His hypothesis is that capitalists in all countries have available to them the same technical production possibilities, regardless of the level of development of the productive forces in each country. In other words, Emmanuel's premise is that in every country, in corresponding branches of industry, production is carried out with the same techniques. In addition he assumes that the costs of the means of production are the same throughout the world, and that the productivity of labor does not vary as much as do wage levels between developed and underdeveloped countries. Given these assumptions and the premise that capital is completely mobile internationally, it follows that production costs will be lower in countries where the wage is lower; and the rate of profit will be higher where wages are lower. Therefore, Emmanuel deduces that unequal exchange occurs in the movement of capital between countries in search of a higher rate of profit. His argument is that as a result of competitive struggles commodity prices fall relatively in low wage countries as capital enters to take advantage of higher profit rates; and commodity prices rise relatively in high wage countries as capital flees in pursuit of more attractive profit rates elsewhere.

Emmanuel concludes that as a consequence of the equalization of the rate of profit achieved through these price movements, international exchange occurs at rates which do not correspond to the labor time embodied in commodities. He maintains that the ratio of prices in the advanced countries to prices in the backward countries is greater than the ratio of the labor time embodied in commodities produced in the advanced countries in relation to the labor time embodied in the commodities produced in the backward countries. Therefore, Emmanuel argues, advanced countries appropriate more labor time in exchange than they generate in production. In a parallel fashion, through exchange backward countries lose labor time that they generate in production. As a result of this process a surplus is transferred from backward to advanced countries, reducing the rate of growth in underdeveloped countries while increasing accumulation in developed countries.

There are many grounds for criticizing Emmanuel's theory of unequal exchange.[27] In the first place, the assumptions upon which the theory is based cannot be presumed. If we assume that all capitalists in all countries have available to them the same technical production possibilities, then in essence we are assuming away the uneven development of the productive forces—the very process that we are attempting to explain.

Like Marini's, Emmanuel's entire argument derives from his theory of wages. Also like Marini, it implicitly defines development in terms of living standards rather than in terms of the development of the productive forces. For both Emmanuel and Marini wage levels are equated to the standard of living on the international level and a lower standard of living translates directly into a lower wage. This view casts aside the important analytical distinctions within Marxist theory among the standard of living, the value of labor power, and the wage.

The standard of living of the working class is determined by the quantity and quality of the products that workers consume. From the point of view of the working class the use value of the wage sets the standard of living. The value of labor power is the abstract socially necessary labor time required to produce the products that workers consume—the products that comprise the standard of living. The value of labor power is determined by productivity in the economy as a whole. The price of labor power, or the cost of labor power to capital, tends to reflect its value. As productivity rises and commodities are produced more efficiently (their production requiring less labor time), then the value of labor power declines for a given standard of living. From the perspective of capital, the wage is the price of labor power. As such the wage tends to reflect the exchange value of the commodities that workers consume. As productivity rises and the value of the commodities that workers consume declines, the value of labor power falls, and the wage cost to capital tends to decline as well.[28]

With the development of capitalism there is an inherent tendency for increases in productivity to lead to a fall in the value of labor power. As a result of this process the wage, which reflects a given mass of use values (a given standard of living), correspondingly falls.[29] Therefore, although it is evident that the working classes in underdeveloped countries have a considerably lower standard of living than the working classes in developed countries, it is not possible to establish theoretically that this lower standard of living automatically translates into lower labor costs to capital, relative to unpaid labor or profits.

The forces of production are not as highly developed in the backward countries as in the advanced countries. As a consequence, in the Third World productivity in the production of the commodities that workers habitually consume is generally lower than in the developed capitalist countries. Therefore, it is likely that more labor time that is recognized as productive may be devoted to producing the commodities that workers consume in the backward countries than in the advanced countries. This provides the possibility that in underdeveloped countries the relative wage cost to capital (relative to profits) may be higher than in more developed countries. This theoretical conceptualization does not negate the reality that the standard of living of the working classes in underdeveloped countries is considerably below that of workers in the developed countries. Under capitalism, profit is the form that unpaid labor time takes; that is, profits derive from that portion of the working day for which workers are not paid. Therefore, in those countries where the working class as a whole must devote more labor time to producing its subsistence needs, profits may be lower than in countries where higher productivity enables the working class to produce in less time the commodities it consumes.

By maintaining theoretical rigor in conceptualizing the relationship between the standard of living and the wage it becomes clear that we cannot assume that the rate of profit is higher in countries where the standard of living is low, relative to those countries where the working class enjoys a higher standard of living. Therefore, it is also erroneous to assume a movement of capital between high and low wage countries which results in the equalization of the rate of profit. As a consequence, Emmanuel's theory of the unequal exchange of labor time between underdeveloped and developed countries becomes untenable.

If, however, we accept Emmanuel's theory on its own terms, the analysis still proves rather unsatisfactory. Emmanuel's theory of unequal exchange suggests that the main tendency is for foreign investment to flow to backward, rather than to advanced, countries. Yet empirical evidence shows that this has not been the case.[30] Even if we put reality aside, by stressing the equalization of the rate of profit Emmanuel's theory predicts that the worst that can happen is that the relative surplus will be the same in advanced and backward countries. In other words, at the worst, the surplus remaining in backward countries is sufficient to match the rate of accumulation in advanced countries. Moreover, implicit in the theory is the argument that as long as profit rates are not equal, only tending to equalize, production in backward countries will grow faster than in the advanced countries as capital moves from one country to another to take advantage of higher profit rates. So, according to the theory of unequal exchange, this movement of capital generates more rapid accumulation in the underdeveloped than in the developed countries. A theory whose mechanism predicts a faster rate of accumulation in backward countries than in advanced countries is not a powerful analytical tool for explaining underdevelopment.

The writings of Samir Amin are in the theoretical current of surplus extraction through unequal international exchange. Amin assumes the task of proving the validity of Emmanuel's wage theory in order to resuscitate the thesis of unequal exchange. Amin seeks to demonstrate that the values of commodities workers consume are the same throughout the world. He bases his argument on the existence of common world prices, as demonstrated in world market prices for commodities—wheat for example. From this postulation of equivalent prices, Amin deduces that "...the labor-hour in all countries creates the same value."[31] Therefore, he perceives that the exchange value and hence the value of the commodities that workers consume is also the same world-wide. From this formulation Amin concludes that differences in the standard of living among countries do correspond directly to differences in the value of labor power, and by extension to differences in the rate of profit.[32] For Amin it is exchange that determines the values of commodities. Ergo, value becomes indistinguishable from exchange value and from price.[33] The problem with this proposition is that it amalgamates at least two distinct theoretical concepts: value and exchange value, or value and price. It is true that when two products are sold at the same price in the same country equal quantities of value are realized in exchange. However, this does not imply that equal amounts of abstract labor time (value) are produced and embodied in the two products, especially when they are produced in different countries in radically different production processes.

Abstract labor time is created by capitalist production, not by commodity exchange.[34] It is the competition among capitals in the sphere of production that transforms concrete labor (heterogeneous labor-in-production) into abstract socially necessary labor (homogeneous labor-in-exchange), and which governs the quantitative relationship between concrete and abstract labor. The value of a commodity is not determined by exchange, or by its price, as Amin argues; but by the interaction among capitals which brings about a norm in the application of labor in the production process. Therefore, it is the competitive struggle in the sphere of production that both creates value (abstract socially necessary labor time) and determines its quantity.

The value of the same commodity produced in different countries varies, reflecting differences in the competitive struggles within countries and in the development of the forces of production among countries. Amin's defense of Emmanuel's wage theory is flawed because he deduces value from price, thereby assuming that abstract labor time is determined in the process of exchange on the international market, rather than in the process of commodity production. Furthermore, in keeping with the tradition of dependency, Amin devotes little attention to the labor process: the specific manner in which products are produced. Amin looks at the form of the final product, again the example of wheat. He does not analyze the social relations in which it was produced. Finally, since value is a concept unique to capitalist production, and a product of the competition among capitals, a theory that hinges upon the equivalence of values must assume capitalist production world-wide. In other words, Amin's analysis implies that in every country all the products that workers consume are produced in capitalist relations of production. However, even a cursory analysis of the dynamics of the economies of underdeveloped countries indicates that this assumption is invalid. The literature on underdeveloped countries clearly demonstrates that foodstuffs for local consumption are frequently produced outside of capitalist relations of production: by peasants, debt-peons, share-croppers, or tenant farmers.[35]

A theory of the limits to capitalist development in backward countries needs to analyze the endurance of traditional social relations; in particular their persistence in the production of foodstuffs for the domestic market. Rather than negating a phenomenon that characterizes many, if not all, underdeveloped countries, a theory of underdevelopment should incorporate it as a significant element in the explanation of the causes of backwardness.

While the critique until this point has dealt with the fallacies of Amin's theoretical assumptions, there are problems as well with his interpretation of reality, particularly with his treatment of world market prices. The existence of a uniform price in every country for the commodities that workers consume is presented as a given. It becomes the keystone of Amin's defense of Emmanuel, as well as of his own theory of surplus extraction through unequal exchange. But in reality there are no world prices in the sense implied by Amin. While world market commodity prices are quoted, these reflect prices in international trade. They bear little relation to the prices that products sell for within a given country, particularly within the local or national markets of underdeveloped countries. The prices that workers in backward countries pay for basic necessities are not determined by internationally quoted prices for commodities. Rather they reflect the complex reality of underdeveloped countries: the interplay of capitalist and noncapitalist relations of production, the role of state policy, and the influence of the international market. The germ of truth underlying Amin's analysis is that competition among capitalists tends to bring about a norm in the production of the same commodity, as more efficient capitals assert their productive efficiency through underselling the less efficient. But this is a tendency within capitalist production, not within precapitalist or peasant production. Furthermore, Amin's theory is problematical because it assumes that capital is completely mobile throughout the world. Although Amin is attempting to explain the differences in development among countries, in effect his theory does not take into account the existence of national boundaries, of separate states, and of the barriers to the movement of capital among countries.

This critique of the dependency literature suggests that theories of surplus extraction, even in their most prestigious and sophisticated forms, are unable to explain the causes of underdevelopment. This is because the essence of dependency theory, the assumption of the primacy of exchange over production, is erroneous. Nevertheless, dependency writers continue to search for a mechanism that explains how a surplus product is appropriated in the sphere of exchange because they are convinced that the key to understanding underdevelopment lies in distribution. Preoccupation with the terms of exchange and relations of distribution continues to lead dependency writers to disregard the process of production and the class relations that specify how a surplus product is produced and how it is appropriated. This is particularly unfortunate since these are the essential elements that need to be analyzed in order to understand how capitalism develops and the barriers to its expansion.

Why is it that in explaining the barriers to growth in the Peruvian mining industry analysts most often rely upon dependency theory? Could it be that in dealing with an extractive sector dependency theory, with its basic tenet of surplus extraction, appears to be a particularly appropriate analytical framework? While scholars of mining may well have a special affinity for extractive processes, as I suggested earlier, the application of dependency to explain the performance of the Peruvian mining industry largely coincides with the apogee of the theory's popularity.

Numerous authors have endeavored to demonstrate that the extraction of a surplus product by foreign mining companies was detrimental to the Peruvian industry. Furthermore, because of the importance of mining in the Peruvian economy they concluded that surplus extraction in the mining sector was one of the major causes of the underdevelopment of Peru. These analysts of Peruvian mining applied dependency theory as it was formulated by Baran and Frank, arguing that surplus is extracted in the form of profit remittances. Several studies attempt to calculate the net outflow of earnings (money capital) as a result of the mining operations of large North American firms, and its effects on the expansion of both the industry and the entire economy.[36] Scholars also have constructed counterfactual models of a Peruvian mining industry dominated by Peruvian rather than foreign firms. From these models they estimate the economic advantages that would have accrued to Peru.[37] These dependency arguments prove difficult to sustain. Not only is it hard to demonstrate that the foreign mining companies extracted a net surplus from Peru (leaving aside the minerals, of course). It is even more difficult to show that had a higher portion of profits remained in Peru this money capital could or would have been productively invested.

The Theoretical Framework for Analyzing Peruvian Mining

While it is outside the scope of this book to elaborate a general theory of the limits to capitalist development in backward countries, in order to understand the dynamics of the mining sector in Peru it is necessary to present a theoretical discussion of the most important barriers to the expansion of capitalism which constrained the growth of the Peruvian mining industry.[38] In the following chapters I analyze the specific barriers to the growth of the Peruvian mining industry which emerged from the nature of the development of capitalism in Peru and from the persistence of precapitalist relations of production. In this section my intention is to present the theoretical foundation for these discussions.

If the extraction of a surplus product from Peru by foreign mining companies does not explain the periodic stagnation and crises in the industry, nor does the performance of the industry mirror price movements and demand in the international market, what then are the determinants of growth? Neoclassical economists would argue that the mining industry in Peru behaves no differently than any other mining industry. Whether production is located in an advanced capitalist country or a backward country is irrelevant in neoclassical theory. This doctrine maintains that there are no fundamental barriers to growth, nor essential differences between advanced capitalist countries and backward countries. Neoclassical economists argue that the only difference between developed and underdeveloped countries is one of location on a continuum of levels of development.[39] While dependency theory and neoclassical economic theory appear diametrically opposed, they share one striking similarity: the failure to treat capitalism as a unique mode of production. Scholars within the Marxist discourse maintain that an analysis of the causes of underdevelopment should begin with an examination of the nature of precapitalist social relations of production; particularly with the manner in which these social relations emerge as barriers to growth. They ague that theories of underdevelopment that ignore the fundamental distinction between the capitalist mode of production and precapitalist modes and ignore the particular characteristics of capitalism are crippled in their explanatory powers.

The Inflexibility of Precapitalist Social Relations

There are innumerable forms of precapitalist social relations of production. For this reason it is hazardous to generalize about these forms. For the purpose of analyzing the nineteenth and twentieth centuries in Peru, the period covered in this study, my analysis will refer to communal relations and to those precapitalist social relations that might be called feudal. "That might be called feudal" is vague and evasive. It is meant to be so. It suggests that the social relations of the *feudatarios, colonos, huachilleros,* and *yanaconas* of Peru bear certain essential similarities to European feudal relations, although they are clearly not identical to the feudal social relations found in Europe.[40] The common essence of precapitalist relations emerges most clearly when these forms of social relations are compared to capitalist relations of production, rather than when they are compared one to another.

In precapitalist modes of production the direct producers have access to the means of production—to land, tools, and animals— through a complex web of social, political, religious and ideological, as well as economic, relations. These relations are called "extra-economic" because the economic or productive aspect of the structures that insure producers access to the means of production are inseperable from all other aspects of the relationship, both in essence and in form. One significant characteristic of precapitalist relations is that direct producers have direct access to the means of production which allows them to produce their own subsistence needs. A second essential characteristic of precapitalist social relations is that exploitation is undisguised. The dominant class appropriates a surplus product or surplus labor directly. Direct appropriation takes many forms and frequently it is this form that distinguishes one precapitalist social relation from another.

The web of relations that enmeshes the direct producers with the dominant class, and binds producers to the means of production, frequently is a barrier to the reorganization of the production process in precapitalist societies. Because direct producers are not separated from the means of production, but possess or have traditional rights to land, tools, and animals, it is difficult to restructure the labor process in order to expand production, or to introduce technical changes that generate economic growth.

The Innovative Force of Capitalism

The essence of capitalism is that the direct producers have been separated from the land, tools, and animals. The process that "frees" the producers from their access to the means of subsistence also sets free the means of production. Subsequently, the two: the producers and the means of production, can be reunited only through the advance of capital. Emancipated from the constraints of precapitalist social relations and divorced from their access to the means of subsistence, free wage laborers are at the disposal of capital. Their labor power is purchased through the advance of capital. Like any other input into the production process, labor power is put to use when, where, and how it is advantageous for capital, and cast off when it is no longer required. It is the emancipation of the direct producers from precapitalist social relations that gives capital the freedom to reorganize the production process, raise productivity, and expand production, all in the quest for profits. Not only does capitalism provide this possibility, but the competition inherent in capitalism necessitates the restructuring of the labor process, the rise in productivity, and the expansion of production.

Even as the direct producers are progressively separated from the land, and as laborers are freed from precapitalist social relations of production, capital's initial control of the production process is weak. As capitalist relations emerge the labor process itself is not a product of capitalism. Rather, the production process is formed by the tensions and conflicts generated within precapitalist relations, adapted subsequently to capitalist production.[41]

In the early stage of the development of capitalism the credit system is underdeveloped. Credit remains oriented to the needs of commerce or merchant capital, the form of capital that dominated an earlier period. The immaturity of the financial system impedes the redistribution of surplus value among capitals, and the movement of capital from one branch of the economy to another. For this reason, individual capitalists frequently are unable to make the large investments that are required to restructure the production process. In the initial stage of the development of capitalism, the stage Marx called the period of manufacture, the division of labor within production reflects the social relations and technology that evolved with artisanal production. At this stage, the major impact of the development of capitalism is on the social relations of production, not the techniques of the production process. In these early stages of the development of capitalism the accumulation of capital is not primarily a function of the increasing division of labor that results in a rise in productivity. Rather, capital's expansion is facilitated initially by its destruction of traditional social relations, by its incorporation of more and more people into free wage labor, and by its concentration of larger numbers of workers into each work place. By congregating workers into larger production units capital provides the conditions for a basic change in the generation of surplus value and the expansion of production.

At this stage in the capitalist transition the possibilities for increasing the exploitation of the working class are limited. The primary source of expanded accumulation is lengthening the working day and increasing the intensity of work without compensation to the workers. Marx called this process the production of absolute surplus value. While capitalism marks a definitive rupture with earlier forms of social organization, in its initial stages of development capitalism retains many vestiges of the feudal past. The dominant class under feudalism can increase the exploitation of the producing class only by directly appropriating a larger share of the product, or more of the labor time of the direct producers. Similarly, in the stage of manufacture, to expand production and appropriate more of the unpaid labor time of their workers, capitalists are limited primarily to lengthening the working day and intensifying the pace of work. While the form and essence of exploitation under feudalism are qualitatively different than under capitalism in the stage of manufacture, we might say that both rely on absolute means of appropriating more unpaid labor time from the class of direct producers.

As a consequence of the method of raising surplus value that characterizes the period of manufacture, capitalists must employ overtly oppressive measures to increase the production of surplus value. But the process that concentrates workers into larger production units also creates the possibilty for the development of resistance to these undisguised means of increasing exploitation. Through their collective struggles workers have been successful in refusing to submit to increasingly oppressive conditions of work. Of particular importance in the history of capitalism has been the struggle for the eight hour day; or the struggle over which class, the capitalists or the workers, will determine the length of the working day. The success of workers in imposing limitations on the length of the working day ushers in the subsequent stage of capitalist development: the period of modern industry. In the stage of modern industry, capital's effort to increase surplus value and expand production no longer is limited by its ability to prolong the hours and intensify the pace of work. Instead, raising the rate of exploitation primarily becomes dependent upon the ability of the capitalist class as a whole to increase productivity and thereby reduce necessary labor time (the value of labor power).

In the period of modern industry all aspects of production and exchange become increasingly socialized. In the stage of manufacture the appearance of capitalist production as atomized and individualized somewhat corresponds to reality, since the extraction of absolute surplus value is achieved primarily by the domination of individual capitals over their workers. In the period of modern industry, however, exploitation progressively is the relationship of capital as a whole to the working class, as the extraction of relative surplus value comes to dominate the capital-labor relationship.

The interaction among capitals in the competitive quest for profits necessitates raising productivity. This leads to a decline in the value of commodities, a process analyzed earlier in this chapter. With a fall in the value of the commodities workers consume, the value of labor power declines. As a consequence, as productivity rises a smaller portion of the working day of the working class is devoted to the production of the value of labor power (the value equivalent of the commodities workers habitually consume), and a larger portion of working time is devoted to the production of surplus value, which is realized as profit for the capitalist class.

In order for technical change to affect the production of relative surplus value it must occur in a branch of industry that produces either a commodity that workers habitually consume, or the machinery or raw materials that are required for the production of such a commodity. However, technical change and rising productivity alone do not cause the value of commodities to decline. An increase in productivity that is restricted to one company does not affect the production of relative surplus value. It simply allows the pioneering capitalist to earn a higher profit margin than his/her competitors who have not introduced the new technique. The market price of a commodity reflects the costs of production implied by the standard technology in each industry. Therefore, by reducing unit costs of production, the capitalist who introduces a new technique enjoys extra unit profits when selling at the market price.

The value of a commodity declines through the interaction of capitals. The competitive struggle forces other capitalists to introduce new techniques. Through this process the abstract socially necessary labor time (value) embodied in the product comes to reflect a new norm in production. Therefore, surplus value increases through the interaction of all capitals. As capitalism develops to a more advanced stage, raising relative surplus value, which is based on the cheapening of the commodities workers consume, becomes the dominant form of increasing the exploitation of labor. As capitalism matures exploitation becomes increasingly socialized, in that increasing exploitation is a consequence of the growth of capital as a whole. The struggle by each individual capitalist to wring more labor time out of his/her work force no longer is the primary form of raising surplus value. Increasing the exploitation of the working class is achieved predominately by the capitalist class as a whole, as the interaction of capitals precipitates a fall in the value of labor power.

The Interaction Between Capitalist and Noncapitalist Relations of Production

In all societies there are obstacles to lowering the value of labor power. Even in a completely capitalist society labor power is not reproduced entirely in capitalist relations of production. For capitalist societies we can classify the products that workers consume into three categories. A portion of the products that workers consume is produced and distributed within the household—not for exchange. These products are not commodities, and have neither value nor exchange value. In another category are those products that are produced for exchange, but whose production does not involve capitalist social relations. An example of this is peasant production. Such products have no value in the strict sense since the mechanisms inherent in the relations of production of these products do not enforce an adjustment of the labor process to an industry-wide norm. Production in this second category does not involve the formation of abstract socially necessary labor time, nor the cheapening of commodities. The price of such commodities need bear no relation to the labor time required to produce them. Instead price may be a reflection of a number of factors, including supply and demand in the market or the cash requirements of the producers. In the third category are those commodities that are produced in capitalist social relations. Competition among the capitalists who produce these commodities necessitates technical change, a rise in productivity, and a decline in the value and price of these commodities.

With the development of capitalism there is a tendency for production to be characterized increasingly by the social relations of free wage labor, and for products to become commodities. Therefore, as capitalism matures products in the first two categories decline in importance, while commodities that are produced in capitalist social relations progressively dominate consumption by the working class. Since capitalist production generates a decline in the value of commodities, as more and more of the products that workers consume are produced in capitalist social relations this expands the scope for lowering the value of labor power and raising relative surplus value. In summary, a rise in productivity in the production of the commodities that workers consume, accompanied by a fall in the value of these commodities, signifies that for a given standard of living a smaller portion of the working time of the working class as a whole is devoted to producing the value equivalent of the necessities of life for the working class.

Analogously, a rise in the standard of living of the working class does not necessitate either a corresponding rise in the value of labor power, or an increase in the cost of labor power to capital. This is because growth in the quantity or improvement in the quality of the use values consumed by the working class may be offset by an increase in productivity. This would result in a decline in the labor time required to produce that standard of living, and a corresponding decline in the values of the commodities that represent the higher level of consumption. In other words, with the maturation of capitalism, the progressive growth of productivity provides the possibility for increasing the exploitation of labor at the same time as it provides the possibility of raising the standard of living of the working class.

Nevertheless, it is important to stress that the standard of living of the working class is determined neither by capital nor by productivity. The essential point is that the development of capitalism, and of the forces of production, generates conditions that allow capital to intensify exploitation, even in the context of improvements in the material welfare of the working class. To the extent that the standard of living of the working class rises, and the conditions of work become less oppressive, this is accomplished through the collective struggles of workers over wages, hours, and working conditions. Improvements in the material conditions of the working class are not a result of rising productivity as such. Whereas the possibility of increasing the exploitation of the working class is unleashed with the development of capitalism, in developing countries the process of raising relative surplus value remains fettered by the persistence of precapitalist social relations of production. In backward countries many of the products that the working class consumes are not produced in capitalist social relations. This is particularly characteristic of foodstuffs, and reflects the importance of precapitalist social relations in agriculture.

In so far as food and other basic necessities consumed by the working class are produced and distributed within the household or the peasant community, and not exchanged, this may be momentarily advantageous to capital. As long as the working class does not purchase these products, the wage is not the vehicle for their acquisition. Consequently, the level of the wage may be low, because a significant portion of the products consumed by the working class is not monetized. However, in so far as precapitalist and household production monopolizes land and labor power that thereby remain unavailable to capital, the persistence of precapitalist and household production may become an obstacle to accumulation. As long as workers retain access to sufficient land to provide a significant portion of their subsistence needs they are not yet totally "free"—and at the complete disposal of capital.

In developing countries many of the basic necessities of the working class are produced for exchange but outside of capitalist relations of production. The mechanisms to increase productivity within the social relations of peasant production, share-cropping, and debt-peonage are weak; and the interaction among capitals to bring about a decline in the value of commodities is absent. The prices of these products are theoretically "indeterminant"—they are not a reflection of abstract socially necessary labor time. They may be low at one moment, and high at another; with the movement in price bearing no relation to conditions of production. In these social relations of production there is no inherent dynamic that engenders a rise in productivity and a fall in the value and price of the products.

In so far as the wage reflects the value of labor power, the socially necessary labor time required to produce the means of subsistence for the working class, low wages in developing countries may be related to the existence of a large precapitalist sector. Under these conditions wages may be low because a large portion of the products that workers consume traditionally were not monetized, or not valorized (have no value in the strict sense). This theoretical possibility does not deny the brutal reality that low wages in developing countries are associated with a low standard of living and reflect the inability of the working class to win concessions from capital.

Finally, in developing countries, rising real wages do not necessarily indicate an improvement in the standard of living of the working class. As capitalism develops there is a tendency for workers to become more completely proletarianized. As their ties to the land are eliminated, workers must purchase an ever growing portion of their subsistence requirements. Many of these necessities previously may have been acquired through traditional relations, not through capitalist exchange. In these circumstances, progressively the wage must cover a larger portion of the necessities of the working class. Nevertheless, rarely will capitalists raise wages before forced to do so by the collective struggles of workers. Therefore, the working classes in developing countries must continually fight for higher wages, not only to improve their standard of living, but simply to maintain it. The objective of this discussion is to demonstrate that in developing countries a low standard of living of the working class need not imply that the value of labor power is low, and the rate of profit is high. Nor that rising wages necessarily signify an improvement in the standard of living of the working class; or that improvements in the material conditions of the working class necessarily increase the cost of labor power to capital.

As a consequence of the interaction between capitalist and precapitalist social relations of production in developing countries it is not possible to deduce a given relationship between wages and the standard of living, or between improvements in the standard of living of the working class and profits. These are complex relationships. To understand their specific dynamics in a concrete historical situation requires a theoretical framework and empirical research on social and economic conditions in a specific national and cultural context.

An understanding of the role of wages is particularly important to the present analysis of the causes of growth, stagnation and crises in the Peruvian mining industry. Frequently mining companies, the Peruvian Ministry of Energy and Mines, and analysts of the industry attributed the stagnation and crises of mining production to worker

conclusions are somewhat different
to analyze the causes of variations in the level of the wage and to
relate these to transformations in the relations of production of the
work force, to changes in productivity, and to fluctuations in the
cost of labor power to capital.

To this point I have discussed the fundamental distinction
between precapitalist and capitalist social relations of production, the
nature of capitalism as it matures, and the barriers to the
development of capitalism implied by the preservation of
precapitalist social relations. The analysis thus far has not dealt with
the export of capital from the industrialized countries to the
underdeveloped countries, and the impact this has on economic
growth. In other words, it has not dealt with the reality of Latin
America, where the transition to capitalism is occurring, or has
occurred, in the context of a world economy dominated by capitalist
countries. To this point the analysis applies equally to the
development of capitalism in Europe, as well as to the capitalist
transition of the Third World. But these processes are profoundly
different, the major difference being that the capitalist transition of
Europe was the "first" transition. Capitalism in England, France,
and the other European countries developed within feudal societies,
without the influence of more advanced capitalist countries. In
contrast, the transition to capitalism in Latin America, Africa, and
Asia has been profoundly affected by the earlier development and
maturity of capitalism in Europe, the United States, and Japan. A
theory of underdevelopment should not ignore this difference. An
analysis of the causes of backwardness in each country needs to be
rooted in the historical specificity of the preservation of precapitalist
social relations of production, the barriers to the development of free
wage labor, and the impact of the export of capital in different
periods on the transformation of social relations of production.

The Export of Capital from Advanced to Underdeveloped Countries

The export of capital is a highly complex process that has
developed with the development of capitalism itself. Although the
export of capital has been the subject of innumerable valuable
theoretical and empirical studies, still it is little understood. Since
the turn of the century the export of capital, a process frequently
referred to by the general term "imperialism," has been at the center
of highly charged political and ideological debates.[42] While these

debates have clarified some of the fundamental issues surrounding the export of capital, at the same time they have obfuscated other crucial problems.[43] Some scholars felt compelled to uphold what they considered to be the inherited wisdom regarding the export of capital, or "imperialism." This restricted, at times even stifled, both scholarly and political debates.

Although within the theoretical and historical literature on the export of capital the term "imperialism" refers both to the export of capital among capitalist countries as well as to the export of capital from advanced to underdeveloped countries, the term is frequently used to describe only the latter process. However, this use of the term "imperialism" is erroneous and the cause of much of the misunderstanding about the process of the export of capital. Nevertheless, it is outside the scope of this study to enter into a theoretical discussion of all aspects of the process of imperialism. Because this book involves the study of the export of capital from advanced to underdeveloped countries, the theoretical discussion is limited to this aspect of the process.

At the center of recent debates on the nature of imperialism and the causes of underdevelopment is the issue of whether the export of capital contributes to economic development, or the development of the productive forces within underdeveloped countries, or whether it retards or blocks this process. On one side of this debate are the dependency theorists who hold that the process of international exchange between developed and underdeveloped countries prevents, or at best distorts, economic growth. Diametrically opposed to this position is a school of writers that holds that the export of capital inevitably leads to the development of capitalism, the growth of the proletariat, and economic expansion.[44] The logic underlying the second view is that the export of capital to underdeveloped areas is the manifestation of the expansion of capitalism in these countries. Writers who hold this view argue that by its very nature this process is, or at the least provides the precondition for, economic growth.

Advocates of both viewpoints draw upon historical examples to validate their arguments and marshall evidence to support their positions. While studies from both perspectives have made major theoretical and empirical contributions to understanding the mechanisms and effects of the export of capital, nevertheless the arguments of the writers in both of these traditions are flawed. They assume that the export of capital is a uniform and unchanging process characterized by one central dynamic that always creates similar conditions. While apparently diametrically opposed, the two positions share a fundamental assumption. Neither recognizes that capital is exported in different forms and that the form of capital export conditions the effect of this process within underdeveloped countries.

Capital is by its nature expansionary. Value expands in the circuit of capital. Therefore, in order to develop a theory of the export of capital there is no need to postulate a special theory to explain why capital expands in an international versus a national context. Driven by the process of competition, capital must expand. In the circuit of capital (M-C...P...C'M'), at different moments capital assumes the forms of money capital, of commodity capital, and of productive capital. When capital is exported, or expands across national boundaries, it expands in these different forms. The particular form of capital export is conditioned by the level of the development of capitalism in the "exporting" country, by the needs and constraints of the particular capital or firm, and by the nature of the state and the relations of production in the country to which capital is exported.

Some historical references may clarify this point. Following the Spanish conquest of Peru and Mexico, trade between Spain and its colonies was financed and carried out by merchant capital. This trade was not associated with capitalism. It represented exchange among merchants, landowners, and craftsmen from Europe and the New World. It was trade among precapitalist elites conducted by merchant capital. Gradually, with the rise of capitalist production in Europe in the eighteenth and nineteenth centuries, and the expansion of markets for factory-made products, the European-New World trade began to assume the character of the export of capital. In this early stage in the development of capitalism in Europe capital was exported primarily in the form of commodities, or commodity capital. The export of capital primarily took this form in the period of manufacture because the relatively underdeveloped state of credit institutions in the capitalist countries restricted the export of money capital, or capital in money form. At the same time the dominance of precapitalist social relations in underdeveloped countries limited the possibilities for the export of money or productive capital. The latter implies the establishment of production based on wage labor. However, trade progressively developed a world market for the products of capitalist production.

The consequence of this trade for the underdeveloped countries is a matter of considerable controversy. As discussed above, some authors argue that trade alone is sufficient to transform precapitalist societies into capitalist formations.[45] Another position is that trade tended to rigidify and strengthen precapitalist social relations in underdeveloped areas.[46] Authors who subscribe to this latter view argue that expanded opportunities for trade frequently induced landowners to appropriate more labor or a larger portion of the product from direct producers via traditional relations. In addition, trade frequently encouraged the formation of alliances between the ruling classes in the advanced countries and the precapitalist elites in the underdeveloped countries. As a consequence of these alliances there was a tendency for precapitalist elites to strengthen their control over the state, thus preventing an incipient local capitalist class from using the state apparatus to foster the development of capitalism.

The consolidation of capitalism in the advanced industrialized countries enabled capital to become more mobile both among industries within the capitalist countries, as well as internationally. In this stage, generically called the period of modern industry, the development of finance institutions facilitated the export of money capital. As the initial export of money capital often assumed the form of loans to governments of underdeveloped countries, this frequently fortified the rule of precapitalist elites since this class dominated the state and benefitted from an expansion of state revenue.

The export of productive capital, also called direct foreign investment, did not come to dominate the process of the export of capital until the necessary conditions evolved in both advanced and underdeveloped countries. The export of productive capital on a large scale required the maturation of financial institutions in developed countries to facilitate the centralization of capital and its global mobility. In addition, until recently the persistence of traditional forms of production in many countries of the world emerged as barriers to the export of productive capital. However, as the export of capital increasingly assumed the form of the export of productive capital this process progressively undermined traditional social relations and contributed to the necessary but not sufficient conditions for the development of capitalism in underdeveloped countries.

This complex and contradictory process cannot be analyzed in the abstract. The obstacles to the export of capital and to the development of capitalism in underdeveloped countries, and the particular ways in which these barriers are overcome, are determined by concrete historical circumstances. The subject of this book is precisely the particular nature of the export of productive capital from the United States for mining production in Peru, the effect of this process on the transformation of social relations in the mines, and the repercussions of these processes on the development of capitalism in Peru.

This chapter concludes with a caveat. Although I have argued theoretically that the export of productive capital generally fosters the development of capitalism, this is not to imply that the extension of capitalism and wage labor is synonymous with equitable growth, the elimination of poverty, or "development," understood as a process of improvement of the social and economic conditions of existence of the population of a country. Capitalism is a system based on inequality and exploitation, not equality and social justice. In Europe and more recently in the Third World the early stage of capitalist development was, and is, particularly brutal. Generally capitalism destroys precapitalist production at a faster pace than capitalist production expands. This results in the ruination of the peasantry and massive unemployment because the capitalist sector cannot absorb the masses of people who are forced off the land. Also, in the initial stage of capitalist development, in order to increase profits capitalists are driven to extend the length of the working day and intensify the pace of work. As such, the expansion of capitalism at this stage primarily depends upon increasing the oppressiveness of work in each workplace. As capitalism matures, the prime mechanism for raising profits shifts from increasing absolute surplus value at the level of the individual firm to raising relative surplus value in the economy as a whole. This latter process is accomplished not by extending the length of the working day as a whole, but by extending that portion of the working day devoted to the generation of profits for the capitalist class. This is not to imply that as capitalism develops it becomes less exploitative and oppressive; only that the form of exploitation becomes less overt.

CHAPTER TWO

A Comparative Analysis of the Peruvian Mining Industry and the International Metals Market

Scholars of Peruvian mining frequently focus their attention on the relationship between the Peruvian and the world mining industries. In this context it is not uncommon for authors to assume that the Peruvian industry is a microcosm of the world mining industry. From this assumption follows another: that international metals prices and world demand are the primary determinants of change in Peruvian metal production. Without doubt the most common explanation offered in the scholarly literature for the expansion and contraction of the Peruvian mining industry is the fluctuation in world metals prices.

The objective of this chapter is to test this hypothesis and to determine whether there is a statistically significant relationship between conditions in the world mining industry and the performance of the Peruvian industry. First, using relatively simple statistical techniques, I examine to what degree changes in Peruvian production correlate with changes in mining production on a world scale. Secondly I analyze the relationship between changes in world market metals prices and variations in the level of production in Peru. This latter analysis is undertaken to determine whether a direct causal relationship exists between variations in prices and output in Peru. The results of these statistical tests are summarized in this chapter. Details on the statistical methods and the results of the tests, along with the data that I use, are presented in a series of tables and figures in the Appendixes.

Peru's Major Mineral Products

Peru's major mineral products are copper, lead, zinc, iron, silver, and gold. Copper, lead, zinc, and iron are predominately used in the production of machinery, consumer durables, and construction materials. For this reason the demand for these metals on a world scale tends to reflect trends in the expansion and contraction of the world economy. Steady growth in the international economy generally increases the demand for these basic

41

metals. Conversely, a slowdown in the international economy frequently is accompanied by a decline in the demand for copper, lead, zinc, and iron.

Historically the precious metals, silver and gold, have played an important role in the world monetary system. In the nineteenth century the currencies of many countries, including Peru, were based on silver. Therefore, there was a great demand for silver and the price tended to be high. At the end of the century many countries converted their monetary system to a gold standard. This contributed to a sharp decline in the price of silver. Whereas gold continues to play a role in the adjustment of international payments, silver does not. Although silver has important industrial uses, particularly in the photography industry, the primary demand for silver in the twentieth century has been for the production of luxury goods. Until recently, determination of the price of gold differed from that of other metals. World market prices of most basic metals reflect their costs of production and international demand. But the price of gold was fixed by the United States government throughout most of the twentieth century. This, however, does not affect the analysis in this chapter.

Peru's Relative Position in the World Mining Industry

Comparable statistics on world metal production on a country by country basis date from the 1920s. These show a significant shift in the production of the basic, non-precious, metals from the developed to the developing countries in the course of the twentieth century. In 1925 about 30 percent of the world's copper production was mined in the developing countries, the vast bulk of it in Latin America; 70 percent was mined in the developed countries, most of this in the United States. The developed countries' share of world copper production has gradually decreased since that time, in large part due to a decline in U.S. copper production. In the late 1970s, over 50 percent of world copper production was mined in the developed countries and 48 percent in the developing world.

In 1930, 33 percent of world lead production was mined in the developing countries. By the late 1970s this figure rose to almost 50 percent. Lead and zinc ores are frequently found together. Consequently, as one would expect, the pattern of world zinc production is similar to that of lead. The developing countries' share of world zinc production was 22 percent in 1930. By the late 1970s their share of total zinc production was 46 percent, more than double the level of the 1930s. The same shift in production from the developed to the developing countries is characteristic of the production of iron ore. In 1955 over 80 percent of iron ore was mined in the developed countries. By the late 1970s this figure had fallen to just over 60 percent.

Of the minerals treated in this book, only the precious metals—gold and silver—are produced in greater quantity in the underdeveloped countries. The share of world silver production mined in underdeveloped countries has declined steadily since 1930, but remained at 60 percent in the late 1970s. Conversely, gold is increasingly mined in the Third World. In the late 1970s the vast majority of the world's gold, 87 percent, was mined in underdeveloped countries, most of this in South Africa. Although mining dominates the Peruvian economy, and traditionally minerals have been Peru's principal source of foreign exchange, for the world mining industry Peruvian metal production is of relatively minor significance.[1]

Copper has been Peru's principal mineral product throughout most of the twentieth century. Nevertheless, since 1900 Peru has contributed an annual average of only 2.5 percent of world copper production. Peru's share of world copper production fell to an annual average of 1.5 percent from 1945 to 1955. Then, in 1960, as a consequence of the opening of Toquepala, a large open-pit copper mine in the south, Peru's share of world copper production rose to a high of 5.4 percent. However, following the inauguration of new pits and the expansion of old copper mines in Chile and Africa, Peru's share of world production soon declined. In the late 1970s Peru's share of world copper production again increased in the wake of the inauguration of the Cuajone mine, another large open-pit operation in southern Peru. At that time Peru was the seventh largest copper producing country in the world, trailing considerably behind the top six producers.[2]

The decades of the 1940s and the 1950s were characterized by an alteration in the composition of Peru's mineral output. From 1948 to 1958 lead surpassed copper as Peru's principal mineral product. However, with the initiation of large scale open-pit copper mining, copper again dominated Peruvian production. The Peruvian share of world lead production reached its peak of almost 7 percent in 1960. Subsequently it declined and hovered just below 5 percent of world lead output.

Due to the absence of local smelters and refineries capable of processing zinc, a negligible quantity of zinc was mined in Peru prior to the 1930s. In 1940 the Cerro de Pasco Corporation established a pilot plant for the electrolytic refining of zinc. The opening of this plant marked the initiation of large-scale zinc production in Peru. The plant was enlarged and entered into full-scale production in 1952, encouraging the further expansion of zinc mining in Peru. At its peak in 1960 Peru contributed almost 10 percent of world zinc production. By the late 1970s Peru's share of world zinc production had fallen to about 6 percent.

Historically Peru was one of the world's leading silver producers. In the colonial period the Viceroyalty of Peru encompassed the richest silver mines in the world, and was renowned for its wealth of precious metals. The name "Peru" is no longer synonymous with vast mountains of silver and hoards of gold, as it was in the sixteenth century. Yet Peru remains a significant source of silver. Since 1900 Peru has steadily increased its share of world silver production, contributing almost 15 percent of the total silver mined in the world each year since the mid-1960s.

Peru's share of world production of the other two metals included in this study is very small. At its peak in 1970 Peru produced almost 2 percent of the world's iron ore. More recently this has declined to under 1 percent. Finally, an insignificant portion of the world's gold production is mined in Peru—less than 1 percent per year. The Spanish conquerors of Peru discovered large quantities of gold objects and adornments. This led them to believe that there remained undiscovered rich mines gold. They and succeeding generations of adventurers have searched in vain for these fabled mines. The mythic treasure of gold has yet to be found. It seems likely that it never existed. While Peru is not a major world producer of any one metal, one of the strengths of the Peruvian mining industry is the extreme diversity of its products. Peru produces a broad range of minerals, both industrial and precious.

The Influence of the World Mining Industry on Peruvian Metal Production: 1900-1945

Before analyzing the extent to which fluctuations in demand and price in the world metals market have influenced the performance of the Peruvian mining industry, I compare the pattern of growth of metal mining in Peru and in the world industry as a whole.[3] This is done by constructing indexes of real (constant price) output for both Peruvian and world production. Then year-to-year movements in these indexes are compared. Next, I estimate the simple relationship between changes in world production and changes in Peruvian production. This makes it possible to measure the correlation between changes in world production and changes in Peruvian production and to measure statistically the extent to which Peruvian production fluctuates with world production.[4]

From 1900 to the late 1970s the Peruvian mining industry grew extremely rapidly. At the beginning of the twentieth century, with the notable exception of silver mining, large scale mining in Peru was in its infancy. In thirty years, from 1900 to 1929, the current revenue received by the Peruvian mining industry (revenue in *soles*) increased six-fold. This expansion was momentarily and abruptly halted in the early 1930s, with the fall in metal prices (see Figure 2.1). The volume of metal production in Peru expanded almost as fast as the value of production (see Table 2.1 and Figure 2.2). Figures 2.1 and 2.2 indicate that the expansion and contraction of the Peruvian mining industry was generally in rhythm with world mining production, though the extent to which this was the case is somewhat difficult to assess in these figures because Peruvian production begins in 1900 from a very low base.[5]

By using trend analysis the correlation between world and Peruvian production can be analyzed more precisely because the variations in Peruvian and world production are measured relative to predicted trend values for each. This statistical technique makes it possible to evaluate, for each separate time series, when production is high or low compared to the long-run performance of that time series.[6] Trend analysis of the volume of production in the world mining industry and in the Peruvian mining industry for the period 1900-1945 is presented in Figure 2.3. This analysis indicates that in general the world industry and the Peruvian industry shared the same good and bad years. For the most part, when the mining industry on a world scale was enjoying relative expansion, so was the Peruvian industry. In other words, Peruvian production had much the same growth pattern as world production from 1900-1945.[7] For both Peru and the world industry the first half of the twentieth century was one of expansion in metal production. This overall growth was interrupted by two major downturns: between 1917 and 1920, and in the first half of the 1930s. Thus far I have not dealt with the issue of causality. The objective simply has been to analyze the correlation between patterns of growth in the Peruvian and the world mining industries.

TABLE 2.1 Indexes of the Volume of Production in the Peruvian and the World Mining Industries[a], 1900-1945

| | (1903 = 100) | |
Year	World[b]	Peru
1900	84.2	n.a.
1901	88.2	n.a.
1902	94.4	n.a.
1903	100.0	100.0
1904	106.7	90.8
1905	111.5	115.6
1906	116.9	137.8
1907	120.8	163.0
1908	129.1	154.8
1909	135.7	154.0
1910	138.3	199.4
1911	141.2	212.1
1912	147.5	226.0
1913	145.0	223.2
1914	131.1	216.2
1915	143.8	250.9
1916	153.5	300.6
1917	153.3	309.0
1918	149.0	294.4
1919	125.3	275.0
1920	117.1	238.0
1921	96.9	252.4
1922	116.7	251.4
1923	144.6	386.6
1924	153.3	342.5
1925	181.6	380.0
1926	191.5	454.7
1927	194.9	418.9
1928	200.8	489.7
1929	214.6	508.0
1930	196.7	400.5
1931	176.4	302.2

(continued)

TABLE 2.1 (cont.)

Year	(1903 = 100) World[b]	Peru
1932	151.5	182.2
1933	160.7	212.2
1934	181.4	268.0
1935	200.8	374.2
1936	226.8	440.2
1937	266.1	455.1
1938	260.9	530.9
1939	272.0	500.3
1940	292.8	545.6
1941	297.6	485.9
1942	289.8	474.2
1943	264.1	461.4
1944	242.6	511.2
1945	211.3	492.8

SOURCES: Computed by the author from data presented in *Statistische Zusammenstellungen Über Aluminium, Blei, Kupfer, Nickel, Quecksilber, Zink und Zinn* (Frankfurt Am Main: Metallgesellschaft, 1907, 1913, 1931); Robert H. Ridgway, *Summarized Data of Gold Production* (Washington, D.C.: U.S. Department of Commerce, Bureau of Mines Economic Paper No. 6, 1929) p. 6; *Metal Statistics: 1965-1975* (63rd edition) (Frankfurt Am Main: Metallgesellschaft, 1976); *Statistical Yearbook* (New York: United Nations, 1949, 1955, 1965, 1976); Pablo Macera and Honorio Pinto, *Estadísticas históricas del Perú: sector minero II (volumen y valor)* (Lima: Centro Peruano de Historia Económica, 1972); and *Boletín del cuerpo de ingenieros de minas* (Lima: 1902, 1903).

[a] Volume of production measured in constant prices.

[b] In order to facilitate the comparison, data for the world mining industry include only those metals produced in Peru in the respective years, i.e., data on output in the world mining industry include copper, lead, silver, and gold for the years 1900-1945. Zinc is included from 1925.

n.a. - data not available.

48

FIGURE 2.1 The Value of Production in the World and Peruvian Mining Industries, 1900-1945

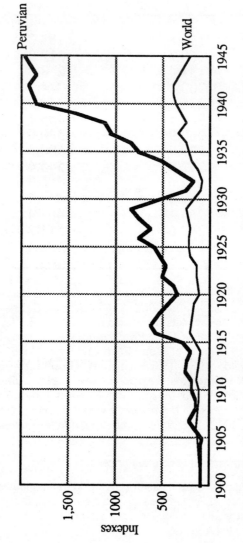

SOURCES: *Statistische Zusammenstellungen Über Aluminium, Blei, Kupfer, Nickel, Quecksilber, Silber, Zinc und Zinn* (Franfurt Am Main: Metallgesellschaft, 1907, 1913, 1931); Robert H. Ridgway, *Summarized Data of Gold Production* (Washington, D.C.: U.S. Department of Commerce, Bureau of Mines Economic Paper No. 6, 1929), p. 6; Pablo Macera and Honorio Pinto, *Estadísticas históricas del Perú: sector minero II (precios)*; and *Estadísticas históricas del Perú: sector minero II (volumen y valor)* (Lima: Centro Peruano de Historia Económica, 1972).

Having established that the pattern of growth of the Peruvian mining industry is similar to that of the world industry, I now turn to the more contentious issue. To what extent can fluctuations in Peruvian production be explained by world market prices and the international demand for metals? To measure the influence of the world mining industry on the mining sector in Peru I employ a variety of statistical methods. Each of the statistical techniques is designed to highlight or measure a different aspect of the comparison between the Peruvian and the world mining industry. First, I compare the annual rates of change of real output in the Peruvian and the world mining industries.[8] This measures causality in a particular and indirect way. Obviously, a given change in world output of metals does not cause a change in Peruvian production. Rather, each changes for specific reasons, some of which are common to both, such as world demand, and some of which are unique to Peru, such as domestic supply factors and social and political conditions.

In estimating the statistical correlation between changes in world output and Peruvian output, the correlation between the two can be interpreted as the portion of the Peruvian variation that is explained by demand, or world market forces—external factors.[9] A simple linear regression, with Peruvian changes specified as the dependent variable, indicates that the estimated relationship is statistically significant. However, although the relationship is significant, only 33 percent of the variation in Peruvian production is associated with variations in world production.[10] Therefore, taking the period as a whole, two-thirds of the variation in Peruvian production do not conform to the variations in the weighted average changes for all producers throughout the world. This is *prima facie* evidence for the impact of internal factors on the growth of Peruvian mining.

Since analysts of the Peruvian mining industry generally argue that the prime factor determining the performance of the Peruvian mining industry is the international price of metals, I undertake an analysis of the correlation between prices and the pattern of change in Peruvian mining.[11] The effect of world prices on Peruvian production can be estimated directly by specifying changes in

50

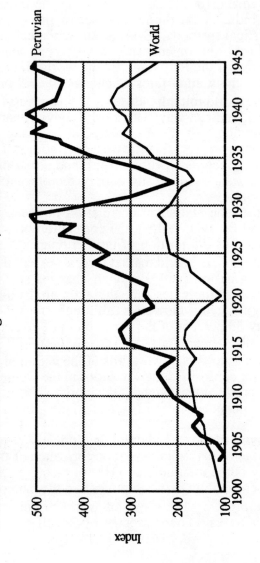

FIGURE 2.2 Indexes of the Volume of Production[a] in the World and Peruvian Mining Industries, 1900-1945

SOURCES: The same as Figure 2.1.

[a]The volume of production is measured in constant 1963 prices.

FIGURE 2.3 Trend Analysis of the Volume of Production [a] in the World and Peruvian Mining Industries, 1900-1945

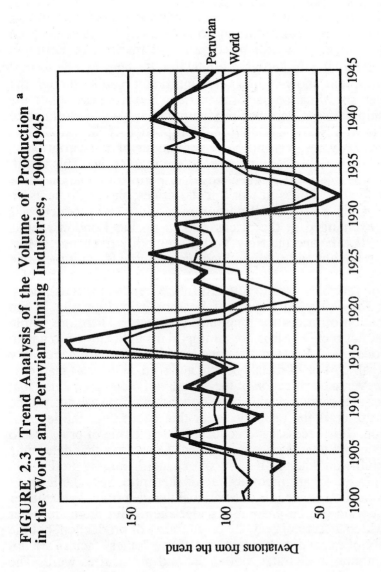

SOURCES: The same as Table 2.1.

[a]The Volume of production is measured in constant 1963 prices.

Peruvian production as the dependent variable and changes in a index of relevant world prices as the independent variable.[12] This is done by correlating the changes in world prices and fluctuations in Peruvian production in each year. In addition, to incorporate the possibility that Peruvian producers cannot adjust production immediately, but require time to do so, I analyze the correlation between changes in world prices and fluctuations in Peruvian production by lagging Peruvian production changes by one year.[13] Both regressions show statistically significant results, though the non-lagged specification performs better. Nevertheless, while the relationship between Peruvian production changes and world price changes is significant, a relatively small portion of the variation is explained, only 28 percent. The remainder of the variation is explained by variables not included in the regression. This result, that less than one-third of the changes in Peruvian metal output is correlated with changes in world metal prices, should come as no surprise. Only a very small portion of world metal production is actually exchanged at the prices quoted on the London Metals Exchange (LME) and the New York Commodity Exchange. Most metals are bought and sold via long-term contracts, with the price stipulated in advance. World market metals prices are one of a number of variables used to forecast future trends in metals prices. As such they play an important but not exclusive role in the determination of prices for long term contracts. Therefore, while world market metals prices are an important indicator of trends in metals prices, they represent the price at which metals exchange only for the small portion of metals bought and sold on the spot market.

However, a clarification of the quantity of metal production that exchanges at the world market price does not make a case against the view that price is the primary factor that determines the level of production. It is necessary to conceptualize the role of price and to see price as but one amongst a number of variables that determine the possibility and the profitability of expanding mining production. Price is obviously an important factor that influences the level of metal production, since it is one variable that determines whether or not production can be profitably undertaken. But there are other factors which affect not only the profitability of production, but the possibility of expanding production. These "other" factors are not only economic in charater, but social and political as well. The determinants of mining production vary considerably from country to country, and can be understood only by analyzing the particular economic, social, and political conditions in the mining sector in each unique country context.

In summary, the statistical results support the hypothesis that in the period 1900-1945 variables internal to the Peruvian economy and society were more important than external variables influencing the volume of metal production in Peru. There significant correlation between variations in production in the mining industry and in the Peruvian industry, and in fluctu~   ιn world market prices and output in the Peruvian mini~   ～ector. However, these correlations account for less than one-t.ιrd of the year-to-year changes in the Peruvian industry. In conclusion, during the period from 1900 to 1945 one cannot explain the performance of the Peruvian industry in terms of fluctuations in world market metals prices or the international demand for metals.

The Influence of the World Mining Industry on Peruvian Metal Production: 1945-1977

The analysis of the performance of the Peruvian mining sector from 1945 to the middle 1970s begins with an investigation of the pattern of growth of the volume of production for the world and the Peruvian mining industries. A comparison of the indexes of real output (the volume of production measured in constant prices) is presented in Table 2.2. The table shows that both the world and the Peruvian mining industries were expanding relatively rapidly in this period of more than thirty years.

A graphic presentation of these indexes is more revealing. Figure 2.4 indicates that metal mining in Peru and on a world scale was expanding in this period, although the pattern of growth is somewhat different in each case. Expansion in the world mining industry was relatively steady, with no quantum leaps or falls in production in any one year. This pattern of incremental growth in the world mining industry is what we might anticipate. The index of world production represents a double aggregation: an aggregation of six metals, and an aggregation of mining production in many countries. For this reason, barring any major crisis, such as the great depression, one would expect that fluctuations in output peculiar to any one country or to any one metal would be smoothed out in the aggregation of the mining industry on a world scale.

The pattern of growth in Peru was substantially different from that of the world industry. The Peruvian mining industry did not expand and contract incrementally, but in bursts and plunges. In the

FIGURE 2.4 Indexes of the Volume of Production[a] in the
World and Peruvian Mining Industries

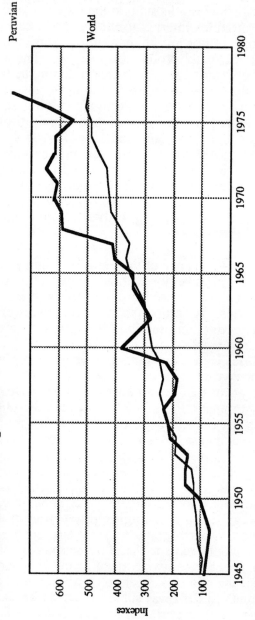

SOURCES: Computed by the author from data presented in *Metal Statistics: 1965-1975* (63rd edition),
(Frankfurt Am Main: Metallgesellschaft, 1976); *Statistical Yearbook* (New York: United Nations, 1949,
1955, 1965, 1976); Ministerio de Energía y Minas, *Anuario Minero del Perú* (Lima: 1966-1972); Ministerio
de Energía y Minas, *Anuario de la Minería del Perú* (Lima: 1973-1975); Ministerio de Fomento, *Anuario de la
Industria Minera en el Perú* (Lima: 1945-1949); Ministerio de Fomento y Obras Públicas, *Anuario de la
Industria Minera en el Perú* (Lima: 1950-1965); *Anuario Minero Comercial* (Lima: 1977); unpublished data
from the Ministerio de Energía y Minas, Area de Estadística, Archives; and "Declaraciones Anuales
Consolidadas de Concesionarios, Empresas y Empresarios Mineros" (Lima: Archivos de la División de
Estadística, Dirección General de Minería, Ministerio de Energía y Minas, 1945-1975).

[a]The volume of production is measured in constant 1963 prices.

TABLE 2.2   Indexes of the Volume of Production in the Peruvian and the World Mining Industries[a], 1945-1977

Year	(1945 = 100) World[b]	Peru
1945	100.0	100.0
1946	92.4	87.6
1947	105.6	80.7
1948	110.0	71.4
1949	111.1	91.0
1950	121.2	106.2
1951	125.1	150.9
1952	132.1	160.9
1953	198.8	155.3
1954	195.7	201.6
1955	218.4	213.7
1956	233.9	228.9
1957	244.9	199.4
1958	235.1	182.9
1959	247.6	214.3
1960	278.1	373.9
1961	283.9	329.8
1962	296.8	271.7
1963	305.1	310.6
1964	333.3	338.5
1965	352.0	340.1
1966	365.7	404.3
1967	362.1	411.5
1968	387.1	588.5
1969	409.1	590.1
1970	436.8	630.4
1971	441.5	611.6
1972	457.0	662.5
1973	481.2	632.6
1974	499.4	633.6
1975	499.4	547.7
1976	511.5	643.7
1977	502.4	779.8

SOURCES: Computed by the author from data presented in *Metal Statistics:*
(continued)

mid-twentieth century major technological changes revolutionized the mining of copper throughout the world. Selective mining methods, associated with underground shaft mining, were superceded by non-selective methods, generally associated with open-pit mining. Shaft mining involves continual exploration for mineral veins, construction of shafts and tunnels to follow the veins, and the drainage and ventilation of the tunnels. The techniques of underground mining in Peru were associated with the gradual expansion or contraction of output, as old veins were exhausted and shafts and tunnels were dug to follow richer new veins. Opening new underground mines increased output. But as individual mines in Peru were relatively small, the start-up or closing of a mine would not result in a large and sudden change in the level of total production.

The pattern of growth of the Peruvian mining industry significantly altered with the introduction of non-selective, open-pit mining. Open-pit mining is profitable only if the volume of output of each mine is very large. The open-pit technique involves the use of non-selective mining methods to exploit a huge deposit of low-grade ore. Large machinery removes massive quantities of earth and rock, which is processed to extract the ore. Subsequently the rubble is deposited at another location. Great leaps in the volume of production are associated with the opening or major expansion of an open-pit mine. Figure 2.4 shows that when the Peruvian mining

---

1965-1975 (63rd edition), (Frankfurt Am Main: Metallgesellschaft, 1976); *Statistical Yearbook* (New York: United Nations, 1949, 1955, 1965, 1976); Ministerio de Energía y Minas, *Anuario Minero del Perú* (Lima: 1966-1972); Ministerio de Energía y Minas, *Anuario de la Minería del Perú* (Lima: 1973-1975); Ministerio de Fomento, *Anuario de la Industria Minera en el Perú* (Lima: 1945-1949); Ministerio de Fomento y Obras Públicas, *Anuario de la Industria Minera en el Perú* (Lima: 1950-1965); *Anuario Minero Comercial* (Lima: 1977); unpublished data from the Ministerio de Energía y Minas, Area de Estadística, Archives; and "Declaraciones Anuales Consolidadas de Concesionarios, Empresas y Empresarios Mineros" (Lima: Archivos de la División de Estadística, Dirección General de Minería, Ministerio de Energía y Minas, 1945-1975).

[a]Volume of production measured in constant prices.

[b]In order to facilitate the comparison, data for the world mining industry include only those metals produced in Peru in the respective years, i.e., data on output in the world mining industry include copper, lead, silver, and gold for the years 1900-1945. Zinc is included from 1925.

industry was expanding in the period 1945 to 1977, the expansion was frequently by leaps and bounds. Spurts in output in the early and late 1960s, and the middle 1970s, were each the direct result of the opening or expansion of a mine based on non-selective mining methods, predominately the open-pit technique.

In Figure 2.5 the indexes of the volume of production in the world mining industry and in the Peruvian mining industry are normalized for their trends. This figure is not intended to suggest causality. Rather, it is presented as a visual method of distinguishing periods of relative expansion and prosperity from normal or average years and sub-normal years. Although the Peruvian and the world mining industries did have almost the same trend rate of growth for the post-1945 period, trend analysis substantiates the conclusion that the pattern of growth from year-to-year was considerably different. For the pre-1945 period it is evident that the statistical (regression) results support the hypothesis that external variables were not most important in explaining changes in Peruvian production. This conclusion emerges more strongly for the years 1945-1977. An analysis of year to year changes in world and Peruvian output reveals that the differences between changes in world and Peruvian production are considerably greater in the latter period.

Applying the same statistical tests to the data from the latter period as I applied to the data from the earlier period reveals that the relationship between changes in Peruvian output and in world output in the post 1945 period is not significant.[14] When the explanatory value of changes in world prices is tested, the regression indicates that there is no relationship at all between changes in world metals prices and mining production in Peru, both using a non-lagged and a lagged specification. That is, taken alone, changes in world prices are not significantly related to changes in Peruvian output. These statistical results indicate that it is the "other things" besides world price that are most important in explaining changes in Peruvian production.

This surprising result contradicts theory, whether neoclassical or Marxian. Other things being equal, higher prices should induce greater production and vice versa. In the real world, however, other things are not equal.[15] Price is but one among a number of factors that condition the profitability of mining production. Statistical analysis reveals that throughout most of the twentieth century factors other than short-term fluctuations in prices have been most important in conditioning the development of the mining industry in Peru. For

58

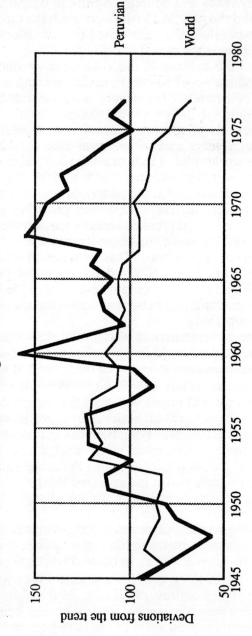

FIGURE 2.5 Trend Analysis of the Volume of Production [a] in the World and Peruvian Mining Industries, 1945-1977

SOURCES: The same as Table 2.2.

[a]The volume of production is measured in constant 1963 prices.

the most part, mineowners were unable to adjust the level of production within a period of several years to fluctuations in world metals prices.

Although statistical tests reveal no significant correlation between the movement of world metals prices and total world mineral output on the one hand, and total mineral production in Peru on the other, it is possible that the construction of composite indexes of the volume of mineral output obscures a significant relationship between the Peruvian and the world mining industry for each particular metal, taken individually. To determine whether this is indeed the case, I test the correspondence between the movement of world metals prices, world mineral output, and mineral production in Peru for the three major metals produced in Peru in the post-1945 period: copper, lead, and zinc. These tests also reveal that the relationship between changes in world prices and world-wide production on the one hand and Peruvian production on the other hand for each of the three metals is not significant. In other words, changes in Peru's output of copper, lead, and zinc cannot be explained by changes in the world prices or the world output of these metals.[16]

The discontinuous pattern of growth of Peruvian copper production is revealed with striking clarity in Table 2.3 and Figure 2.6. The latter graphically illustrates the contrast between the steady, incremental expansion of world copper production and the irregular, spasmodic growth pattern of copper production in Peru. The great leaps in Peru's output of copper coincided with the inauguration of the large open-pit copper mines, not with short-term changes in metals prices or world production. Copper production in Peru almost quadrupled between 1959 and 1960, the year the Toquepala mine opened. When Cuajone, another large open-pit copper mine, came on-stream in late 1976, the output of copper in Peru increased by 60 percent.

Extensive exploration, followed by the construction of the mine, processing plants, and transport facilities, involved in the exploitation of a large scale, low-grade copper deposit requires a large investment. Frequently it is beyond the financial capabilities of one company alone, even one of the largest mining companies in the world, to develop an open-pit mine. In the case of the copper deposits in southern Peru, the scale of investment required to bring the mines into operation necessitated the formation of a consortium of four of the world's largest mining companies. This consortium, which took the name Southern Peru Copper Corporation, put

60

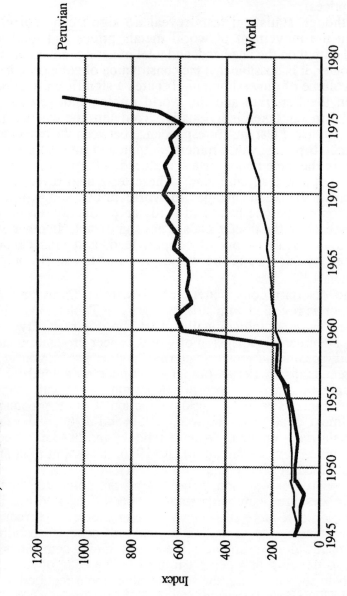

FIGURE 2.6 Indexes of Peruvian and World Copper
Production, 1945-1977

SOURCES: The same as Table 2.2.

TABLE 2.3 Copper Production in the Peruvian and the World Mining Industries, 1945-1977

Year	(Thousands of Metric Tons) World	Peru
1945	2172	31.6
1946	1848	24.3
1947	2229	22.3
1948	2323	17.6
1949	2268	27.6
1950	2525	33.3
1951	2662	35.4
1952	2766	30.3
1953	2802	33.6
1954	2852	40.1
1955	3112	41.4
1956	3470	45.4
1957	3556	54.8
1958	3449	51.9
1959	3693	50.5
1960	4242	184.0
1961	4394	197.5
1962	4555	165.4
1963	4624	180.1
1964	4799	176.4
1965	4963	180.3
1966	5216	200.0
1967	5057	192.7
1968	5456	212.5
1969	5942	198.9
1970	6384	220.2
1971	6459	207.3
1972	7042	219.1
1973	7509	202.7
1974	7653	211.6
1975	7317	181.0
1976	7854	220.3
1977	7981	350.4

SOURCES: The same as for Table 2.2.

together a financial package to develop the Cuajone and Toquepala mines.[17] In general, once funds are raised it takes years to construct the mine, processing, and transport infrastructure that must be in place before production can begin. In the case of the Cuajone mine almost a decade elapsed between the initiation of negotiations between the Peruvian government and the Southern Peru Copper Corporation and the inauguration of the mine. Therefore, as a consequence of the size of the financial commitment required to develop a major open-pit mine, as well as of the long period that elapses between the conception and the inauguration of a mine, in the second half of the twentieth century there occurred a major transformation in the nature of the mining industry on a world scale.

Conclusion

Statistical analysis indicates that world market prices and production in the world mining industry did not determine the pattern of growth of metal production in Peru. Between 1900 and 1945, prior to the advent of open-pit mining in Peru, there is a statistically significant, though not high, correlation between movements in world metals prices and world mineral production and the growth of the mining industry in Peru. However, after 1945 there is no correlation between the level of metal output in Peru and world prices and world production. Following the initiation of open-pit mining, conditions in the world market exert little direct influence on the level of metal production in the short and medium term. To the extent that prices and demand influenced the level of metal production in Peru in the second half of the twentieth century, it was as one among a number of statistical indicators that are used to forecast long-term trends in world prices and world demand. Decisions by mining companies to expand or contract mining capacity are based on these predictions. Once companies establish production targets the actual level of mining output depends largely upon local political, social, and economic conditions.

The purpose of this chapter has been to consider the relationship between Peruvian metal production and the world market, and specifically to test the hypothesis that changes in Peruvian production can be explained in large part by external factors. That is, I have sought to test the proposition that the Peruvian industry can be treated as an extension of the world market for metals. The result of testing that proposition is to reject it. For the pre-1945 period, world prices play a significant but minor explanatory role. For the latter period, they play no significant explanatory role whatsoever. On this basis, I proceed to analyze factors internal to the Peruvian economy and society that may have exerted considerable influence on the growth of the Peruvian mining industry.

CHAPTER THREE

The Transformation of Highland Society and the Historical Roots of Industrial Mining

The mineral reserves of Peru have been worked since pre-Hispanic times. Nevertheless, there is little information about how the mines were exploited, how artisan miners were integrated into *ayllus* or communities, or how precious metals were distributed prior to the Spanish conquest. However, because the search for silver and gold was the driving force for Spanish colonization in the New World, there is a relative abundance of information on mining throughout the period of Spanish rule. One of the principal objectives of the Spanish colonial administration was to secure an adequate labor force to work the mines. This proved to be exceedingly difficult in the sixteenth century and remained so for the three centuries of colonial period and through the nineteenth century. During these years the size and characteristics of the labor force were conditioned by the multiple forms of resistance to forced labor in the mines as well as by demographic trends. Nevertheless, there was no fundamental change in the availability of labor for mining until the middle of the twentieth century. Over the course of four hundred years succeeding generations of colonial administrators, mineowners, and managers of large foreign mining companies confronted the formidable task of maintaining a work force in the mines. From the time of the Spanish conquest until the 1940s the scarcity and transience of labor for the mines were the major barriers to the expansion of mining production in Peru.

Potosí: The Magic Mountain of the Viceroyalty of Peru

The Spaniards discovered the great silver mines of Potosí in 1545.[1] The richness and accessibility of the veins immediately attracted a wave of prospectors, both Spanish and Indian, who sought to make their fortunes. The Spanish crown moved quickly to regulate the chaos that accompanied the rush to Potosí. Under Spanish law all minerals within the Empire belonged to the Crown, which leased concessions at Potosí to Spaniards to exploit particular sections of the mineral vein. In exchange for royal concessions the Spanish mineowners, or *azogueros* as they were known in colonial Peru, paid a royalty of one-fifth of the silver they produced.

From the outset one of the major problems besetting the first Spanish mineowners was the difficulty of securing laborers to work in the mines. The Spanish conquest of Peru engendered havoc in Indian society, causing widespread population relocation and social disruption. However, despite major upheaval the vast majority of the native population retained its ability to produce its own subsistence needs in much the same way as it had for generations. Through traditional social networks virtually the entire indigenous population had access to land, seeds, and the primitive tools that were used to plough the earth, harvest the crops, and construct dwellings. With these resources the *ayllus* managed to sustain themselves through farming, grazing, seasonal migration, and barter.[2]

To alleviate the scarcity of labor that was crippling their nascent enterprises, the Spanish settlers pressured the Crown to impose tributes and taxes in kind, in silver, and in labor upon the conquered Indian communities. The *encomienda*, a royal grant of rights to Indian tribute, enabled Spanish settlers to institutionalize their control over a portion of the labor and the products of the Indian communities. For example, the Spanish *encomenderos* appropriated a part of the harvest of the Indian communities under their jurisdiction. Furthermore, communities were obliged to provide laborers to carry out tasks assigned to them by their *encomendero*. In addition to these tributes the colonial administration levied taxes in labor, cash, and in kind for the benefit of the Crown. These early forms of tribute were the catalyst that produced the first labor force at Potosí. By 1549 *encomienda* Indians from all parts of the Viceroyalty of Peru were forced to work in the mines by their Spanish masters.[3] Other laborers in the Potosí mines were sent there by *kurakas*, the local indigenous chiefs, who needed silver to meet the royal tribute and tax obligations levied on their *ayllus*. In the sixteenth century payment at the mines was in raw or coined silver. This silver was appropriated by the *kurakas*, from whom it was claimed subsequently by the colonial administration.[4]

In the first decades after the Spanish conquest silver mining at Potosí was carried out predominately by laborers who were forced to work in the mines to fulfill obligations to Spanish *encomenderos* and the indigenous elite. However, the work force was not composed entirely of forced laborers. A small minority of the Indians who labored in the Potosí mines did so without compulsion. The turmoil of the conquest created a small number of displaced persons without ties to land or to an *ayllu*. Some of these *yanaconas*, as they were called, were lured to Potosí, attracted by tales of mountains of silver. The more fortunate *yanaconas* became skilled miners, proficient at identifying minerals, following the veins, and refining ore. These craftsmen were in great demand because their skills were exceedingly rare in colonial Peru.

For almost twenty-five years following the Spanish discovery of the silver mines at Potosí these informal methods of compulsion for the many and enticement for the few sufficed to mine and process the rich ore bodies. However, by the 1560s silver production began to decline because of social and technological constraints. Once the high-grade ores close to the surface were depleted it was necessary to deepen the shafts and extend the tunnels to follow the veins. This required a larger number of workers than could be provided by the networks of *encomenderos* and *kurakas*. As the horrors of work in the mines became known, *kurakas* refused to send men to labor at Potosí. In the 1560s sabotage and subversion disrupted the Indian labor draft as Andean communities resisted the Spanish imposition of forced labor. The Crown was particularly concerned by the decline in silver production because its portion of the product, the *quinto real* (or royalty of one-fifth of total silver produced) was central to the solvency of the royal treasury.

By 1572 the King's supreme representative in Peru, Viceroy Francisco de Toledo, concluded that there was an inadequate number of workers at Potosí. He was convinced that more silver could be produced if the mineowners were assured a steady stream of laborers. Concluding that the task of maintaining a large work force at the mines could not be left to the *encomenderos*, the *kurakas*, or to chance, Toledo determined that the state should assume the responsibility for securing labor for the mines at Potosí. He determined that there was no viable alternative to forced labor in the mines.[5]

Forced Indian labor for mineral extraction already had an unfortunate history in the New World. The first Spanish colonizers of the Caribbean compelled the natives of the islands to excavate and pan for gold. Within several decades the indigenous population of the Caribbean was virtually extinct. Although now it is believed that the decimation of the Caribbean population was not the result of forced labor alone, the Spanish authorities believed otherwise. Consequently, in 1542 Charles V of Spain decreed that the Indians of the New World should not be compelled to labor in mineral extraction.[6] Notwithstanding this royal decree, thirty years later Viceroy Toledo designed a draft labor system to force the male population of the Andean highlands to work in the mines of Potosí.

Committed to forced labor, Toledo nonetheless was aware of the disastrous precedent of the Caribbean. Therefore, the forced labor system that he created was designed to protect the lives of the miners, to preserve the indigenous population. The first *mita minera*, as the forced labor system for the mines was called, was implemented in 1573.[7] According to its provisions Indian laborers were drawn from sixteen "obligated" communities, all at extremely high altitudes, comparable to Potosí. The rationale for the selection of the communities was that the population in these areas was accustomed to working at high altitudes; consequently the Indian men would adjust to the work in the mines of Potosí, located at approximately 15,000 feet above sea level. The viceroyal decree required one-seventh of the tribute-paying males in each of the designated communities to work in the mines for a period of one year. During his year of service each laborer was to work one week out of every three. Toledo decreed that *mitayos* (the Indian men drafted under the *mita*) should be paid for their work, as well as for their travel to and from the mines. Finally, to provide minimum health protection to the miners, Toledo prohibited the imposition of production quotas. While the formulation of these regulations was no doubt motivated by some humanitarian concern, the primary impetus for this protective legislation was that the Spaniards endeavored to avoid the genocide that accompanied the conquest in the Caribbean. The riches of the New World, the silver of Potosí, was accessible to the Spaniards only if they could harness the labor of the native population.

With the arrival at Potosí of the first *mita* Indians in 1573 the labor force at the mine was composed predominately of forced laborers. There were 4,300 *mitayos*, compelled to work in the mines under Toledo's new decree. There was an almost equal number of *ayllu* Indians, sent to the mines by their *kurakas* to earn silver to pay the taxes and tributes levied by the royal treasury on each Andean community. In addition, there were approximately 900 *yanaconas* who apparently worked in the mines voluntarily.[8] This suggests that at the inception of the *mita* most workers in the mines were forced rather than free laborers. Evidence indicates that of the ten percent of the labor force that worked voluntarily in the mines, most were artisans who performed skilled work, not unskilled laborers. As an enticement, artisans received wages that were approximately double those purportedly paid to *mitayos*. In addition, they were allowed to extract and process silver for their personal benefit when not laboring for the Spanish mineowners.

In its early years the *mita* appears to have accomplished its objective. With approximately 8,500 Indians laboring in the mines as a result of the direct and indirect coercion of the Crown, the mineowners were able to increase the output of silver substantially. In 1592 silver production at Potosí reached its peak.[9] Thereafter production declined. In large part the fall in silver production reflected the inability of the colonial administration to enforce the *mita*. In addition, the readily accessible veins of high-grade ores were depleted. Finally, a shortage of mercury, a vital ingredient in the silver processing techniques of the day, exacerbated the decline in the quantity and the quality of the ores. Although mercury was mined in Huancavelica in the central highlands of Peru and transported to Potosí, there was not enough mercury to process all of the silver extracted from the magic mountain at Potosí.

The *mita* suffered great transformations in the course of the seventeenth and eighteenth centuries, in large part because the draft labor system intensified the metamorphosis of Indian society. The establishment of the *mita* accentuated the disruption of the indigenous social order as families fled their communities to evade the labor draft, flight being the primary form of resistance. Some fugitives settled in communities exempted from the *mita*, while others escaped into regions yet to be pacified by the Spaniards. Still other Indians fleeing the labor draft sought the protection of landowners who, like all Spaniards in Peru, were plagued by a scarcity of laborers. Ironically, in its later years, the forced labor policy for Potosí provided a labor force for the haciendas. Many Indians preferred to settle on a hacienda, where they owed tribute only to the *hacendado*, rather than remain in communities that were subject not only to the *mita minera* but to additional tributes and taxes levied by the Crown.

Throughout the seventeenth century there was an acute shortage of workers at Potosí. The fundamental cause of the labor shortage was that the Indian communities retained access to land and maintained their subsistence economy. Under these conditions there was no economic imperative driving Indians to seek work in the mines. Ultimately only by resorting to violent enforcement of the *mita* could the colonial state force masses of Indians to go to the mines. In part the shortage of laborers was the result of widespead evasion of the *mita*. In addition, the scarcity of labor reflected a dramatic decline in the indigenous population. In the wake of the social dislocation and the epidemics of disease that accompanied the Spanish conquest there was a demographic crisis throughout Peru. Population decline was particularly drastic in the highland regions that were subject to the labor draft for the mines. The reduction in the population in these communities was caused by flight to evade the *mita*, the high mortality rate in the mines, and the ravages of disease.

In the seventeenth century Spanish mineowners continually appealed to the Viceroy and the Crown to reorganize the *mita* in order to guarantee them more labor. In response to these pleas each succeeding Viceory adjusted, extended, or reorganized the labor draft to compel more Indians to work in the Potosí mines.[10] At the best of times these adjustments were ineffective. Frequently they aggravated the very problems they were designed to redress. Evasion of the *mita* was so rampant throughout the seventeenth century that in practice increasingly it became a money tribute obligation rather than a labor draft. As early as 1600, *kurakas* frequently were unable to deliver the required number of *mitayos* to Potosí. In consequence, it gradually became accepted practice for *kurakas* to send a money payment in lieu of an Indian laborer. Some mineowners used this income to pay a free or *minga* worker to carry out the tasks of a *mitayo*.[11] Although *minga* workers were not formally classified as forced laborers or *mitayos*, many of them were not free laborers, at the mines of their own volition. Some (perhaps most) of the *mingas* were obliged to labor in the mines by their *kurakas* to earn silver that would be used by the *kuraka* to make the *mita* payment. In other words, while the *minga* workers were not, stricly speaking, draft laborers, they were *mita* Indians once removed, driven to the mines by compulsion, not drawn there voluntarily by the enticement of a money wage.

The transformation of the forced labor draft into a monetary tribute appears to have worked to the advantage of the mineowners, at least on occasion. Increasingly mineowners would forgo production. Instead of mining silver they would "mine" the *kurakas*. Mineowners frequently closed down their mining operations and simply collected the *mita* payments that *kurakas* were forced to make. This suggests that mineowners might have found it more profitable simply to collect the *mita* payment than to mine for silver. As this practice became more common, the *mita* transformed, in custom though not in law, into a personal tax levied by the mineowners on the *kurakas*. If a *kuraka* proved unable to pay the sum of silver that was demanded by a mineowner, it was not uncommon for the *kuraka* and his family to be imprisoned and tortured for his debts.[12]

Over the course of the seventeenth century the shortage of workers became increasingly acute, and silver production continued to decline. Even though the silver payments extracted from the *kurakas* could be used to pay wages, mineowners were unable to attract a sufficient number of workers to sustain the production levels of the previous century. As the seventeenth century progressed the implementation of the *mita* diverged more and more from the idealized construct of Viceroy Toledo. As the silver boom at Potosí receded further and further into the past, so did the legislation protecting the welfare of the *mitayos*. Conditions became more oppressive as *mitayos* were forced to work every other week, at the minimum, instead of one week in three. Production quotas were instituted and *mitayos* worked excessively long hours to fulfill their quotas. On top of this, the meager wage stipulated by Toledo frequently was not paid, either for work or travel. Even at the best of times, when *mitayos* received the stipulated money wage, this stipend was insufficient to feed and clothe the *mita* Indians. Therefore, despite the money wage, communities had to provision their *mitayos* throughout their year at the mines. Some particularly enterprising mineowners sold or rented the workers they received through the *mita* to other Spaniards in desperate need of laborers. This deterioration of the working conditions of *mitayos* provoked more Indians to evade the labor draft or to flee from the mines.

By the latter half of the seventeenth century the labor shortage was so dire that the viceroys took drastic action. First they expanded the number of communities subject to the *mita*. In addition, they decreed that all male residents of a region would be subject to the draft, instead of only the tribute-paying males of each *ayllu*, as previously stipulated in law. In response there was a vicious cycle of flight, evasion, and fewer *mitayos*.[13] As the colonial administration endeavored to force more workers to labor in the mines more Indians found ways to evade the draft.

In the eighteenth century silver production expanded at Potosí. This revival coincided with the establishment of a new dynasty in Spain. The Spanish throne passed from the House of Hapsburg to the Bourbons of France. This dynastic change brought a transformation of the administration of the colonies as the Bourbons implemented reforms to revitalize their overseas empire. Historians have argued that the Bourbon reforms were responsible for the expansion of silver production in Spanish America, though the impact of the reforms actually was rather mixed.[14] A royal decree of 1736 halved the Crown's share of the silver produced in the New World from one-fifth to one-tenth. This reduction in the royal tax (royalty) on silver has been interpreted as a particularly significant incentive to mineowners to expand output. Later in the century the Spanish Crown made efforts to re-exert its authority over the mining sector, by centralizing important activities under royal control. The Crown sought to safeguard the expansion of silver production and to guarantee its share of the output by establishing a *Tribunal de Minería* and a royal bank in Potosí. The bank monopolized the marketing of silver and the extension of credit for mining activities. No longer were the mine operators permitted to sell silver to independent merchants, nor to receive credit from private sources. By establishing the royal bank the Crown attempted to reduce the flourishing contraband trade in silver that evaded the royal tax, and to provide more credit to loyal and law-abiding mine operators.[15] There can be little doubt that the reduction of the royalty was beneficial to the mineowners. However, the more important issue is how the mineowners were able to raise production after a century of decline. Recent scholarship demonstrates convincingly that the expansion of output was primarily the result of increasing the exploitation of *mita* labor.[16]

The labor shortage at the mines intensified in the eighteenth century, despite the growth in the indigenous population after one hundred and fifty years of decline. In the almost fifty years between 1692 and 1740 the number of *mitayos* declined from about 4,000 to 2,800. Successive reorganizations of the *mita* were undertaken to recruit more workers, but these efforts were largely futile. The vigilance of colonial administrators to ensure enforcement of the labor draft was unsuccessful. The number of *mitayos* remained approximately the same from 1740 until the end of the century. Mineowners continually complained that there were not enough workers, neither *mitayos* nor *mingas*, to satisfy their demand for labor.[17] Therefore, the mineowners used the *mitayos* at hand to the fullest extent, which meant imposing production quotas on each worker. In their efforts to maintain the overall level of production, the mineowners raised the quotas incrementally as the number of *mitayos* declined. Between 1740 and the end of the century the volume of silver ore that each *mitayo* was required to extract from the mine approximately doubled.[18] In order that *mita* Indians might fulfill their quotas, the prescribed weeks of rest were eliminated and *mitayos* labored long hours throughout the year. Frequently women and children relatives of *mitayos* worked in the mines and processing plants alongside the draft laborers to meet the tribute obligation. The Bourbon "reform" that proved crucial to the revitalization of the mining sector was the tacit acceptance of the mineowners' right to use and abuse their *mita* Indians in the way they chose.

Increasing output in the mining sector was achieved primarily by extending the length of the period of work and pressing relatives to assist in meeting production quotas. In addition, there were technological changes that raised productivity. At the end of the eighteenth century, with the assistance of the Crown, the mineowners arranged for the Nordenflict Mission of European mining experts to visit the mines. The Mission recommended changes in mining techniques, some of which were adopted.

Despite the acute labor shortage in the mines the proportion of *minga* workers at Potosí remained constant from the middle seventeenth century to the end of the eighteenth century— approximately one half of the labor force.[19] Few *mingas* worked voluntarily. Many were *mitayos* who worked in the mines beyond the obligatory year of service in order to complete their production quotas. Others were from the families of *mita* Indians, laboring to assist relatives. Although classified as *minga* or free laborers, there was little freedom of choice for these laborers in the mines. Many *mingas* were men who accumulated debts while they worked as *mitayos*. Indebtedness was not unusual as *mita* indians were required to supply candles to light their way underground, and often resorted to purchasing food from the mineowners. Because the meager wage that *mitayos* nominally were paid (though rarely saw in practice) was insufficient to cover the cost of their basic survival needs, *mita* Indians frequently had no choice but to remain working in the mines after they completed their year of forced labor in order to pay off their debts. At the end of the eighteenth century an observer wrote,

> With all this [the *mita*], the unhappy Indians cannot find the relief which the King wishes them to have...because during the time that the *mita* lasts, they themselves and their families spend much more on their keep than they can earn. Consequently, they are in debt and when they leave this has to be paid off, so that they are poorer than before; and forced to beg or steal or to hide in the town, to get jobs as domestics or *minga* (that is to say, to work as free laborers)...[20]

Finally, as in earlier periods, the *minga* workers included *ayllu* Indians who were sent to the mines by their *kuraka*. Although many of the men and women who were classified as receiving wages, few or none were free wage laborers. Undoubtedly among the *mingas* were some who had ties neither to Indian communities nor to haciendas. Their labor was motivated by the economic compulsion to earn enough money to support themselves and their families (or, as is alleged by contemporary observers, to support their drinking and carousing). These *mingas* were predominately artisans who became highly-skilled in mining techniques, and who were in great demand at the mines.

With few exceptions the Indians who labored in the mines of colonial Peru were forced to do so by the combined authority of the colonial state, the *kurakas*, and the mineowners. When Indians or *kurakas* attempted to evade their obligations, the violent enforcement of the *mita* soon reminded them of the necessity of fulfilling the tribute and tax obligations imposed by the Spanish Crown.

For centuries the *mita* has generated great debate. Throughout its reign of two hundred and fifty years, which was more often than not a reign of terror for the Indian population, the *mita* was a source of contention. Its critics pleaded with the Crown for its abolition, both on humanitarian and practical grounds. Critics argued that the *mita* was decimating the indigenous population, itself one of the greatest riches of the New World. They argued as well that the labor draft for the mines was robbing other enterprises of workers. Advocates of the *mita*, generally the viceroys, colonial administrators, and the mineowners themselves, demanded that it be expanded and enforced as the only method to secure a labor force in the mines.

The debate about the *mita* continues to this day. At present the primary issue is not whether the *mita* was good or bad, but whether the labor force in the mines of colonial Peru was predominately forced or free. A decade or two ago most historians agreed that the Indians who worked in the mines of Potosí were compelled to do so.[21] More recently some scholars of colonial Peru, possibly influenced by dependency theory, have suggested that a large number of the workers in the mines were free wage laborers. They argue that these workers were not forced to labor at Potosí, but did so voluntarily; attracted by the incentive of money wages.[22] These studies fail to capture the essence of the labor relations that characterized the mining sector, suggesting that free wage labor existed in the mines in colonial Peru. This comes close to the position that the mines were capitalist enterprises, characterized by the co-existence of capitalist production relations and forced labor. Some scholars explicitly embrace this view.

An analysis of the nature of the labor force in the mines is important not only for a history of the mining sector. It forms a crucial part of our understanding of the nature of colonial society in general in the Viceroyalty of Peru. The view that the labor force was characterized in large part by free wage labor creates a vision of colonial society that is erroneous. It implies the generalization of a complex of social structures that did not characterize colonial society. The view that free wage labor predominated in the mining sector in colonial Peru suggests that there was an extended labor market, that peasants and Indians generally were free to seek wage employment, and they were driven to do so by economic necessity. In addition, this position assumes the separation of a large portion of the Indian society from access to land and from the ability to reproduce their households and communities.[23] These conditions were to develop very slowly and unevenly in the course of the nineteenth and twentieth centuries. As I argue in Chapters Four and Five, the mass of the highland peasantry of Peru did not lose its access to land until the mid-twentieth century. Consequently it was not until quite recently that the mining sector, and highland society in Peru more generally, was predominately characterized by free wage labor.

Money payment alone signifies little about the nature of production relations. *Mitayos* received a monetary payment, in theory if not always in practice. Nonetheless, they were forced laborers: compelled to work in the mines by the authority of the colonial state. Likewise, the occasional incidence of labor for wages does not indicate that production is organized according to capitalist principles. Throughout most of recorded history some sectors of society have had to work for money payment. However, this alone does not generate the conditions for the spread of free wage labor and capitalist production. Conditions are present for the development of capitalism only when large numbers of direct producers are displaced from the land, and when the traditional ties that unite them to landowners disintegrate. These conditions allow large numbers of laborers to search for wage employment; and forces them to do so in order to survive.

The *mita minera* was legally abolished in 1812. However, state sponsored labor drafts for the mines continued to function unofficially for several more decades due to a shortage of workers. The succeeding chapters describe how this shortage continued unabated throughout the nineteenth and well into the twentieth centuries. Through the first decades of the twentieth century most peasants and Indians in highland Peru produced their own foodstuffs, clothing, tools, seeds, and other necessities within the household, the community, and the hacienda. In this social order the offer of a money wage was insufficient to recruit large numbers of workers to the mines.

Mining in the Central Highlands of Colonial Peru

Only two mining centers in the Viceroyalty of Peru had the legal right to workers recruited through the *mita minera*: Potosí and Huancavelica. Huancavelica was of great importance because it was the site of a large mercury mine. Mercury was the key element in the *patio* process, a method invented in the sixteenth century to extract silver from low-grade ores. The mines of Huancavelica were the only major source of mercury in the New World. When mercury production declined at Huancavelica it was necessary to import mercury from Spain to process silver.

Although the other mining centers in the Viceroyalty were legally excluded from the *mita minera*, owners of mines in these regions frequently collaborated with local colonial administrators and *hacendados* to implement a regional labor draft. Cerro de Pasco in the central highlands, not far from Huancavelica, had been a mining center since 1630. However, mining at Cerro de Pasco languished throughout the seventeenth century and for most of the eighteenth century, in large measure for lack of official support.

While the colonial administration fostered mining production at Potosí and Huancavelica through the *mita*, credit facilities, and official marketing institutions, it all but neglected the other mining centers. Mineowners at Cerro de Pasco complained that colonial administrators were not responsive to the needs of the lesser mining regions. Beset by a series of obstacles ranging from an acute shortage of workers to insufficient funds to invest in maintenance and expansion of the mines, production at Cerro de Pasco was barely profitable and output was of little significance until the last third of the eighteenth century.[24]

In 1776 the Viceroyalty of Río de la Plata was carved out of the Viceroyalty of Peru, and Potosí passed to this new jurisdiction. This administrative restructuring had a major impact on the regional economy as the transport and commercialization of silver passed from Lima to Buenos Aires. However, the administrative change did not signal the demise of mining production in the territory that remained in the Viceroyalty of Peru, for it coincided with the expansion of silver production in the mines of the central and northern highlands. Between 1777 and 1812 silver production in the then-reduced Viceroyalty of Peru more than tripled.[25] Most of this growth took place in the mines around Cerro de Pasco.

Throughout the eighteenth century the mines in the Pasco region were plagued by drainage problems. In 1760 a mineowner built a drainage tunnel which initially facilitated the deeper exploitation of the mineral veins. However, in the early 1770s production began to decline as the veins above the water level were exhausted. In 1780, fifty mineowners at Cerro de Pasco collaborated to build a major drainage tunnel. This reduced the immediate flooding problem and output increased significantly. Nevertheless, little by little renewed flooding again began to plague operations.[26]

Though production increased in the Peruvian mines at the end of the eighteenth century and in the first decades of the nineteenth century, expansion was greatly restricted by an acute shortage of labor. There is evidence that the endemic scarcity of labor in the mines intensified in the last decades of the viceroyalty as the mechanisms for forcing Indians to work in the mines deteriorated.[27] The termination of the *repartimiento de mercancías* in 1784 reduced the Indians' need to work in the mines to earn cash.[28] Although legally the *mita minera* did not directly benefit the mineowners of Cerro de Pasco, its legal abolition in 1812 made it more difficult (though not impossible) to impose the customary local labor drafts. At the same time as the mineowners were appealing to the Crown to reinstate and expand the scope of the *mita*, they were collaborating with colonial officials to implement unofficial labor drafts that bore such ironic names as *socorro voluntario* (voluntary assistance).

In 1791 a mineowner wrote "the shortage of workers [is the] principal, first, and most severe cause of the decline in Peruvian mining."[29] In 1786 the Intendent, the local colonial administrator in Huancavelica, wrote that it was necessary to use "violent measures" to force the Indians to perform wage labor. He explained that the Indians were refusing to perform light tasks in the mining centers even when they were offered good salaries and payment in advance. In this document the Intendent lamented that the mines were full of rich ores but the mineowners and colonial administrators had been unsuccessful in forcing Indians to cooperate to extract the metal.[30]

At the close of the colonial period the mass of the population of Peru retained its access to the land, continued to directly produce its own subsistence requirements, and consequently had little need of a cash income. For this reason money wages alone did not attract large numbers of workers to the mines. Mineowners relied on forced recruiting imposed by the colonial apparatus to generate their work force. But even these methods failed to provide an adequate number of workers to exploit the mines to their full potential.

Obstacles to Mining Production in the Nineteenth Century

The central highlands of Peru became one of the major battlefields for the wars of independence from Spain. Fighting disrupted mineral production in the regions surrounding Huancavelica, Cerro de Pasco, and the mineralized zones closer to Lima. The success of the independence wars, secession from Spain in 1824, and the ensuing struggles within the landowning class for control of the feeble government of the new Republic ensured continuation of the general economic upheaval that began with the wars. The fragile banking system of Peru was completely disorganized. The mule and llama trains organized by local merchants and muleteers that provided transport in the central highlands were reduced in number and became more unreliable.[31] In addition, commercial links with European markets were in momentary disarray. Both exporting metal and importing the materials needed to mine and process the ores became difficult and expensive. But the principal barrier to the expansion of mining production, the problem that continually plagued mineowners and the Spanish colonial administrators since the sixteenth century, remained unresolved: the scarcity of laborers to work in the mines.

In the middle nineteenth century successive national governments exerted sporadic and usually ineffectual efforts to introduce liberal reforms. Although the government decreed the abolition of the Indian labor draft, in practice *caudillos* and local landowners and mineowners continued to compel Indians and the rural poor to perform paid and unpaid labor in much the same manner as in previous centuries. As a result of the abolition of the *mita*, labor drafts became more localized as well as more disorganized than before; and labor obligations decreased.

In the mid-nineteenth century there was a movement which called for the elimination of the protected status of Indian communities. This status nominally gave Indian communities the inalienable right to their land. Out of this movement came legislation that legalized the commercialization of the lands of Indian communities. But the successive passage and repeal of these laws had only a limited effect upon the alienation of land in the highlands. By the middle nineteenth century some community lands in the central highlands were privatized, but relatively few; there was yet to be a generalized market in land in that region.[32] At that time Indians, peasants, and *colonos*, or tenants in servitude on haciendas, retained direct access to land, animals, and tools. For this reason mineowners and other would-be entrepreneurs still faced great difficulty in recruiting workers.

Commercial mining in Peru was extremely depressed in the middle of the nineteenth century. The little mining that occurred was for silver. Production units were small, generally including the mineowner, relatives, and perhaps several artisans who worked on a basis similar to share-cropping. The product of their labor was divided between the artisans and the owners of the mine. Some *hacendados* organized mining activities on their estates, basing production on the labor tribute of their *colonos*. Things had changed very little since the end of the colonial period.

In the middle nineteenth century guano, or bird excrement, was exported from Peru to Europe to be used as fertilizer. By the 1840s guano became the major Peruvian export and the source of substantial state revenues. The guano was found on islands that were the property of the state. Consequently, for a fixed share of the total value of guano sales the government of Peru leased out the right to exploit guano. The 1870s was a period of change in Peru as state revenues from the guano boom were used to develop an infrastructure to facilitate the expansion of commercial activities in different sectors of the economy. At this time commercial production was primarily for export, in large part because the vast majority of the Peruvian population had little necessity or ability to participate in the marketplace. The urban population, the one group that purchased the bulk of its consumption requirements, was exceedingly small. For this reason the internal market in Peru, particularly in the highlands, was extremely restricted.

Government revenue from the exploitation of guano was spent to initiate the construction of a railway from Lima into the foothills of the central highlands and to build roads. The improved transportation system facilitated the movement of products, both to Lima and to the ports for shipment abroad. The tremendous increase in state funds and the construction projects initiated by the government necessitated the expansion of the state bureaucracy and the reorganization of the financial system.[33] These activities promoted the expansion of the population of Lima and demand by urban residents for an array of products, particularly foodstuffs.

This commercial expansion affected the central highlands. *Hacendados* attempted to take advantage of the improved transportation system and the growing internal market by expanding market-oriented production. They sought to accomplish this by exacting more tribute from their *colonos* and enlarging the area of land devoted to commercial crops. Often this resulted in reductions in the size of the plots allocated to *colonos* for subsistence production. At the same time *hacendados* sought to purchase or appropriate land belonging to peasant communities. Concurrently, the increasing commercialization of highland society engendered social differentiation within peasant communities. Some community members endeavored to control more land at the expense of their neighbors. The claim to land alone was of little use, however, unless it was accompanied by the ability to command more labor in reciprocal exchange relationships. Therefore, fundamental to the social differentiation within peasant communities was the emergence of differences in access to labor. The nature and extent of these transformations varied considerably from one hacienda and community to another.[34] Evidence indicates that as early as the 1870s, due to loss of access to land, the poorest peasant families in some communities found it more and more difficult to sustain the members of their households through self-provisioning alone. For these families it became necessary to supplement subsistence production with paid labor.[35]

The commercial boom of the 1870s was brief and had little or no lasting effect upon the vast majority of the population of Peru, particularly of the highlands. For the most part the social networks and economic activities of peasants and *colonos* were unchanged. They remained subsistence producers. Although some of the constraints on mining that beset the industry in the early decades after independence were partially resolved, there remained a critical shortage of labor throughout the nineteenth century.

The gradual abolition of the Indian labor draft required mineowners to employ new methods to secure control over labor. The expanding commercialization of highland society in the late nineteenth century facilitated the adaptation of debt servitude to the needs of mineowners. Debt servitude had been used to compel the Indian and *mestizo* poor to work on haciendas and in the mines since the early years of Spanish rule. However, the commercialization of the 1870s contributed to the relative impoverishment of the poorer members of rural society; those families with access to land of an inferior quality or in lesser quantity than others in the community. As more and more families were obliged to supplement their subsistence household economy with cash, the possibilities of using debt servitude to gain access to labor expanded. This possibility was quickly seized upon by *hacendados* and mineowners.

Hacendados, local merchants, and richer peasants became the creditors and the labor contractors of highland society. In the case of the mines, mineowners advanced cash to influential members of the local community. These local notables became labor contractors and in turn advanced money to peasants in need of cash. The peasants agreed to repay their debt by working for the mineowner. In the nineteenth century this system of debt servitude was known as *contrata*. With the expansion of the mining industry in the twentieth century, and the legalization and institutionalization of this form of debt servitude, the system came to be referred to by the more invidious term *enganche*.[36] Again, labor recruitment was achieved through a combination of influence, reciprocity, indebtedness, and force.

During the nineteenth century indebtedness resulted in forced labor. But this was a result specific to conditions in Peru. In other contexts, where direct producers were separated from the land, indebtedness has led to proletarianization of the rural population.[37] This process had not begun in the highlands of Peru in the late nineteenth century. Forced indebtedness resulted in debt servitude, or forced labor; not in free wage labor. For the moment, at least, most of the coerced laborers retained access to land.

The economic expansion of the early 1870s was short-lived. Although state revenue from guano declined, state expenditures continued to soar, forcing the Peruvian government to default on its bonds. This touched off a financial crisis that was intensified by the defeat of Peru by Chile in the War of the Pacific (1879-1881). After the war Peru's bondholders agreed to cancel their claims in exchange for control of the railroads and the remains of the guano trade, and other concessions. This agreement, the Grace Contract that was signed in 1890, aroused the interest of British businessmen who considered buying and developing the mineral deposits of the central highlands. Peru's bondholders, who were mostly British, formed the Peruvian Corporation in order to develop their newly acquired assets.

As a response in part to British interest in investing in silver mining in the central highlands, the Peruvian Corporation resumed construction of a central railroad. In 1893 the rail line was extended to La Oroya, a village eighty-three miles from Cerro de Pasco, in the heart of the mineral region of the central highlands. The opening of the rail head at La Oroya sparked a flurry of mining activity. It significantly reduced the cost of transporting ores from the central highlands to the port of Callao. Nevertheless, fearing a renewal of political and economic instability in Peru, the British entrepreneurs decided against making the large investments that were required to develop the mines. Mining continued to be the domain of Peruvian mineowners, characterized by relatively small production units.[38]

In the last decades of the nineteenth century copper began to replace silver as Peru's most profitable mineral product. The expansion of the railroad, innovations in processing techniques, and rising world prices combined to generate interest in copper. In 1887, before the extension of the railroad to La Oroya, a sudden increase in world copper prices sparked a boom in production known as the *boya del cobre*. During the brief copper bonanza high-grade ores were extracted and exported with little or no processing. However, given the difficulties and expense of transporting unprocessed ores by mule and llama to the rail head just outside of Lima, once the high-grade ores were depleted copper mining became unprofitable. For copper mining in the central highlands to become profitable it was necessary to smelt the ore to reduce its weight and increase its value. Because copper was more bulky and less valuable than silver, even after smelting, commercial production required a greatly improved system of transport. The reverberatory furnace, a new technique for processing ores, and the railroad, were crucial for the profitability of copper production. This smelting process made it economical to reduce the bulk of the mineral ore, facilitating its transfer to the rail head at La Oroya. By 1900 there were 17 smelters operating in the Cerro de Pasco region alone.[39]

Just when improvements in transportation and processing rekindled interest in copper production, profitability in silver mining declined. Beginning in 1885 world silver prices began a steady fall, dropping precipitously in 1892. In 1897, in the wake of the collapse of the world market for silver, the Peruvian government followed the lead of other countries and converted its currency from a silver to a gold standard, and discontinued coining silver. These measures proved disastrous for silver mining in Peru and forced many companies to close. By the turn of the twentieth century the search for precious metals ceased to dominate the Peruvian mining industry. Subsequently, the extraction of silver was generally a by-product of copper, lead, and zinc mining.

The enthusiasm for copper mining continued throughout the 1890s with intense exploration, a rush to stake claims, and the inauguration of new mines. However, serious technical and social constraints limited the expansion of production. While the extension of the Central Railway in 1893 reduced transportation costs between the central highlands and the port of Callao, the transportation network in the mineral region remained inadequate. Mineowners continued to contract mule and llama trains to transport ore to the rail head. For entrepreneurs in Cerro de Pasco this meant transporting bulky ore over eighty-three miles of mountain paths to La Oroya. Worse still was the difficulty in acquiring fuel to run the new smelters. There were coalfields about fifty miles from Cerro de Pasco, but no road or railroad from the coalfields to the mines. It was cheaper to import coal from Britain than to transport it from the coalfields in the highlands. Even if the problems of transport could be solved, there were others, equally serious, that plagued mineowners in the Cerro de Pasco region. The veins above the water table were nearly exhausted. But before the existing shafts could be lowered it was necessary to drain the mines.

Another barrier to the expansion of production was the nature of the installed capacity for smelting copper ores. In the last decade of the nineteenth century the expansion of copper production was facilitated by the proliferation of small smelters, most of which served one or two mines. Initially the construction of these smelters represented a major technological innovation, for without them the commerical mining of copper ore would not have been possible. However, by the beginning of the twentieth century the limited capacity and somewhat primitive techniques of these smelters restrained the expansion and more rational organization of mining activity. The mineowners of the Cerro de Pasco region concluded that it would be advantageous to build a large smelter that could process their combined production more efficiently.

Finally, the shortage of labor for the mines remained endemic. Impoverishment and indebtedness within highland communities compelled a growing number of peasants to seek remunerated work outside of their communities. This allowed mineowners to continue to use debt as a means of forcing peasants to labor in the mines. But *contrata* was used not because it was the preferable form of recruiting workers.[40] It was the most readily available method of compelling peasants to labor in the mines. Nevertheless, mineowners found *contrata* highly unsatisfactory for many reasons. The demand for workers outstripped the supply that was provided through debt servitude. In addition, peasants frequently abandoned the mines before completing their contracted obligation. Since there was no recognized legal authority to enforce *contrata*, it was difficult to pursue fugitive workers and to force them to return to the mines. Finally, most peasants bound by *contrata* worked in the mines only for several months. In this brief period they did not become skilled at extracting and processing the ore.[41] Therefore, the possibilities of introducing new techniques, reorganizing the production process, and raising productivity were limited by the unskilled and transient nature of the labor force.

In 1898 two North American mining engineers, Jacob Backus and J. Howard Johnston, submitted a proposal to the Peruvian government to develop the mining region around Cerro de Pasco. Backus and Johnston proposed to extend the Central Railway to Cerro de Pasco and to build a tunnel to drain the mines. In return they requested extensive rights to exploit the mines around Cerro de Pasco. The Sociedad Nacional de Minería, an association of Peruvian mineowners, urged the government to reject this proposal on the grounds that the terms were disadvantageous to the nationals who operated mines. It was clearly not in their interests to forfeit the rights to exploit the minerals in the Cerro de Pasco region, they argued. The government acceded to the wishes of the Peruvian mineowners.[42]

Over the next few years Peruvian mineowners, in collaboration with entrepreneurs, bankers, and merchants based in Lima, established a series of companies with the intention of developing the Cerro de Pasco mineral region. They endeavored to construct a drainage tunnel, a railroad to the coalfields, and a large processing plant that would use the most advanced smelting techniques of the day.[43] The companies floundered for several years, none of them able to make substantial progress. The syndicates of Peruvian mineowners faced two obstacles that proved insurmountable. The investment required to develop the infrastructure for the region exceeded the capacity of the immature Peruvian banking system. In addition, competition among the mineowners impeded collective action. Fears that the location of the drainage tunnel, railway, and smelter might benefit competitors at their own expense engendered conflicts among the mineowners.

The last years of the nineteenth century saw a period of intense competition among Peruvian mineowners. They expected that the constraints on copper production would be overcome quickly and the necessary infrastructure built that would provide adequate fuel, drainage, and transport. Consequently, many mineowners pursued an aggressive policy of buying out smaller mining companies, some of whose assets were little more than the legal claim to a mineral deposit. By 1901 there were seven mining companies which recently had expanded dramatically through the purchase of smaller companies. The largest of these held the claims to ninety mines.[44] Prospectors and investors, both Peruvian and foreign, were active in the region. There was widespread confidence that impending technological changes were about to transform the central highlands of Peru into one of the world's major mining centers.

Consolidation of the Mining Industry and the Emergence of a Free Wage Labor Force

Foreign Capital Transforms the Industry

At the close of the nineteenth century mineowners, prospectors, and speculators in the central highlands of Peru were predicting a boom in mining. They anticipated the construction of roads, railroads, smelters, and drainage tunnels that promised to overcome the obstacles to the development of the mining region. However, as the veins above the water table around Cerro de Pasco neared depletion, local entrepreneurs began to fear that ore extraction would come to a halt. Fear subsided in 1900 when local mineowners joined with entrepreneurs in Lima to form the Empresa Socavonera, (the drainage tunnel company). The Empresa Socavonera won a contract from the Peruvian government to construct a drainage tunnel in Cerro de Pasco. This brought renewed faith in the imminent prosperity of the region. Nevertheless, optimism again turned to pessimism when it became clear that rivalry among associates of the Empresa stymied the undertaking. Each shareholder in the Empresa was primarily concerned with the drainage of his/her own mines and was vigilant lest the tunnel bring greater benefits to his/her competitors. For this as well as other reasons the Empresa was unable to forge ahead with the construction of the proposed drainage tunnel.

At the turn of the century the failure of the Peruvian syndicates to improve the inadequate infrastructure convinced many mineowners that the barriers to the expansion of production would not be easily and quickly overcome.[1] Even if they were able to resolve their disputes over the location and specifications of the railway, smelter, and drainage tunnel, sufficient funds for investment were not available to them. From the middle of the nineteenth century the financial system in Peru was controlled by merchant capitalists, many of whom were European immigrants. Banking houses were established to facilitate foreign trade between Europe and Peru. Habitually the banks extended credit to *hacendados*, who organized production for export, and to the state to promote the construction of the infrastructure that was required to transport and store agricultural export products.

In the later part of the nineteenth century sugar emerged as the major export crop, grown in the valleys of the northern coast.[2] The complementary activities of the banking houses and the *hacendados* gradually developed into informal alliances.[3] By the later part of nineteenth century some of the leading merchant families became landowners and produced sugar for export. Increasingly it became difficult to distinguish between these two groups. Notable cases of merchant capitalist turned *hacendado* were the Gildemeister family and W. R. Grace. By the early twentieth century Gildemeister and Grace were among the largest sugar producers in Peru.

At the close of the nineteenth century, when mining was reviving in the central highlands, Peruvian mineowners sought to raise funds to develop the mineral region. However, banks and merchant capitalists were debilitated by the War of the Pacific which ravaged Peru from 1879 to 1881. After Peru suffered a humiliating defeat at the hands of Chile its economy collapsed. The Peruvian banking system was in ruins, and the mineowners' efforts met with scant success. Little large-scale credit was available in Peru. Investment funds were scarce and monopolized by the *hacendados* of the northern coast. Because capitalism in Peru was in embryonic form at the beginning of the twentieth century there were few alternative sources of investment funds within the country. Capitalist enterprises were few and far between, production units were small, and so were profits. Mineowners of the Cerro de Pasco region tried to raise money in Lima in order to develop the mining potential of the zone, but they met with little success.[4] Confronted with these difficulties, many of the mineowners welcomed the opportunity to sell their properties to a North American firm that rapidly was buying up mines in the area.

In 1901 a New York mining syndicate purchased approximately 80 percent of the mines in the Cerro de Pasco region in the space of three months.[5] The syndicate soon assumed the name Cerro de Pasco Mining Company in recognition of the location of its mines.[6] The prior centralization of the ownership of mines in the region in the last decade of the nineteenth century facilitated the take-over by the Cerro de Pasco Corporation. The Corporation purchased seven relatively large mining companies in 1901 and 1902, and another six companies in the next few years. With these thirteen purchases the

Corporation controlled the major mines of the central highlands of Peru.[7] The entrance of North American capital marked a major leap in the centralization of ownership in the Peruvian mining industry, but it did not initiate the process. The more successful Peruvian mineowners had been buying out smaller mining companies since the 1880s.

The centralization of ownership by the Cerro de Pasco Corporation intensified competition in the industry. Several Peruvian capitalists, among them Eulogio Fernandini, Lizandro Proaño, and Manuel Mujica, refused to sell out to the North American firm. Instead they continued to compete with the Corporation through the purchase of mines and the expansion of their processing plants.[8] In addition, the Empresa Socavonera made a last-ditch attempt to exert its influence by quickly constructing a drainage tunnel under one of the Corporation's mines. Citing the terms of an old agreement, the Empresa claimed 20 percent of the mine's ores. After claims, counter claims, and considerable violence, the Corporation and the Empresa reached an agreement whereby the Empresa renounced its right to a percentage of production in exchange for shares in the Cerro de Pasco Corporation.[9]

While the competitive struggles mounted by the Peruvian entrepreneurs were fierce and sometimes successful, the Cerro de Pasco Corporation had an insurmountable advantage: access to large investment funds in the United States. The precursor of the Cerro de Pasco Corporation, the New York Syndicate, was formed by the leading capitalists in the United States, among them J. P. Morgan, Henry Clay Frick, and Cornelius Vanderbilt. With such powerful and illustrious backers it is little wonder that the Corporation was able to raise the capital it required from financial institutions in the United States. It is estimated that by 1910 the Cerro de Pasco Corporation invested US$ 25 million in Peru in the purchase of mines and the construction of roads, railroads, and a smelter.[10] For that period this was a large investment, even by New York standards.

The entry of the Cerro de Pasco Corporation into Peru coincided with the Peruvian government's application of a laissez-faire policy in the mining sector.[11] In 1901 the government of President López de Romaña enacted a new mining code designed to stimulate the industry and encourage investments. This legislation provided a favorable legal framework and political climate for investment in mining. In keeping with Spanish legal heritage, Peru's mineral resources were owned by the state prior to 1901. Rights to exploit minerals were leased from the Peruvian state upon payment of an annual fee. This legal structure created uncertainties for investors, whose rights to extract minerals were not guaranteed for an indefinite period. This risk discouraged foreign investors in particular, who lacked confidence in the stability of the Peruvian government.

The Mining Code of 1901 resolved these problems. Its most significant measure altered the legal status of mineral rights. Under the provisions of the code mineral rights acquired the status of private property. Upon payment of an annual tax the possession of mining property became perpetual and irrevocable. This allowed mining companies to purchase large mineral reserves that could be brought into production at such time as their exploitation became profitable. In addition, mining property, like real estate, could be freely disposed of at the discretion of the owner. The code also provided investment incentives and exempted from import duties all tools, machinery, and materials used in mining, railroads, and related construction.[12] This liberal legislation largely abolished the existing legal and administrative barriers to the expansion of the industry and encouraged large investments.

Following its initial purchase of mines, the Cerro de Pasco Corporation invested in the construction of the infrastructure that the Peruvian mineowners had been struggling to provide. The Corporation purchased the concession to continue the rail line from La Oroya to Cerro de Pasco and to extend the railway to Huancayo, in the heart of the Mantaro Valley. Upon acquiring the railroad concessions the Corporation immediately built wagon roads to bring in heavy machinery and initiated construction of the rail lines. The Corporation purchased nearby coal mines to provide fuel for its smelter, and began construction of a railroad to the coalfields. Finally, it constructed two electric power plants and a large smelter which utilized the Bessemer process. The Corporation's new smelter at Tinyahuarco had the capacity to process more than five times the volume of ore as Peru's next largest smelter. The Corporation also modernized the existing shafts and tunnels by introducing ventilation systems and water pumps to drain the mines. In addition, it created a network of lifts, cars, and railways to transport the ore from the face of the mine to the smelter.[13]

With this new infrastructure the Cerro de Pasco Corporation overcame many of the obstacles that constrained the growth of the

Peruvian mining industry during the preceeding decades. But money alone could not supply laborers to mine the ores, operate the processing plants, and run the railways in the central highlands of Peru. The increased smelting capacity created a greater demand for ore and fuel, and a need for more workers to mine the copper and coal. The smelter at Tinyahuarco alone required between 1,500 and 2,000 workers in order to operate at full capacity.[14] Not only did the Corporation need a large number of workers, but the new machines and modern infrastructure required workers with skills that were completely unknown to the population of the highlands of Peru.

There is no direct evidence to indicate whether the directors of this consortium of the leading capitalists of the United States assumed that the Corporation could attract a sufficient number of workers by offering a "decent" wage, or if from its inception the executive officers of the Corporation recognized that the company would need to coerce peasants to labor in the mines and processing plants. However, intentions are of little importance. The fact is, more often than not during the first three decades of the century the Cerro de Pasco Corporation, and the other mining companies in Peru, were plagued by a shortage of workers. In order to mine the ores and operate the processing plants and transportation network the mining companies in the central highlands were obliged to resort to various forms of forced labor.

The Growing Commercialization of Highland Society

The reactivization of the mining industry in the 1890s followed by the Cerro de Pasco Corporation's massive investments contributed to the growing commercialization of highland society.[15] The extension of the railroad and the proliferation of mining ventures brought more people into the region, and expanded the local market for foodstuffs. In addition, the extension of the railway made the shipment of foodstuffs from Huancayo and Cerro de Pasco to Lima practicable for the first time. *Hacendados* and wealthy peasants were able to take advantage of these new commerical opportunities.   ＼

By 1910 the process of social change within peasant communities enabled some peasants to acquire control over lands that formerly were the collective property of the community. Using reciprocal exchange relationships or hired labor these peasants began producing foodstuffs for the local, regional, and urban markets.

Frequently those peasants who gained access to land and labor were local political authorities or peasants who already controlled more or higher quality lands. They could use their position, or call upon more powerful regional politicians, to legitimate usurpation of land or use of communal labor for personal enrichment. Through these processes the increasing market for foodstuffs intensified pressures for the privatization of community lands.

Most of the tensions that surfaced in highland society in the early twentieth century had been smouldering since the last commerical boom of the 1870s. The expansion of local and regional markets for food contributed to the intensification of the exploitation of *colonos*. *Hacendados* attempted to increase the tribute and labor obligations of *colonos* in order to appropriate more products that could be marketed. Similarly, in their efforts to expand commercial production, *hacendados* often tried to reduce the size of the plots that *colonos* controlled directly and on which they produced their subsistence requirements. Where successful, *hacendados* used these lands and the extra labor tribute they demanded to produce commerical crops.

With the increasing commercial value of land, conflicts over rights to and ownership of land intensified. This drew peasants and *colonos* into struggles at the community, regional, and the national level to preserve their traditional access to land. Nevertheless, pressures for the privatization of land were at this time still comparatively weak, and the vast majority of the rural population in the highlands retained direct access to land, animals, and tools. The process of the expulsion of the direct producers from the land had barely begun in the Peruvian highlands in the early years of the twentieth century. Nevertheless, encroachments upon subsistence economies made it necessary for some peasants to seek wage work. Some poorer households were obliged to supplement farm production with a small cash income earned during one or two months of the year. The peasants of the central highlands naturally looked to the mines when they needed cash. The mining region was relatively close, transportation available, and the region abounded with labor contractors or *enganchadores* offering cash advances to any man ready to sign a fixed-term contract to work in the mines.

The entry of the Cerro de Pasco Corporation and the expansion of productive capacity in the mining industry intensified the demand for labor. To operate the mines and smelters the mining companies continued to rely on traditional methods of acquiring workers: *contrata* and *enganche*. In the first decades of the twentieth century *contrata* implied subcontracting the work of extracting the ore. Frequently the mining companies, including the Cerro de Pasco Corporation, contracted an individual, usually a merchant or former owner of a small mine, to extract ore. The contractor would organize production and provide the workers and tools. In return the mining company would pay the contractor for each ton of ore extracted.

By the early twentieth century debt peonage in the mines was generally known as *enganche*.[16] *Enganche* involved a complex network of social relations as *enganchadores*, under contract to a mining company to supply workers, would subcontract recruitment to local merchants, shopkeepers, *hacendados*, and village political authorities. These people were in positions to use their influence and contacts to cajole or compel peasants and peons to enter into contractual agreements to work in the mines in exchange for a cash advance. A recent study of capitalist transition in the central highlands shows how *enganchadores* and their local agents manipulated traditional reciprocal relationships such as the frequently studied "patron-client" relation of the Andean peasant community to gain access to labor for the mines. In this manner *enganche* involved the "commercialization of traditional relations of reciprocity."[17]

The precapitalist social relations of highland society, and the rarity of free wage labor that these implied, continued to retard the expansion of the mining industry. *Enganche* was incapable of providing an adequate labor force for the mines. The *enganchadores* could not secure a sufficient number of workers, and lacked the power to enforce the contracts. Many peasants who contracted a debt (*enganchados*), and signed a contract to amortize the debt by working for a mining company, reneged on their contractual obligations and abandoned the work to return to their communities.[18]

Until the early twentieth century this form of debt servitude had no legal status. Therefore, mineowners and *enganchadores* encountered problems when they attempted to compel fugitive workers to return to the mines. The pursuit of fugitives was costly, time consuming, and frequently unsuccessful. Even if a case were brought to court, it was uncertain whether the judge would decide that the contract was legally binding. Consequently the enforcement of *enganche* largely depended upon the power, prestige, and ruthlessness of the *enganchadores* and their agents. In time the informal and personal underpinnings of *enganche* proved too weak to support the heightened demands on the system. In response to pressures from the mining companies the Peruvian government legalized and institutionalized the use of *enganche* for the mining industry. The Mine Labor Law of 1903 sanctioned the use of *enganche*, allowing political authorities to actively pursue fugitive *enganchados*, bringing the coercive apparatus of the state to impose debt servitude in the mines.[19] Even intervention by the state was incapable of enforcing *enganche*. It is estimated that in 1910 nearly half of the labor force of the Cerro de Pasco Corporation violated contracts with *enganchadores* and fled from the mines.[20]

Historians of Peru debate the role of *enganche* in the mines. Some argue that by the early twentieth century there was an adequate or even abundant supply of labor, contending that peasants wittingly and willingly became debt peons in the mines in the hope of making their fortunes through the hoarding of wages. From this perspective there is little *de facto* difference between *enganche* and free wage labor because it was economic compulsion alone that drove workers to the mines. Some scholars who make this argument also contend that *enganche* was the labor recruitment system selected by mineowners who preferred to establish contractual relationships with labor recruiters rather than directly with workers. In other words, mineowners purposefully and preferentially encouraged *enganche* instead of free wage labor, though they could have had the latter if they had perceived it in their interests.[21] This suggests that there was little fundamental difference between *enganche* and free wage labor.

Another view is that the preservation of precapitalist relations of production, that necessitated the use of *enganche*, was advantageous to the mining companies, at least in the first decades of the twentieth century. Peasants' continued access to land and seasonal return to their communities helped to maintain low wages because the wage was a supplement to household subsistence production, not the sole means of ensuring the survival of the miners and their families.[22] While this is true, it is possible that the disadvantages associated with a chronic shortage of workers may have come to outweigh the advantages which accrued to the companies. Evidence suggests that except in periods of severe recession *enganche* was unable to satisfy the mining companies' demand for labor, for there was a continual shortage of workers. This shortage was aggravated by the transience of the labor force, with the brevity of *enganche* contracts exacerbated by the high number of fugitives. The rapid turnover in the labor force made it difficult to adequately train workers to perform their tasks. This retarded the rationalization of the labor process and the implementation of new techniques. In addition, not only was *enganche* a hopelessly inadequate method of recruiting workers for the mining companies, it was also expensive. *Enganchadores* were paid a commission for every day worked by each laborer they supplied. These considerations suggest that *enganche* may not have been preferred by the companies, but used in the absence of a viable alternative. As long as peasants and hacienda peons had access to land and remained enmeshed in a network of social relations that facilitated their production of their subsistence requirements, the mining companies found it necessary to use force to recruit workers.

A Watershed in the Economic Development of Peru

The launching of the Cerro de Pasco Corporation in the first decade of the twentieth century marked a watershed in the development of capitalism in Peru. The Corporation was the first major firm to operate in Peru that did not have its roots in mercantile capitalism. From its inception the objective of the company was to establish a modern industrial mining enterprise, and its investments revolutionized the Peruvian mining industry. The modernization of the shafts and tunnels, the construction of a large smelter, and the expansion and innovation of transport for both long and short hauls made the production process more rational and efficient. The transformation of the production process is reflected in data on labor productivity. Table 4.1 indicates that from 1906 to 1921 the volume of output per worker in the mining sector increased erratically. The rise in productivity might be judged modest given the size of Cerro de Pasco's investments. Despite the Corporation's modernization project there existed barriers to raising productivity. Limitations to the expansion of mining production and to capitalist development within Peru originated from the extension of precapitalist social relations. Peasants' access to land, and consequently the scarcity of free wage labor, meant that labor was not at the disposal of capital. To acquire a labor force the Cerro de Pasco Corporation had to ally with local notables, insert itself into the traditional social networks, and ultimately coerce peasants to labor in the mines and processing plants. This form of bonded labor was a fetter on the reorganization and rationalization of the labor process. The nature of the labor

TABLE 4.1 Labor Productivity in the Peruvian Metal Mining Industry, 1906-1921

Year	Labor Productivity[a]
1906	0.84
1907	0.80
1908	0.84
1909	0.88
1910	1.02
1911	1.07
1912	1.02
1913	0.98
1914	0.93
1915	1.02
1916	1.10
1917	1.09
1918	1.18
1919	1.10
1920	0.89
1921	1.08

SOURCES: Computed by the author from data in *Boletín del Cuerpo de Ingenieros de Minas* (1903-1922); and Pablo Macera, *Estadísticas históricas del Perú: sector minero I (precios)*, and Pablo Macera and Horacio Pinto, *Estadísticas históricas del Perú: sector minero II (volumen y valor)* (Lima: Centro Peruano de Historia Económica, 1972).

[a]This is an approximation of labor productivity. It is a measure of production in constant dollars, using average prices for 1906-1921, divided by the number of people employed.

force obstructed maximization of the company's productive and technological potential.

This analysis suggests an obvious but frequently overlooked conclusion. The development of capitalism in Europe and the United States was substantially different from the process of the development of capitalism in Peru. In the incipient stage of capitalist development the relations of production appropriate to capitalism are primitive. At its inception capitalism unleashes productive potential and engenders economic growth in so far as it destroys anachronistic social relations and transforms laborers into free wage laborers, or proletarians. This was characteristic of the early transitions to capitalism in Europe, as well as of its subsequent development in other countries. The essence of the progressiveness of capitalism is this transformation of relations of production.[23] While this fundamental characteristic of the initial stage of capitalist development is common to all capitalist transitions, the different historical circumstances in which capitalism develops affect the nature of the transition. These circumstances vary depending upon local, national, and international conditions. The principal local and national factors that affect the transition are the character of precapitalist production relations, the strength and struggles of antagonistic classes, and the nature of the state. The role of capital in the world economy and the form of the export of capital from advanced to backward countries are the principal international factors that condition the capitalist transition in each country.

Traditional analyses of the initial stage of the capitalist transition, called the period of manufacture, referred specifically to the first capitalist transition. Classical economists analyzed the birth of capitalism as it emerged out of feudal social relations in Europe at a time when capitalism did not exist elsewhere in the world.[24] At that time the expulsion of the peasantry from the land largely predated the emergence of capitalist production. This process, which classical economists called primitive accumulation, was the precondition for capitalist development. While the major restraint on the expansion of capital in this stage was the primitive nature of capitalist social relations, financial and technological constraints significantly fettered the expansion of capital. Most machinery was produced in craft workshops and was in short supply, retarding the pace of technical change. In addition, the immaturity of the credit system and the relatively small size of individual capitals meant capitalists often were unable to make the large investments that technological innovation required. As a consequence the division of labor in the production process and the technology and machinery that characterized the period of manufacture were those that evolved in artisanal production. The dynamism of capital in the period of manufacture was the result of the new social relations of free wage labor, not technical change.[25] Capital's "real" control of the production process was not consummated until the subsequent period of modern industry. In this stage the division of labor, machinery, and the work process all are generated by capital.[26]

While this analytical method is useful for understanding the development of capitalism in the twentieth century in backward countries, this periodization of capital is not valid for all processes of capitalist transition. The capitalist transitions in backward countries, occurring in a world dominated by advanced capitalist countries, are significantly different from the initial transitions in Europe. The form of the export of capital from the advanced countries is singularly important in shaping the transition to capitalism in backward countries. The export of productive capital from the advanced countries generates major changes in the sphere of production in backward countries, even in the absence of capitalist relations of production. In the case of the entrance of the Cerro de Pasco Corporation into Peru, capital from the United States had access to a mature credit system and advanced technology. The Cerro de Pasco Corporation marshalled these financial and technical resources to modernize the production process. This resulted in an alteration of the social division of labor in the central highlands of Peru. Generalizing from this example it can be argued that the export of productive capital to backward countries ushers in a reorganization of the production process along capitalist lines, even when the social relations of production are not capitalist. In the case of Peru the export of productive capital from the United States, in the form of the Cerro de Pasco Corporation, set into motion a process of technical change, accompanied by the increasing social division of labor in the mines. This process began prior to the widespread destruction of traditional social relations of production.

The distinction between the period of manufacture and the initial stage of capitalist development in backward countries is one of degree, not the polarity of opposites. In both periods the persistence of precapitalist institutions and the primitive nature of capitalist social and productive relations retard technical change, division of labor, and rising productivity. As capitalism initially developed in Europe, however, the destruction of precapitalist social relations began prior to, and was a precondition for, the emergence of capitalism. In this process the freedom of the direct producers from traditional obligations, and their separation from the land, generated a generalized market in labor power. These were the dynamic forces of the early stages of capitalist production in Europe.

In backward countries the early stages of capitalist development frequently are characterized by major technical change. The export of productive capital revolutionizes the production process. This may occur before the decline of traditional social relations, before the direct producers massively are separated from the land, and before the proliferation of free wage labor. In these circumstances technological innovation and the social division of labor generated by the export of productive capital becomes a driving force in the expansion of production and in the destruction of traditional social relations of production.

Consolidation of Foreign Control

The Peruvian mining industry grew rapidly during the first three decades of the twentieth century. The volume of output doubled from 1903 to 1910, and almost doubled again from 1910 to 1923 (see Table 2.1). This expansion reflected innovations in the mining and smelting of copper. Silver mining was not neglected, however, and remained an important source of revenue in the industry. Occasionally the value of silver production exceeded that of copper (see Appendix G).

Following its initial spate of investment, the Cerro de Pasco Corporation attempted to consolidate its position of hegemony in the mining regions of the central highlands. From 1910 to 1918 the Corporation made major investments to purchase mines and land in the areas surrounding the mines. The Corporation had many advantages over its Peruvian competitors: its large capital stock, the facility with which it was able to raise investment funds, and its ready access to advanced technology. Nonetheless, for almost twenty years it faced bitter competition over control of mines and ore. Several tenacious local mineowners refused to sell out, surviving by combining collusion with competition. They competed with the Corporation in the purchase of mines and custom ores, ores produced by smaller mining companies and sold to larger companies for further processing. At the same time several Peruvian mineowners collaborated with the Corporation in ingenious ways. They leased mines and infrastructure to the Corporation, entered into

TABLE 4.2 Index of World Market Prices[a], 1901-1945

(1963 = 100)	
Year	Index
1901	50.4
1902	39.7
1903	43.3
1904	43.3
1905	49.8
1906	59.8
1907	60.6
1908	43.1
1909	42.5
1910	42.6
1911	41.7
1912	51.7
1913	48.2
1914	43.6
1915	51.2
1916	77.0
1917	82.3
1918	78.1
1919	66.7
1920	64.9
1921	43.7
1922	47.8
1923	51.3
1924	49.8
1925	53.5
1926	51.2
1927	45.9
1928	48.3
1929	55.0
1930	40.1
1931	28.0
1932	21.4
1933	27.1
1934	32.3

(continued)

TABLE 4.2 (cont.)

Year	(1963 = 100) Index
1935	35.8
1936	35.4
1937	44.7
1938	35.8
1939	37.7
1940	39.0
1941	41.6
1942	43.7
1943	44.7
1944	44.5
1945	45.8

SOURCES: Computed by the author from data presented in Appendix C, Table C.2.

[a]The price index is weighted to reflect the composition of output in Peru.

partnerships in the exploitation of veins, sold it custom ores, and staked claims that they subsequently sold to the Corporation.[27]

World War I increased the demand for metals and prices rose dramatically from 1915 to 1917 (see Table 4.2). The prices of copper and silver increased by about 60 percent (see Appendix C, Table C.2). In response to these favorable world market conditions metal production expanded in Peru.

Following the war, the United States and Britain established a ceiling on metal prices so that by 1921 they were at pre-war levels. At the same time the United States imposed trade restrictions banning the importation of copper concentrates with a low ore content. This combination of falling prices and restricted access to the U.S. market proved disastrous for metal producers in Peru, with the exception of the Cerro de Pasco Corporation. The volume of metal production in Peru declined in 1918 and fell precipitously from 1921 through 1923 (see Table 2.1 and Figure 2.3). At this time the costs of production in the mining industry in Peru increased because of rising prices for imported raw materials, parts, and machinery. As a result of declining product prices and rising import prices most mining companies in Peru suffered several years of crisis.

The Cerro de Pasco Corporation was the only mining company in Peru that had the technical capability to produce copper concentrates which were eligible for the U.S. market. As a consequence Cerro's share of the U.S. market expanded at the expense of its competitors in Peru. From the time that the Corporation initiated operations it had tried to buy out the mines and smelter of its major competitor, the Backus and Johnston Company. In 1919 Backus and Johnston could not hold out any longer and capitulated to Cerro. After this takeover the Cerro de Pasco Corporation produced 72 percent of the value of Peru's mineral concentrates (see Table 4.3).

At the height of copper prices in the late 1910s the Corporation made the decision to develop the most technologically advanced metal processing complex in the world. In 1918 construction began at La Oroya and a new smelter and refinery for copper was completed in 1922. The inauguration of the processing complex at La Oroya effected a leap in the volume of metal production in Peru. Table 2.1 shows that from 1922 to 1923 output rose by more than 50 percent. A few years earlier, in 1920, the company opened two new gravity concentration plants. This network of processing plants more than doubled the Corporation's processing capacity and made it one of the lowest cost copper producers in the world.[28]

The small and medium sized mining companies in the central highlands that formerly processed ores in their own concentrators were unable to compete with the Corporation and closed down their processing plants. By 1923, only one year after the opening of the La Oroya plant, all smelters in the central region other than those owned by the Corporation had discontinued operations. The smaller mining companies had little alternative but to sell their ores to the Corporation for further processing. Through its control over the smelting and refining of minerals the Corporation was able to exercise control over the entire mining industry in the central highlands. This is demonstrated clearly in Table 4.3, which shows Cerro's share of Peruvian metal production. In 1922 the Corporation produced 88 percent of the final output of the Peruvian metal mining industry, and averaged over 80 percent from 1922 to 1928.

At about the same time as Cerro concluded its takeover of the central mining region, the Northern Peru Mining and Smelting Company expanded in the province of La Libertad in the northern highlands of Peru. Northern Peru was a wholly-owned subsidiary of the American Smelting and Refining Company (ASARCO), one of the largest U.S. mining companies. In the 1920s Northern Peru bought a number of mines, constructed roads and an aerial cableway to transport ores, and installed a concentrator and a large smelter. As a result the company expanded copper production in the north of Peru.[29]

In the late 1920s the Cerro de Pasco Corporation and the Northern Peru Mining and Smelting Company monopolized the smelting and refining of metals in Peru. It is estimated that by 1929 these two companies, together with a third U.S. firm, accounted for more than 97 percent of Peru's mineral exports.[30] Peruvian-owned mining companies were unable to continue processing their own ores and their existence depended upon their ability to forge alliances with the larger firms. Those Peruvian mining companies that survived became suppliers of custom ores to the foreign companies.

Proletarianization in the Central Highlands

Within a year after the inauguration of the processing complex at La Oroya it became evident that the pollution from the plant was lethal. The smelter and refinery dumped waste into the air and waterways. Crops withered, animals died, and people became ill in the valleys and *puna* within twenty miles of Oroya. By the middle 1920s thirty peasant communities and twenty-eight *hacendados* filed legal claims against the Cerro de Pasco Corporation for damages. As part of the agreement to what was known as the *Los Humos* or Smoke Controversy the Corporation purchased more than 200,000 *hectares* of land in the central highlands.[31] These lands, combined with several haciendas acquired previously, made the Cerro de Pasco Corporation the largest landowner in Peru.

The massive damage to land and crops and the decimation of animal herds accelerated the transformation of highland society. About fifty years earlier highland society had begun to change in significant ways. Through the final decades of the nineteenth century and the first two decades of the twentieth, increased commercialization engendered conflicts within peasant villages and between villages and haciendas over access to land, labor, and

104

TABLE 4.3 Percentage of the Final Output of the Peruvian Metal Mining Industry Produced by the Cerro de Pasco Corporation[a], 1906-1945

Year	% of Final Output[b]
1906	5.8
1907	30.9
1908	46.1
1909	56.6
1910	54.3
1911	54.5
1912	54.5
1913	55.1
1914	52.3
1915	62.3
1916	61.0
1917	63.8
1918	66.0
1919	64.2
1920	64.4
1921	71.7
1922	88.2
1923	83.0
1924	78.2
1925	80.8
1926	75.7
1927	81.6
1928	85.8
1929	73.1
1930	78.4
1931	79.6
1932	72.7
1933	72.7
1934	75.6
1935	74.4
1936	70.0
1937	70.8
1938	68.4

(continued)

TABLE 4.3 (cont.)

Year	% of Final Output[b]
1939	69.9
1940	63.6
1941	63.7
1942	71.0
1943	75.6
1944	59.8
1945	60.8

SOURCES: Computed by the author from data presented in *Boletín del Cuerpo de Ingenieros de Minas del Perú* (1903-1922); *Boletín Oficial de Minas y Petróleo* (1924-1932); Jorge Hohagen, *La Industria Minera en el Perú* (1932-1939), and Anuario de la Industria Minera en el Perú (1940-1945); Pablo Macera, *Estadísticas históricas del Perú: sector minero I (precios)* (Lima: Centro Peruano de Historia Económica, 1972); and Pablo Macera and Honorio Pinto, *Estadísticas históricas del Perú: sector minero II (volumen y valor)*(Lima: Centro Peruano de Historia Económica, 1972).

[a]Final output is the product of smelters and refineries.

[b]The volume of final output is measured in constant prices (U.S. dollars). This is a measure of physical production. Weight cannot be used since the metals are of different qualities. To construct the index, average prices for 1906-1945 for the five major metals (copper, lead, zinc, silver, and gold) were applied to the quantities produced in each year. This eliminates changes in the value of production that are purely due to price changes and isolates changes in production.

animals; and over the appropriation of tributes and rents.[32] As peasants and hacienda peons struggled against increasing encroachments on their household production, the more disadvantaged families had to complement production for self-provisioning with work for monetary payment in order to survive. Peasants and peons resisted the confiscation of land, the intensification of tribute obligations, and limitations on their traditional rights. Frequently this resistance flared up into local struggles.[33] The process of the dissolution of the peasantry, the separation of direct producers from the land and from their access to the means of production, advanced unevenly in the decades preceeding 1920. However, the inauguration of the La Oroya processing complex greatly accelerated this process. Because the contaminated area could not be used for cultivation or grazing, increasing numbers of peasants and hacienda peons were forced to abandon their lands and sought wage employment. Since the mines traditionally offered work, indeed for decades the companies forced peasants to labor under *enganche* contracts, many recently proletarianized peasants migrated to the mines as a means of survival.

Several authors have pointed out that the effect of migration to the mines was not the same for all workers.[34] The impact of *enganche* and labor in the mines varied, depending upon a peasant's access to land and other resources and upon the period in which the migration took place. The majority of peasants who went to the mines were driven by impoverishment. To sustain their household economy they needed a cash supplement to their subsistence production. However, even before commencing work these peasants became indebted to *enganchadores* or to the company store for advances of cash, food, clothing, and the mining tools that workers were required to provide. These poor peasant-miners were skilled agriculturalists, herders, and craftsmen. But they possessed none of the skills valued by the mining companies. Therefore, they worked in the lowest-paid jobs. Novice miners, who retained no access to land or to community networks that could supply food and clothing, had difficulty in repaying the loans they contracted. Many found themselves further and further in debt. For these miners wage labor perpetuated, even accentuated, their impoverishment.[35]

The inauguration of the La Oroya complex represents a milestone in the transition to capitalism in the central highlands of Peru. The ecological destruction that accompanied the opening of the processing plant accelerated the expulsion of the peasantry from the land and the proletarianization of the rural poor in the areas surrounding La Oroya. Formerly there were cases of the dispossession of individual families and numerous households that required a complementary monetary income to sustain their subsistence economy. But a free wage labor force is not characterized by isolated and occasional wage workers. The massive destruction of land, animals, and crops wrought by contamination from the new smelters and refinery created a mass of persons who were completely separated from the land. In this process the inauguration of the La Oroya plant created the preconditions for the development of a proletariat in central Peru.

Not all of the migrants to the mines were completely dispossed, or "smoked out," by pollution from the processing plant at La Oroya. For many peasants in the areas surrounding La Oroya the effects of the contamination were less dramatic. They could continue to cultivate their lands, but the yields were smaller. Their cattle lived, but were less fertile and more susceptible to disease. The subsistence economy of these peasants became more precarious, and wage employment became a necessary complement to self-provisioning. Their household economy came to depend upon the monetary supplement that was provided by wages. One author argues persuasively that seasonal migration to the mines prolonged the viability of subsistence production in the central highlands by infusing peasant households with the small amounts of cash that were necessary for the perpetuation of economies based primarily upon self-sufficiency.[36]

Some members of highland society prospered by migrating to the mines. In the years prior to the 1920s, merchants, former mineowners, and more prosperous and well-connected peasants worked as contractors for the Cerro de Pasco Corporation under the *contrata* system. Often this relationship proved lucrative for the contractors, who amassed a degree of wealth by extracting ore for the Corporation. By the 1920s the Corporation limited subcontracting to the construction of tunnels and shafts, because increasingly it was able to hire workers directly.[37] After *contrata* was curtailed, some of the migrants still prospered through work in the mines. Because of their class, their personal contacts, or their higher educational level they were given administrative or office positions. These "white collar" workers or *empleados* were paid better than the *obreros* who worked in extraction, transport, or processing. As Table 4.4 indicates, from 1924 through 1945 less

TABLE 4.4 Employment of *Obreros* and *Empleados* in the Peruvian Mining Industry[a], 1912-1945

Year	Obreros	Empleados
1912	14,435	4,175
1913	n.a.	n.a.
1914	n.a.	n.a.
1915	n.a.	n.a.
1916	17,768	4,991
1917	19,003	4,735
1918	16,674	4,636
1919	n.a.	n.a.
1920	n.a.	n.a.
1921	n.a.	n.a.
1922	n.a.	n.a.
1923	n.a.	n.a.
1924	20,238	2,420
1925	23,378	2,674
1926	27,263	3,133
1927	25,389	3,042
1928	25,430	3,045
1929	29,457	2,864
1930	25,336	2,801
1931	16,160	n.a.
1932	13,004	1,193
1933	14,350	1,201
1934	16,357	1,377
1935	17,855	1,504
1936	29,428	1,589
1937	n.a.	n.a.
1938	n.a.	n.a.
1939	33,889	2,232
1940	35,486	2,186
1941	42,121	2,135
1942	32,589	2,352
1943	40,577	2,451
1944	39,950	2,632
1945	33,833	2,876

(continued)

than 10 percent of the work force in the mining industry was classified as *empleados*. It was a small minority of the migrants to the mines who were in the higher pay brackets. For the vast majority of the workers, particularly for the *obreros*, wage labor in the mines usually brought with it continued impoverishment.

In summary, the effect of migration to the mines appears to have been contradictory, largely dependent upon the social and economic circumstances of the particular group of migrants and the period in which they worked in the mines. In general migration accelerated and accentuated the continuing process of the social differentiation of highland society. In the vast majority of cases poor peasants were driven to the mines as part of their attempt to alleviate indebtedness. Nevertheless, frequently they found themselves mired further and further in debt, as the pay was so low that they contracted new loans while unable to pay off the old ones. As said, a few prospered, those who controlled large plots of land or other resources that could be profitably managed in their absence. These few more affluent migrants were able to save some of their salary. Then they might use their hoard to purchase a truck, store, lumber mill, or similar equipment with which to initiate or expand small enterprises.[38] In particular circumstances migration appears to have retarded the process of the social differentiation of highland society by staving off immiserization and proletarianization. Some impoverished peasant families were able to sustain their household economy as a small cash income earned in temporary wage employment at times postponed the loss of land through indebtedness.

By historical accident the inauguration of the processing plant at La Oroya accentuated the need for stable workers at the same time as

---

SOURCES: Computed by the author from data in *Boletín del Cuerpo de Ingenieros de Minas* (1903-1922); *Boletín Oficial de Minas y Petróleo* (1924-1932); Jorge Hohagen, *La Industria Minera en el Perú* (1932-1939); Jorge Hohagen, *Anuario de la Industria Minera en el Perú* (1940-1945); Pablo Macera, *Estadísticas históricas del Perú: sector minero (precios)* (Lima: Centro Peruano de Historia Económica, 1972); Pablo Macera and Horacio Pinto, *Estadísticas históricas del Perú: sector minero (volumen y valor)* (Lima: Centro Peruano de Historia Económica, 1972).

[a]These data are for the entire mining industry including the petroleum sector. For this reason they are not comparable with data in Table 4.5.

n.a. - not available

it accelerated the supply. The new metallurgical complex intensified the demand for workers who could operate the sophisticated machinery in the new smelter and refinery. With the need for permanent skilled workers, traditional forms of labor recruitment became increasingly inadequate. The Cerro de Pasco Corporation needed the flexibility to hire and fire workers readily and relocate them from one division of the company to another. More than ever before, the mining industry needed laborers who were readily at the disposal of capital. In launching the Oroya processing plant the Cerro de Pasco Corporation hastened the transformation of the labor force, probably unwittingly.

Not only was *enganche* cumbersome, expensive, and ineffective, it was also under attack on humanitarian grounds. Intellectuals and social reformers drew attention to the miserable working and living conditions of the miners, focusing on the plight of the workers of the Cerro de Pasco Corporation. This unleashed a campaign against the most flagrant abuse of all: *enganche*.[39] In 1914 the Mine Labor Law of 1903 that legalized debt servitude in the mining sector was repealed.

The La Oroya complex had a profound impact on the entire mining industry. In 1923, its first complete year of operation, the volume of production in the industry as a whole was 50 percent higher than it had been a year earlier (see Table 2.1). This leap in output was not accompanied by significant growth in employment. Employment in the industry as a whole remained virtually unchanged (see Table 4.5). In the Cerro de Pasco Corporation employment increased by 6 percent from 1922 to 1923 (see Table 4.6). Growth in output with little change in the size of the work force indicates a significant rise in productivity. Between 1921, the year before the inauguration of the Oroya plant, and 1923 productivity in the Cerro de Pasco Corporation increased by more than 50 percent (see Table 4.7). Expansion in the size of the labor force did not occur until the second half of the decade, several years after the inauguration of the Oroya metallurigical complex.

Throughout the 1920s mineral output increased in Peru. This was not a response to favorable world market conditions because in the decade of the 1920s metal prices were markedly lower than they had been during World War I, as a result of price ceilings established by Britain and the United States (see Table 4.2). The expansion in output reflected the major technical innovations in the mining and processing of ores. In the late 1920s the Corporation constructed a second major mining shaft at Cerro de Pasco. In addition, the company introduced a new mechanical flotation concentration process that allowed for the processing of different metals within the same process. Soon the Corporation converted two older concentrators to this new process.[40]

Following the ecological disaster that resulted from the contamination of the region surrounding La Oroya, the Cerro de Pasco Corporation agreed to install pollution control devices to treat the exhaust fumes that were the major cause of the damage to land, crops, and animals. In 1927, when lead prices were high, the Corporation installed a Cottrell flue to capture lead and zinc particles. The next year the Corporation opened a lead circuit at the Oroya plant that processed the lead dust captured in the Cottrell flue (see Appendix B, Table B.2, for lead production in Peru).

The installation of the pollution control devices and the inauguration of the lead circuit proved exceptionally profitable. They enabled the Corporation to expand its level of output and raise productivity. With the reduction of pollution in the region the surrounding lands gradually regained their fertility and became productive grazing zones again. However, for the most part these improvements did not benefit the peasant communities and *haciendas* because they already had forfeited their lands to the Corporation.

Union Organizing and the Crash of 1929

In 1928 the level of output in the mines and processing plants of the Cerro de Pasco Corporation was greater than ever before and prices were moderately high. As usual, however, the Corporation was short of workers. Recruitment policies were changing in response to transformations in the social conditions in the areas surrounding the mines. As peasants sought more permanent wage work the Corporation's dependence upon *enganchadores* decreased. Instead, more workers were directly hired. These workers, called *maquipureros*, were given specialized training and paid higher wages. The Corporation expected that these workers would remain employed for longer periods than the *enganchados*.[41] The increasing presence of stable workers in the late 1920s laid the basis for the organization of a trade union.

The first recorded attempt to organize miners into a trade union was in 1918 at the Morococha mine of the Backus and Johnston Company. The following year a policeman shot a man in Morococha, an incident not related to the mines. However, the

TABLE 4.5 Total Employment in the Peruvian Mining Industry[a], 1905-1945

Year	Total No. Employed
1905	8,266
1906	11,444
1907	12,828
1908	12,950
1909	12,192
1910	13,652
1911	13,818
1912	15,506
1913	16,032
1914	16,410
1915	17,334
1916	19,295
1917	20,056
1918	17,632
1919	17,818
1920	18,975
1921	16,640
1922	15,475
1923	15,902
1924	16,221
1925	17,362
1926	20,395
1927	19,710
1928	20,591
1929	25,508
1930	21,730
1931	13,724
1932	9,785
1933	10,713
1934	12,205
1935	13,755
1936	25,339
1937	22,264
1938	27,039

(continued)

TABLE 4.5 (cont.)

Year	Total No. Employed
1939	29,421
1940	30,305
1941	36,756
1942	27,081
1943	34,965
1944	34,139
1945	27,867

SOURCES: Compiled by the author from data in *Boletín del Cuerpo de Ingenieros de Minas* (1903-1922); *Boletín Oficial de Minas y Petróleo* (1924-1932); Jorge Hohagen, *La Industria Minera en el Perú* (1932-1939); Jorge Hohagen, *Anuario de la Industria Minera en el Perú* (1940-1945); Pablo Macera, *Estadísticas históricas del Perú: sector minero (precios)* (Lima: Centro Peruano de Historia Económica, 1972); Pablo Macera and Horacio Pinto, *Estadísticas históricas del Perú: sector minero (volumen y valor)* (Lima: Centro Peruano de Historia Económica, 1972).

[a]Data on total employment in the metal mining industry from 1905-1919 are derived by subtracting the number of people employed in the exploitation of petroleum from the number of persons employed in the entire mining industry.

TABLE 4.6 Number of Persons Employed by the Cerro de Pasco Corporation, 1920-1945

Year	Employment
1920	7,915
1921	7,856
1922	7,856
1923	8,412
1924	7,153
1925	8,128
1926	10,449
1927	9,363
1928	10,392
1929	13,066
1030	5,686
1931	5,680
1932	4,330
1933	4,375
1934	5,643
1935	7,642
1936	8,917
1937	9,900
1938	10,231
1939	10,568
1940	10,875
1941	10,350
1942	10,332
1943	9,927
1944	9,080
1945	9,053

SOURCES: *Boletín del Cuerpo de Ingenieros de Minas* (1903-1922); *Boletín Oficial de Minas y Petróleo* (1924-1932); Jorge Hohagen, *La Industria Minera en el Perú* (1932-1939); Jorge Hohagen, *Anuario de la Industria Minera en el Perú* (1940-1945); Pablo Macera, *Estadísticas históricas del Perú: sector minero (precios)* (Lima: Centro Peruano de Historia Económica, 1972); Pablo Macera and Horacio Pinto, *Estadísticas históricas del Perú: sector minero (volumen y valor)* (Lima: Centro Peruano de Historia Económica, 1972).

TABLE 4.7 Labor Productivity[a] in the Peruvian Metal Mining Industry and in the Cerro de Pasco Corporation, 1920-1945

Year	Total Mining Industry	Cerro de Pasco
1920	0.89	1.38
1921	1.08	1.77
1922	1.14	1.99
1923	1.72	2.69
1924	1.49	2.64
1925	1.54	2.65
1926	1.57	2.32
1927	1.50	2.58
1928	1.67	2.84
1929	1.42	2.02
1930	1.31	3.92
1931	1.58	3.04
1932	1.35	2.23
1933	1.45	2.58
1934	1.59	2.60
1935	1.94	2.60
1936	1.25[b]	2.49
1937	1.50	2.38
1938	1.44	2.61
1939	1.26	2.45
1940	1.33	2.36
1941	0.99	2.24
1942	1.31	2.43
1943	0.99	2.24
1944	1.11	2.50
1945	1.33	2.48

SOURCES: Computed by the author from data in *Boletín del Cuerpo de Ingenieros de Minas* (1903-1922); *Boletín Oficial de Minas y Petróleo* (1924-1932); Jorge Hohagen, *La Industria Minera en el Perú* (1932-1939); Jorge Hohagen, *Anuario de la Industria Minera en el Perú* (1940-1945); Pablo Macera, *Estadísticas históricas del Perú: sector minero (precios)* (Lima: Centro Peruano
(continued)

miners directed the anger of the population against the mining company and converted the protest movement into a strike demanding higher wages. The Backus and Johnston Company refused to grant the wage increase and the workers retaliated by flooding the mines. The company reciprocated with a three-month lockout. A local newspaper reported that the workers were all peasants who returned to their lands.[42] Following these events, there was no concerted attempt to organize miners for another decade.

In 1929 a wave of union organizing swept the mines, initiated again at Morococha. By this time conditions at Morococha had changed. The Morococha mines were owned by the Cerro de Pasco Corporation, which had bought out Backus and Johnston, and there were more *maquipureros* in the labor force than before. In 1929 miners in Morococha created a Comité *Central de Reclamos* or grievance committee, that called a strike to demand better working conditions and higher wages. The miners at Morococha won some concessions and the strike spread to other mining centers.

The start of the Great Depression of 1929 undermined union organizing in the mines. After the crash international demand for metals declined sharply. From 1929 to 1932 world metal prices dropped by approximately 60 percent (see Table 4.2), and output in the world industry declined by about 30 percent (see Table 2.1). In Peru, where mineral production fell by about 65 precent in these same years, the repercussions of the depression were particularly severe. In the late 1920s the large foreign firms that dominated mining in Peru were principally copper producers, and the crisis devastated the market for copper. Copper prices plummeted by almost 70 percent from 1929 to 1932. The Cerro de Pasco Corporation responded by reducing the level of production. Labor

---

de Historia Económica, 1972); Pablo Macera and Horacio Pinto, *Estadísticas históricas del Perú: sector minero (volumen y valor)* (Lima: Centro Peruano de Historia Económica, 1972).

[a] This is an approximation of labor productivity, measured in production in constant dollars using average prices for 1920-1945 divided by the number of people employed.

[b] For a consistent analysis of productivity for the mining industry as a whole it is necessary to divide the data into two discontinuous time series, with the break at 1936. In that year there was a significant increase in the number of *lavaderos* panning for gold. This continues to affect the data through 1945.

contracts that provided job stability were rare in this period, and enforcement of a company's obligations rarer still, so it was not difficult for the Corporation to respond to the fall in demand by reducing the size of its labor force by more than two-thirds. Throughout the mining sector companies reduced salaries, fired workers, lengthened the duration of shifts, and intensified the pace of work. When miners organized to present their grievances, frequently the companies responded with violent repression.

In the depression years the trade unions in the mining sector were unable to protect workers' jobs and pay. The weakness of the incipient trade unions in large part was a reflection of the nature of the labor force. Few miners were full-time, permanent workers. The majority were peasants who occasionally or seasonally migrated to the mines. The peasant-miners did not view their employment as long-term, nor did their families' subsistence primarily depend upon wages. Therefore, these miners were reluctant to participate in prolonged and potentially dangerous struggles to improve employment conditions in the industry.

Despite the unfavorable circumstances, in 1930 the Communist Party of Peru (PCP) convened the Congreso Minero del Centro (Miners' Congress of Central Peru).[43] The goal of the congress was to establish one trade union in the mining sector that could later join the national trade union federation. When delegates from the mines assembled for the congress they were arrested. Miners demanded the release of their leaders and organized massive violent demonstrations. These demands were echoed in Lima, where workers were resisting lay-offs and pay cuts brought on by the depression. The government yielded to pressure and released the imprisoned miners. When the leaders of the miners' unions returned to the central highlands they organized occupations of the Oroya metallurgical complex and of several mines. In response the government declared a state of seige, imprisoned many miners, and declared all trade union activity illegal. There was no further legal organizing in the mines until 1945. To break the momentum of worker militancy in the mines the Cerro de Pasco Corporation declared a lockout and subsequently fired its entire labor force. The lockout was particularly convenient in light of the recent fall in demand for metals. Several months later there were less than half as many workers on the Corporation's payroll as before the lockout (see Table 4.6). Productivity in the Cerro de Pasco Corporation appears to have increased dramatically in 1930 and 1931 (see Table 4.7). This reflects a drastic decline in employment, as well as a substantial, though less extreme, fall in output. Growth in output per worker was not the result of innovations in the production process. Instead it reflects the lengthening of the working day and the intensification of the pace of work, measures the Corporation was able to impose on the work force it rehired in 1930. By 1932 productivity in the mines and plants of the Cerro de Pasco Corporation returned to the level of the middle 1920s and remained more or less unchanged through 1945. Although the Corporation continued to expand its infrastructure, it experienced stagnation in productivity. During this period it introduced few changes in the structure of production that significantly altered the labor process. The Cerro de Pasco Corporation and the rest of the Peruvian mining industry began to recover from the depression in the mid-1930s. The recovery was weak, based on rising prices rather than on restructuring and modernizing the production process. As a result, when prices stagnated or fell, as they did in the late 1930s and early 1940s, growth in the industry was sluggish.

During the depression output declined dramatically in those export-based enterprises throughout Peru that traditionally provided short-term employment. Consequently many peasants who migrated to the mines, highland haciendas, and coastal plantations for several months each year found these sources of employment closed off. For many peasant families the elimination of a cash income eroded the viability of household production. Poorer households borrowed cash, produce, or seeds from more prosperous neighbors to weather the crisis. As the depression dragged on many families became mired in debt and were forced to sell or forfeit their land and animals. This caused peasant households to become more dependent on cash for their survival at a moment when less wage employment was available. Through this process the depression accelerated the proletarianization of peasants in Peru.[44] Mining companies expanded production in the late 1930s in response to a revival in the international market. In this process they discovered that the shortage of labor that traditionally plagued the industry had abated. After the depression peasants tended to remain in the mines for longer periods than they had a decade earlier.[45] Working in the mines had become a way of life. For greater numbers of peasants wage labor in the mining sector was not a supplement, but the primary means of household survival.

Transformation of the Corporation's Haciendas

Work in the mines was oppressive and dangerous. In the early decades of the twentieth century it was not uncommon for miners to work fifteen hours, or even longer, on one shift; and to stay underground for lengthy periods. Accidents occurred frequently. Safety precautions were inadequate, shafts and tunnels collapsed, explosives were unreliable and often improperly used, and many miners were mutilated by machinery. Even if a miner was fortunate and escaped sudden death or injury, prolonged work underground or in the processing plants frequently caused acute and chronic ailments. Like underground miners almost everywhere, the workers in the Peruvian mines suffered from an array of occupationally-related diseases. Because of the hazards associated with extracting and processing minerals, the mining companies had to offer higher pay than peasants could earn in temporary employment on an hacienda. Therefore, through the early 1940s wages in the mining sector were slightly above wages paid for temporary work in agriculture.[46]

Despite this, the level of pay increasingly was inadequate. In the past wages earned at the mines tended to supplement household production. In the late 1930s and 1940s diminished access to land and weakening community ties forced miners and their families to depend on wage labor in the mines to a far greater extent than ever before. Collective action and strikes were still illegal. However, in the wake of the lockout by the Cerro de Pasco Corporation miners tried to protect their standard of living by pressuring the companies to pay higher wages. While data on wages prior to 1945 are inconsistent, there is evidence that wages rose in the years following the depression.[47] The Cerro de Pasco Corporation was in a more fortunate position than its competitors in Peru, however, because it was able to palliate the struggle for higher wages by selling products from its haciendas to its workers at prices below the market prices in the surrounding areas.

In past years the Corporation had administered its extensive haciendas in much the same way as did the former owners. The Corporation allowed the *colonos* and *huachilleros* who resided on its lands to continue their traditional activities. Whatever meat, wool, and dairy products the Corporation received in exchange for use of its land were sold to its workers. Following the depression, however, the Corporation embarked upon a program to rationalize and modernize its estates. To accomplish this the Corporation created a separate División Ganadera (Ranching Division) which at its peak owned about 325,000 *hectares* of the most productive pastureland in the central highlands.[48]

In the 1930s and 1940s the Corporation installed additional pollution control devices at its metallurgical complex at La Oroya. The new flues captured bismuth and sulphuric acid, in addition to finer lead and zinc particles. By the early 1940s the environmental contamination in the region was significantly reduced and the pasturelands around La Oroya were relatively fertile again. To raise productivity on its estates the Corporation gradually replaced traditional production relations with wage labor. From this period, and continuing until its lands were nationalized under the Agrarian Reform of 1969, the Corporation was involved in constant struggles with peasants who resisted attempts to reduce their traditional grazing rights on the Corporation's lands.[49]

In the 1940s the Corporation began to hire wage workers in the División Ganadera. By preventing local peasants from herding their animals together with those of the Corporation, the Corporation improved its breeds of sheep and cattle, and raised its output and quality of meat, dairy products, and wool. Also, by hiring and firing workers in response to the seasonal labor demands of livestock production, the División Ganadera lowered the costs of production. The best wool produced by the Corporation's herds was exported. The rest of the wool, meat, and milk was sold to the Corporation's labor force below market prices.[50] Through the 1960s the company used its provision of relatively low-priced foodstuffs to counter workers' demands for higher wages.

La Compañía

All members of highland society, miners and peasants, landlords and merchants alike, believed that the Cerro de Pasco Corporation dominated every aspect of life in the region. Until the 1960s people throughout the central highlands refered to the Corporation as *La Compañía* (the company). In the early years of the century *La Compañía* opened the economy of the region by extending the central railroad into the heart of the highlands and through the Mantaro Valley. Next it manipulated *enganche* to compel peasants to labor in its infernal underground domain. Then *La Compañía* extended its empire to include the most productive farming and pasture lands in the central highlands. *La Compañía* seemed to own everything in the zone: roads, water, electrical energy, politicians, even the priests.

By the 1920s the Corporation was the largest employer in Peru. It even had its own monetary system, paying its workers in company scrip and accepting this alone in its network of company stores. Since there were few government services in the mining zones the Corporation built its own housing, schools, and hospitals. In the early decades of the twentieth century *La Compañía* was the political, economic, and military authority in the mining region.

CHAPTER FIVE

Restructuring Ownership and Transformation of the Labor Process

The Revitalization of Peruvian Firms

For the first three decades of the twentieth century mining was the most dynamic sector of the Peruvian economy. In this period an industrial mining complex replaced artisanal production. The work force was increasingly characterized by free wage labor rather than by debt peonage, and the chronic scarcity of investment funds was superceded by a deluge of foreign capital that transformed the mineral zones of the central highlands. The early years of this century were characterized by a boom in mining that centered around the production of copper. This resulted in a sweeping denationalization of ownership in the industry.

In the 1930s the predominance of copper and the hegemony of foreign mining companies in Peru were eroded by the world economic crisis. Although the world market price of copper fell relative to the prices of other metals, this was not the primary cause of the decline in the importance of copper production in Peru. Low prices were aggravated by a shift towards protectionism in the developed countries. In 1932 the United States imposed a high tariff on copper imports and France and Great Britain established systems of preferential tariffs for their colonies and spheres of influence. These measures reduced demand for Peruvian copper. As a consequence, the second largest foreign mining company operating in Peru, the Northern Peru Mining and Smelting Company, discontinued the production of copper in 1931. The next year the Cerro de Pasco Corporation decreased production to 40 percent of its installed capacity and decided to reduce investments in copper mining and processing. Further, the Corporation's output of copper declined throughout the next three decades.

Although the expansion of the Peruvian mining industry since the turn of the century depended upon an abundance of high-grade copper ores, in the 1930s there was a significant change in the composition of mineral output. From 1903 through 1931 copper accounted for over 50 percent of the value of Peru's metal

123

production. This fell to an average of 30 percent from 1932 through 1945 (see Appendix G), and continued to decline for the next fifteen years. It was not until 1960, after a revolution in mining technology made the exploitation of low-grade copper ores profitable, that copper became Peru's premier mineral once again.

The world economic crisis of the 1930s devastated demand for industrial metals, but had the opposite effect on the markets for precious metals. From the late nineteenth century until 1932 the price of gold was fixed by the United States Treasury at US$20.67 per troy ounce. In February, 1934, the U.S. raised the price of gold to US$35.00 per troy ounce. This fueled an already feverish gold rush in Peru, led by local firms and individual prospectors or *lavaderos*, who panned for gold. Gold prospecting intensified in 1936 after the Peruvian Congress passed a bill that opened state gold reserves to private exploitation. In the 1930s gold became one of Peru's leading mineral products, for the first time in recorded history. From 1932 to 1939 Peruvian gold production increased by approximately 220 percent, and its value increased by 430 percent. From 1903 to 1930 gold accounted for less than 7 percent of the average annual value of mineral production in Peru. For the next fifteen years, until 1945, gold accounted for almost 25 percent of the average annual value of Peruvian mineral production (see Appendix G).

Silver, lead, and zinc production also expanded in the 1930s, while copper was on the wane. The decline in the importance of copper affected the structure of ownership in the industry. Despite three decades of expansion by foreign capital, many silver, lead, and zinc deposits remained in the hands of Peruvian entrepreneurs. This is because initially the Cerro de Pasco Corporation sought to develop its mining complex on the basis of copper. In the 1920s Peruvian mineowners also tended to neglect lead and zinc deposits. They did not have the machinery to process these metals for the export market, and little profit could be made by selling the ores to *La Compañía*. Prior to the 1930s the only flotation concentrators in Peru capable of treating lead and zinc ores belonged to the foreign mining companies. In the 1930s conditions changed. Many Peruvian mineowners reactivated and renovated their processing plants by installing flotation concentrators to process silver, lead, and later zinc ores. The flotation concentrator was a crucial innovation that contributed to the expansion of lead and zinc production. It was easily installed at almost any location and could be run by water power. This reduced the need for fuels. More importantly, unlike earlier smelters the flotation concentrator could process zinc. In 1935 there were nine flotation concentrators in Peru. By 1942 the number had grown to seventeen.[1] Most of these were operated by mining companies in the *mediana minería*, the subsector dominated by Peruvian entrepreneurs who owned medium scale mining firms.

In addition to the proliferation of the flotation concentrator, relative price movements favored lead and zinc production in the 1940s. International market prices of lead and zinc recovered from the effects of the depression before the revival in copper prices. Copper did not recover its pre-depression world market price until 1947, whereas the prices of lead and zinc exceeded their pre-crisis highs by the early 1940s (see Appendix C, Table C.2). The shift away from copper in the 1930s and 1940s had a major impact on the structure of ownership in the Peruvian mining industry. From early in the century through the 1920s large foreign firms dominated the production of copper. However, the expansion of gold, silver, lead, and zinc production, relative to copper, reflected growth by locally owned firms of the *mediana minería*. For decades Peruvian mineowners had pressured their government to promote the expansion of small and medium scale mining. By the late 1930s this lobby had generated a modicum of official support. In 1939 the Ministerio de Fomento (Ministry of Economic Development), which regulated the mining sector, inaugurated a smelter to process the ores of the small and medium scale firms. Two years later, in 1941, the government established the Banco Minero. This development bank was designed to assist the *pequeña* (very small scale) and *mediana minería* through the provision of credit and the establishment of processing plants. The bank also facilitated the export of ores produced by the smaller mining companies.[2]

Expansion of production by the *mediana minería* and its enhanced capacity to process and export its products led to changes in the relationship between the Cerro de Pasco Corporation and some of the Peruvian-owned firms. Several firms in the *mediana minería* severed the ties that bound them to the North American giant. Instead these firms processed and marketed their ores with the assistance of the Banco Minero. However, the larger Peruvian mining firms tended to maintain their traditional relations of dependence and reciprocity with the Cerro de Pasco Corporation. They sold custom ores to *La Compañía* and endeavored to benefit from their association with Cerro in numerous creative and singularly individual ways.

Despite the rise of the *mediana minería*, the Cerro de Pasco Corporation remained the largest single producer of lead and zinc in Peru. Copper, lead, and zinc ores were frequently mined together because of the characteristics of the mineral deposits in the central highlands and the techniques of underground shaft mining. Consequently, although the Corporation placed a priority on copper production in its early years, it produced lead and zinc as by-products of copper mining. However, by the mid-1930s the Corporation no longer completely dominated the industry. The majority of lead and zinc exports were produced by firms in the *mediana minería*. The reorientation of production away from copper to other metals, and the corresponding expansion of locally-owned firms, resulted in a decline in the Corporation's share of production. In 1922, at the peak of its direct control of mineral production in Peru, the Cerro de Pasco Corporation produced eighty-eight percent of the output of the mining sector. By 1945 this figure had fallen to approximately sixty percent (see Table 4.3).

The Cerro de Pasco Corporation attempted to reverse this trend. It introduced modern techniques for lead and zinc processing so that the firms of the *mediana minería* would find it advantageous once again to sell their ores for further processing. In 1934 the Corporation opened an electrolytic processing plant for lead and bismuth. This was followed by the inauguration of a lead refinery, a pilot plant for producing electrolytic zinc, and a plant to process sulphuric acid; all at La Oroya. In 1936 the Corporation opened another hydroelectric plant that produced energy for its expanding complex and the following year it installed an additional flotation concentrator. To complete this phase of expansion and to augment its own mineral output, the Corporation opened a new mine at San Cristóbal in 1935.

The Crisis of the 1940s

World War II engendered economic expansion, based largely on the production of armaments. Despite general economic growth, the early 1940s were characterized by a downturn in the world mining industry and a decline in mining production in Peru (see Table 2.1). War preparations began in the 1930s and had fueled the earlier expansion of mineral production. By the time war was declared the industry was stagnating. The United States and several European countries reimposed price controls. As a result, metal prices remained relatively stationary from 1941 through 1945.

127

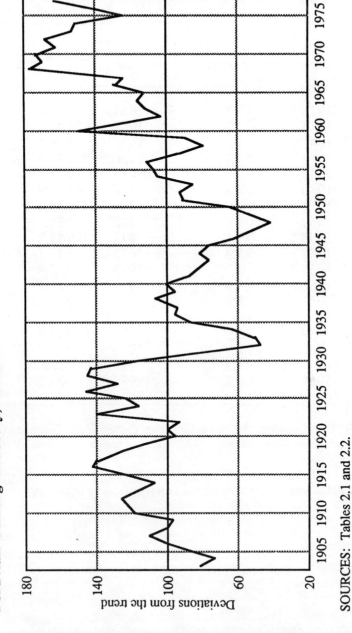

FIGURE 5.1 Trend Analysis of the Volume of Production[a] in the Peruvian Mining Industry, 1903-1977

SOURCES: Tables 2.1 and 2.2.

[a]The volume of production is measured in constant 1963 prices.

TABLE 5.1 Index of World Market Metals Prices[a], 1945-1980

		(1963 = 100)		
Year	Price Index		Year	Price Index
1945	45.8		1963	100.0
1946	57.7		1964	108.2
1947	75.8		1965	118.2
1948	85.1		1966	138.2
1949	75.2		1967	137.4
1950	78.5		1968	149.8
1951	98.0		1969	165.4
1952	104.4		1970	168.3
1953	94.1		1971	143.7
1954	93.3		1972	148.1
1955	110.4		1973	215.3
1956	115.3		1974	291.7
1957	93.8		1975	242.3
1958	86.2		1976	256.0
1959	95.9		1977	262.4
1960	97.7		1978	283.4
1961	93.1		1979	436.6
1962	94.8		1980	598.2

SOURCES: Computed by the author from data in *Metal Statistics* (Franfurt Am Main: Metallgesellschaft, 1907-1977); and unpublished data from the U.S. Bureau of the Mines.

[a]Price index is weighted to reflect the composition of mineral output in Peru.

Demand was depressed further because many European metals markets were closed. Also, the industry was plagued by commercial difficulties stemming from problems with transport and financing.

The recession in mining lasted until the middle of the decade. With the end of the war and the subsequent economic recovery efforts in Europe, the United States and Japan spurred expansion in mining production. However, the performance of the industry in Peru did not reflect this general recovery. In 1945 the Peruvian mining industry was in the midst of a severe crisis that lasted the entire decade from 1940 to 1950. Figure 5.1, which presents the results of trend analysis of mineral production in Peru from 1900 through 1977, shows the depth and duration of the crisis. Production bottomed out in 1948, and began to recover in 1949. An analysis of price movements suggests that the depth and duration of this crisis[3] of Peruvian mining had little to do with changes in the price level on the international market. World market prices rose rapidly from 1945 to 1948, the same years that the Peruvian industry was depressed (see Table 5.1 and Appendix J). The symptom of the crisis in Peruvian mining was the decline in copper production.[4] The cause, however, lay buried in more than a decade of stagnating productivity.

From the late 1930s through the 1940s the ore content of the copper concentrates produced by the Cerro de Pasco Corporation progressively declined. When it became apparent that the Corporation's copper reserves were seriously depleted the Corporation developed plans to revitalize copper production. To lower costs and increase its installed capacity to process copper Cerro opened a flotation plant at Cerro de Pasco in 1943. This plant raised the ore content from approximately 2.7 percent at the mine head to a concentrate with a fifteen to twenty percent copper content.[5] Prior to 1948 only blister copper was produced in Peru. The blister was exported to the United States where the purifying process was completed. Cerro's reliance on refining capacity in the United States, and its failure to build a complete copper refinery in Peru generated criticism among Peruvians. Although Peru was a major copper producer, refined copper for industrial uses had to be imported. In part to placate this criticism the Corporation inaugurated a large electrolytic copper refinery at La Oroya in 1948. In the 1940s the Corporation also developed the Yauricocha mining complex which included a railway and an aerial tramway. Mining at Yauricocha was inaugurated in 1947 and reached full production in

1949. Notwithstanding these attempts to revitalize the copper industry, copper production continued to decline in importance. The doubling of copper prices from 1947 to 1956, and the demand for copper generated by the Korean War, had little impact on copper production in Peru. Copper output stagnated from 1940 through 1959 (see Table 5.2).

It is clear that the crisis of the industry was in the production of copper, because throughout this period lead and zinc production expanded. From 1947 to 1954 the value of lead surpassed the value of copper (see Table 5.3). While this was unusual for an industry that purportedly rested on its copper reserves, it is particularly surprising because it coincided with years when the world market price of copper was rising faster than the price of lead (see Appendix C, Table C.2). Stagnation in the output of copper indicates underlying constraints on the expansion of the copper industry in Peru.

The primary cause of the crisis in the industry was the long-term stagnation in productivity. The inauguration of the processing complex at La Oroya in 1922 effected a large increase in output per worker. However, from 1923 through the mid-1940s there was little sustainable change in productivity in mining and mineral processing in Peru.[6] This problem soon grew worse. The period from 1945 to 1949 was characterized by a sharp decline in productivity (see Table 5.4). This underlined the necessity to fundamentally reorganize the labor process in the industry. However, political and social conditions in Peru had changed and the labor force of the 1940s was not as easily controlled as it had been a generation earlier.

In 1930 trade unions had been banned, and all organizing activity remained illegal until the mid-1940s. Workers in the industry had neither job security nor legislation protecting health and safety. In the mid-1930s they began, illegally, to agitate for improvements in wages and working conditions and for the right to organize trade unions. In 1944 the Cerro de Pasco Corporation legally recognized a trade union of miners for the first time. The following year a union was established at the plant in La Oroya. Following these successes the Aprista Party launched a campaign to organize the miners of the central highlands.[7] By 1947 thirty-eight unions of miners were granted legal status in the central region alone.[8] This encouraged APRA to create a trade union federation, the Federación del Trabajadores Mineros del Centro, to unify these unions.

TABLE 5.2 Peruvian Copper Production and the World Market Price of Copper, 1940-1959

Year	Copper Production (metric tons)	World Price[a]
1940	43,965	11.30
1941	36,882	11.80
1942	35,332	11.78
1943	33,407	11.78
1944	32,396	11.78
1945	31,916	11.78
1946	24,592	14.80
1947	22,492	20.96
1948	18,069	22.27
1949	27,959	19.20
1950	30,050	21.34
1951	31,988	26.07
1952	30,448	31.74
1953	35,401	30.84
1954	38,425	29.89
1955	43,403	39.12
1956	46,236	40.43
1957	57,174	27.16
1958	53,619	24.12
1959	50,686	28.89

SOURCES: Compiled by the author from data in Ministerio de Fomento y Obras Públicas, *Anuario de la Industria Minera del Perú: 1959* (Lima), p. 116; and Appendix C, Table C.2.

[a]Price for electrolytic copper on the New York Metals Exchange, cents per pound.

TABLE 5.3   Current Value of Copper and Lead
Production in Peru, 1940-1959   (in thousands of
Peruvian *soles*)

Year	Copper S/.x1000	Lead S/.x1000
1940	64,408	33,015
1941	57,516	38,978
1942	59,711	40,061
1943	55,140	44,147
1944	54,315	44,775
1945	53,510	46,012
1946	52,068	50,027
1947	67,376	110,770
1948	57,600	120,577
1949	169,730	311,419
1950	209,901	251,691
1951	281,587	444,996
1952	330,757	493,045
1953	404,193	509,834
1954	491,072	588,557
1955	716,367	695,445
1956	782,729	766,908
1957	633,048	745,424
1958	646,370	725,674
1959	713,334	585,017

SOURCES: Ministerio de Fomento y Obras Públicas, *Anuario de la Industria Minera del Perú: 1959* (Lima), pp. 116 and 132.

TABLE 5.4 **Labor Productivity in the Peruvian Mining Industry[a], 1945-1975**

Year	(1945 = 100) Output Per *Tarea*	Index
1945	304	100
1946	287	94
1947	244	80
1948	203	67
1949	230	76
1950	276	91
1951	405	133
1952	393	129
1953	355	116
1954	297	131
1955	396	130
1956	440	145
1957	372	122
1958	455	149
1959	517	170
1960	761	250
1961	755	248
1962	627	206
1963	505	166
1964	679	223
1965	n.a.	n.a.
1966	786	258
1967	659	216
1968	890	293
1969	950	312
1970	976	321
1971	969	318
1972	957	315
1973	841	277
1974	805	265
1975	717	236

(continued)

This upsurge in union activity was facilitated by the reformist policies of the government of President José Luis Bustamante, who was elected in 1945 with the endorsement of APRA. In exchange for APRA's support, the government legalized trade unions for the first time in fifteen years. In addition, the government of Bustamante passed legislation that conceded to workers a degree of job security. The law regulated dismissal procedures and required companies to provide severance pay to workers who were fired. However, no effective enforcement apparatus was created and application of the legislation in the mining sector was rare.[9] Nevertheless, the miners' trade unions continued to press for higher wages and improvements in working and living conditions. As a result of union activity money wages rose substantially throughout the industry in the 1940s. The cost of living rose faster than wages, however, so price-deflated wages declined (see Appendix I). Although average money wages paid to workers in the Cerro de Pasco Corporation doubled from 1945 to 1947, miners' families struggled to maintain their standard of living in the face of rapidly rising prices for basic necessities.[10] Declining living standards led to anger and frustration. In 1948 the trade union at Cerro de Pasco protested the scarcity of food and the rising cost of living. In the course of this protest a crowd of people beat and killed the mayor of the town. In retaliation, a state of seige was imposed in the Department of Pasco and the union leaders were prosecuted.[11]

Worker militancy aggravated the crisis of production and profitability in the copper industry in the 1940s. As part of their struggles for higher pay, workers' organizations resisted attempts to

---

SOURCES: Computed by the author from data presented in Ministerio de Energía y Minas, *Anuario Minero del Perú*, 1966-1972; Ministerio de Energía y Minas, *Anuario de la Minería del Perú*, 1973-1975; Ministerio de Fomento, *Anuario de la Industria Minera en el Perú*, 1945-1949; Ministerio de Fomento y Obras Públicas, *Anuario de la Industria Minera en el Perú*, 1950-1965; *Anuario Minero-Comercial*, 1970; and "Declaraciones Anuales Consolidadas de Concesionarios, Empresas y Empresarios Mineros" (Lima: Archivos, División de Estadística, Dirección General de Minería, Ministerio de Energía y Minas, 1945-1975).

[a]Productivity is measured in the volume of output per working shift or *tarea*. The volume of output is measured in constant Peruvian *soles*. For another measure of productivity see Appendix H.

n.a - not available.

prolong the working day and intensify the pace of work without an increase in wages. The companies in the industry had weathered the previous crisis, the depression of the 1930s, by reducing the size of their labor force, extending the working day, and speeding up the tempo of the production   process.   But the militancy and organization of the miners made it difficult for the companies to compensate for stagnating productivity by carrying out these same measures again.

Contemporary analyses attribute the crisis of the 1940s to rising wage costs.[12] However, an examination of the wage as a relative cost to the companies, which I call "the wage cost to capital," demonstrates that this was not the case. The wage cost to capital measures the ratio between movements in metal prices and changes in the money wage. As an indicator of labor costs it is valuable because it shows the relationship between average labor costs (productivity constant) and average revenue. Falling productivity from 1945 to 1949 was a signal of the severity of the crisis in the mining industry. However, the effects of this decline on the companies' profits were mitigated by greater decline in the wage cost to capital (see Table 5.5). Although money wages rose by more than one hundred percent from 1945 to 1949 (see Table 5.6), the companies' balance sheets were cushioned by an even greater increase in the prices of the metals (see Table 5.1). The crisis of the 1940s arose from more fundamental causes than the rise in money wages.

The major problems of the industry had changed significantly since the early years of the century. Stagnating productivity, rising money wages, and increasing worker militancy were the hallmarks of the 1940s. Nevertheless, the directors of the Cerro de Pasco Corporation, still the most powerful company in the industry, were convinced that the primary obstacle to the expansion of production remained a shortage of labor. The Corporation's *Annual Report* for 1946 states that "[t]he low level of production in 1946 is principally due to conditions in the supply of labor. In no month of the year was there a sufficient number of workers to work the mines and the processing plants to full capacity."[13] The depression, rising commercialization, and the privatization of land had all swept through the central highlands in the preceding decades. Nothwithstanding these assaults on traditional society, the social relations on *haciendas* and in peasant communities evidently had not yet changed enough to insure an adequate supply of workers for the mines.

TABLE 5.5 Index of the Wage Cost to Capital in the Peruvian Mining Industry[a], 1945-1975

	(1945 = 100)
Year	Index
1945	100
1946	91
1947	84
1948	82
1949	53
1950	63
1951	82
1952	82
1953	81
1954	99
1955	92
1956	93
1957	89
1958	80
1959	135
1960	135
1961	127
1962	130
1963	153
1964	150
1965	n.a.
1966	237
1967	218
1968	299
1969	294
1970	337
1971	380
1972	443
1973	248
1974	191
1975	221

(continued)

SOURCES: Computed by the author from data presented in Ministerio de Energía y Minas, *Anuario Minero del Perú*, 1966-1972; Ministerio de Energía y Minas, *Anuario de la Minería del Perú*, 1973-1975; Ministerio de Fomento, *Anuario de la Industria Minera en el Perú*, 1945-1949; Ministerio de Fomento y Obras Públicas, *Anuario de la Industria Minera en el Perú*, 1950-1965; *Anuario Minero-Comercial*, 1970; and "Declaraciones Anuales Consolidadas de Concesionarios, Empresas y Empresarios Mineros" (Lima: Archivos, División de Estadística, Dirección General de Minería, Ministerio de Energía y Minas, 1945-1975).

[a]The wage cost to capital meaures the ratio between movements in the prices of the metals and movements in the wage in current Peruvian *soles*. This is an index of the ratio of average labor costs to average revenue in the industry. Appendix K presents the index of the wage cost to capital using wages converted into U.S. dollars at the official exchange rate. The two indexes are very similar.

n.a. - not available

TABLE 5.6   Average Annual Money Wages in the Peruvian Mining Industry[a], 1945-1975 (in Peruvian *soles*)

Year	(1945 = 100) Average Wages	Index
1945	1,709	100
1946	2,020	118
1947	2,593	152
1948	2,886	169
1949	3,725	218
1950	4,612	270
1951	5,793	339
1952	6,269	367
1953	7,425	435
1954	8,811	516
1955	9,182	537
1956	9,866	577
1957	10,542	617
1958	11,527	675
1959	14,172	829
1960	16,053	939
1961	17,241	1,009
1962	20,397	1,194
1963	24,242	1,419
1964	26,537	1,553
1965	n.a.	n.a.
1966	47,843	2,800
1967	49,052	2,870
1968	64,582	3,779
1969	72,719	4,255
1970	81,678	4,779
1971	93,952	5,478
1972	109,510	6,409
1973	145,031	8,486
1974	131,163	7,675
1975	208,313	12,189

(continued)

The Shift from Underground to Open-Pit Mining

The mining crisis of the 1940s coincided with a major revolution in the methods of copper mining in the world industry. Open-pit mining was replacing traditional underground mining techniques. Open-pit mining has been described as precipitating a "fundamental change in the conditions determining the cost of producing copper."[14] In the century prior to the introduction of open-pit mining there were no radical changes in the technologies of copper mining (as opposed to processing). Traditionally copper mining was based on selective techniques that involved exploitation of high-grade veins, generally with a minimum ore content of four to five percent. Underground mining required exploration of the ore body and construction of shafts and tunnels to follow the veins. Because high transport and processing costs are associated with selective mining techniques, companies using the old techniques attempt to extract only those minerals that possess a high ore content. Prior to the development of open-pit mining, advances in the art of mining generally were concentrated in the transport and processing, rather than in the extractive phase.

In the early twentieth century radical changes in transport and refining techniques fundamentally transformed copper mining. For the first time it became economical to mine and process massive quantities of low-grade ores. Fine grinding and milling, followed by a chemical flotation process to separate the ore from the

---

SOURCES: Computed by the author from data presented in *Metal Statistics: 1965-1975* (63rd edition) (Frankfurt Am Main: Metallgesellschaft, 1976); *Statistical Yearbook* (New York: United Nations, 1949, 1955, 1965, 1976); Ministerio de Energía y Minas, *Anuario Minero del Perú* (Lima: 1966-1972); Ministerio de Energía y Minas, *Anuario de la Minera del Perú* (Lima: 1973-1975); Ministerio de Fomento, *Anuario de la Industria Minera en el Perú* (Lima: 1945-1949); Ministerio de Fomento y Obras Públicas, *Anuario de la Industria Minera en el Perú* (Lima: 1950-1965); *Anuario Minero Comercial* (Lima: 1977); unpublished data from the Ministerio de Energía y Minas, Area de Estadística, Archives; and "Declaraciones Anuales Consolidadas de Concesionarios, Empresas y Empresarios Mineros" (Lima: Archivos de la División de Estadística, Dirección General de Minería, Ministerio de Energía y Minas, 1945-1975).

[a]Average annual wages and salaries paid to *obreros* and *empleados*.

n.a. - not available

surrounding rock, replaced mechanical concentration. As a result of these technological innovations it became possible to profitably mine low-grade porphyry copper deposits using non-selective techniques. Non-selective or mass methods of extraction can also involve underground mining, as it did in Cobriza, a mine developed in the late 1950s by the Cerro de Pasco Corporation. However, non-selective methods usually are associated with the open-pit technique. Open-pit mining involves the removal of the overburden, or surface ground covering, and the extraction of extensive mineral bodies that contain approximately a one percent ore content. In order to be profitable open-pit mining generally is carried out in large scale operations.

The shift from underground to open-pit copper mining occurred rapidly throughout the world. Before 1910 mining copper with open-pit methods was virtually unknown. By the 1920s more than one-third of the copper produced in the Americas derived from open-pit mines.[15] In the United States, the world's leading copper producer, copper extracted with open-pit methods exceeded the total volume of copper mined underground by 1942. By 1950 almost seventy-five percent of U.S. copper production came from open-pit mines. Clearly the world copper industry was becoming increasingly dominated by non-selective mining techniques, and open-pit mining and non-selective techniques reduced the cost of production.

At the time of this transformation in the world copper industry all Peruvian copper was extracted from underground mines utilizing selective methods. Because relatively high costs of production were associated with underground mining, copper producers in Peru found it increasingly difficult to compete in the world market, even in periods of rising prices. Consequently, the leaders of the mining industry pressured the Peruvian government to implement a policy that would facilitate the development of open-pit mining. The foreign mining companies of the *gran minería* as well as the firms of the *mediana minería* collectively petitioned the government to promote open-pit operations by revising the tax structure and removing legal constraints to large-scale investments.

When the severity of the mining crisis became apparent in the early 1940s, producers urged the state to adopt measures that would facilitate the restructuring of the industry. However, the government of President Bustamante was not responsive to pressures from the foreign companies—the loudest voices calling for state promotion of open-pit mining. The Peruvian government under Bustamante enacted no legislation that facilitated the resolution of the crisis in the mining industry, nor measures that promoted large scale investments in new mining ventures.[16] In 1948 President Bustamante was overthrown, replaced by General Odría. President Odría formed a government sympathetic to the interests of foreign capital and large Peruvian exporters. One of the first measures of the military government was once again to outlaw trade unions. Union activity remained illegal throughout the eight years of Odría's rule.

During the Odría administration foreign mining interests and their Peruvian supporters prevailed upon the government to enact a new mining code. The objective of the new legislation was to promote major investments in large-scale mining ventures, particularly open-pit operations. A new mining code was enacted in 1950, drafted by a commission comprised of representatives of both foreign and national firms.

Prior to 1950 the tax structure for the mining industry was convoluted. There were taxes on land, profits, excess profits, and exports. The export taxes were the most onerous for the companies. In the 1940s representatives of the mining companies argued that the export taxes were formulated in such as way as to discourage the expansion of production in periods of rising prices. The tax structure for exports was keyed to the prices of metals on the international market. As prices rose, so did the tax rate.[17] Consequently, the rise in world market prices in the 1940s triggered an increase in the tax rate. This was particularly burdensome for those producers who were suffering from stagnating or falling mine output and declining profits.

The Mining Code of 1950 greatly simplified the tax structure. Taxes were levied on profits, rather than tied to prices.[18] As an incentive to investors, the code established a lower tax rate for the mining industry than the prevailing rates that applied to other sectors of the economy and guaranteed that no taxes, other than those explicitly enumerated in the legislation of 1950, would be levied for twenty-five years.[19] Leaders of the industry were confident that the new tax structure, which greatly reduced levies, would promote the expansion of the sector. Nonetheless, the effective tax rate proved lower even than that implied by the law. The Mining Code reinforced the advantages of the new tax structure with a depletion allowance that permitted as much as one-half of a company's profits to be tax-free.[20] Representatives of the industry justified inclusion of the depletion allowance by arguing that it allowed a company to build a reserve fund that would be used to develop new deposits.

The tax structure and the depletion allowance were extremely favorable to capital in the industry. However, the transformative nature of the decree lay in its promotion of large-scale, open-pit ventures. Article 56 of the Mining Code allowed the Peruvian government at its own discretion to waive taxes on profits if it considered that a proposed mining project would be marginally profitable. In such cases the company would pay the Peruvian goverment between 10 and 20 percent of the profits, the rate to be determined through negotiations between the company and the government. In addition, to protect investments in marginal mining operations, the concessionaire (the mining company) could "apply the entirety of his first profits to the preferential amortization of such capital" in accordance with a contract which would be negotiated with the government.[21] In other words, in cases of marginal operations all taxes could be waived until the original investment was recovered.

Because the underlying purpose of the Mining Code of 1950 was to promote open-pit mining, the Peruvian government considered that all investments in such ventures were marginal. Actually, open-pit mining in Peru promised to be extraordinarily profitable. By enacting the Mining Code of 1950 the Peruvian Government made a commitment to subsidize and protect investments that the mining companies expected would yield an extremely high rate of profit. As a final incentive for capital, the code provided that machinery, equipment, spare parts, and materials for specific use in the mining industry would be free of all import and additional duties, present and future.[22]

For the next twenty-five years the Mining Code generated considerable controversy. At one end of the spectrum, the President of the Cerro de Pasco Corporation lauded the code for creating the most favorable climate for United States investment in the world.[23] Opponents of the code agreed with this assessment, but they were by no means sanguine about its effects on the Peruvian economy. They feared that foreign companies would wield undue political and economic power in Peru. Many owners of small mines, trade unions representing the miners, and politicians who advocated reducing foreign domination of the economy were united in their opposition to the code. They denounced the Peruvian government for capitulating to foreign interests and relinquishing Peru's natural resources to foreign control. Until the code was rescinded in 1970, nullification of the Mining Code of 1950 was one of the major demands of Peruvian nationalists.

Critics focused their opposition to the code on two of its major provisions: the concept of marginal investments and the depletion allowance. They argued that what the Peruvian government defined as marginal investments were in fact the reverse. They objected to the depletion allowance on the grounds that it created windfall savings on taxes; savings which allegedly far exceeded the costs of developing new deposits. Opponents of the code reinforced this position in later years. They pointed out that the Southern Peru Copper Corporation (SPCC), by far the largest producer of porphry copper in Peru, petitioned the government for permission take funds from its depletion allowance and to remit them to the United States as profits. To critics of the code this demonstrated that the depletion allowance was excessively generous, and that the companies were not reinvesting the depletion funds in mineral exploration and development in Peru.[24]

Expansion of the Industry: The Resurgence of Foreign Hegemony

The passage of the Mining Code of 1950 marked the beginning of two decades of expansion in the industry. Much of the growth was in response to the favorable investment climate fostered by the code. Immediately after its passage foreign mining companies swarmed into Peru to search for investment opportunities. The Marcona Mining Company, a United States corporation, initiated the first large-scale open-pit mining venture. In the 1940s the Corporación del Santa, a company partially owned by the Peruvian state, invested about US$ 2 million in developing a large iron deposit near San Nicolás on the coast in southern Peru. However, soon the company was forced to suspend operations for lack of sufficient funds. Following passage of the mining code several U.S. companies became interested in developing these iron deposits. In 1951 the Peruvian government granted the Utah Construction Company rights to exploit the mine. Two years later this enterprise formed a joint-stock company with the Cyprus Mines Corporation, another U.S. firm, to develop these deposits. The new company was incorporated in the United States as the Marcona Mining Company, and immediately began to mine, process, and export iron.

Interest in developing Peru's large porphyry copper deposits dated from the 1940s. After the Cerro de Pasco Corporation and the American Smelting and Refining Corporation (ASARCO) engineered the passage of a mining code that catered to their interests, the two firms rushed to stake claims to large copper deposits in the southern departments of Moquegua and Tacna. There ensued a lengthly legal battle over which of the two companies possessed title to the properties.[25] The Supreme Court of Peru decided in favor of ASARCO in 1948. With its claim resolved ASARCO created a wholly-owned subsidiary, the Southern Peru Copper Corporation (SPCC), to administer its mining operations in Peru.[26] La Southern, as the company in Peru is known, negotiated with the Peruvian government over its rights and obligations. In 1954 the government of Peru and the Southern Peru Copper Corporation signed a contract, the terms of which were extremely favorable to the North American firm.[27]

Southern Peru initiated an exploration program at Toquepala, a mine in the department of Tacna, close to the Chilean border. This revealed an even more extensive deposit than was previously believed to exist, and ASARCO immediately sought additional financing for the project. In 1955, after several years of negotiations, Cerro de Pasco, Newmont Mining, and the Phelps Dodge Corporations purchased shares of capital stock in SPCC and agreed to make cash advances during the construction phase at Toquepala.[28] Construction of the mine and processor began in 1956 and for several years experimental mining and processing was carried out at Toquepala. The complex reached full-scale production in 1960. For the next seventeen years 60 percent of the Peru's copper was mined at Toquepala. With the impetus of the Mining Code, the Cerro de Pasco Corporation experimented with open-pit techniques. In 1957 open-pit mining was initiated at the McCune Pit in Cerro de Pasco. By 1960 approximately 80 percent of the copper ore mined at Cerro de Pasco came from the McCune Pit.

The 1950s was a decade of transition in the Peruvian mining industry. At the beginning of the decade there was no open-pit mining. Ten years later 75 percent of Peru's copper and all of its iron ore were extracted from open-pits. This technological revolution generated rapid growth. The volume of mineral production more than doubled from 1950 to 1959 (see Table 2.2), and the industry continued to grow in the 1960s. In 1965 the Cerro de Pasco Corporation made larger investments in Peru than in any other year in the Corporation's history. Most of the funds were used to expand the McCune Pit and processing capacity at Cerro de Pasco. In 1964 the Corporation enlarged the copper refinery and inaugurated a new copper precipitation plant in 1966.

The 1960s was also a decade of growth for the Marcona Mining Company. In 1961 Marcona built a new port and processing plant at San Nicolás. The next year the company began the construction of a plant that utilized the latest technology for processing iron. With the completion of this plant in 1964 Marcona became one of the most technically-advanced iron ore producers in the world. The pellets and sinter produced at the Marcona complex in Peru were in great demand because they were high-grade, could be transported in pipelines and tankers more easily than traditional iron bars, and were compatible with the changing needs of industry.

The rapid expansion of open-pit mining was a catalyst for the modernization of underground copper, lead, and zinc mines. The Cerro de Pasco Corporation, despite its successful development of the McCune Pit, was compelled by the nature of its deposits to remain tied to underground mining. Therefore, it attempted to combat obsolescence and declining profitability in its underground mines by introducing new techniques in shaft and tunnel mining. In particular the Corporation experimented with methods to reduce the danger of underground fires. New equipment was installed in the mines at Cerro de Pasco that permitted the expansion of mineral exploitation into areas where it had been too dangerous to blast because of the presence of pyrites.[29]

The major innovation in underground mining was the introduction of a trackless mining system at Cobriza, a mine that the Corporation developed in the 1960s. Trackless mining involves a transport system within mines that replaces the traditional trains or carts on tracks with large trucks. This technique makes mining operations more flexible. New veins at Cobriza could be exploited relatively quickly because there was no need to install tracks prior to mining for ore. New drilling techniques, power shovels, and advanced machines for cutting through rock also were introduced at the site. The Cobriza mine was a hybrid that merged two mining methodologies: the shafts and tunnels that were characteristic of selective underground mining techniques and the large trucks, power shovels, and drills that are associated with open-pit non-selective mining.

Cobriza was inaugurated in 1967, when the managers of the Cerro de Pasco Corporation were considering selling the company to the Peruvian government. In anticipation of that sale, Cobriza was exploited intensively. To recover the investment in the mine as soon as possible the richest ores were extracted first. This explains, in part, why labor productivity at Cobriza was four times higher than the company average.[30] Despite the instant success of Cobriza, underground copper mining was increasingly less competitive in the world market. In consequence Cerro converted some of its copper mines into silver and lead-zinc mines; and at the same time expanded its capacity to process lead and zinc ores. In 1962 the Corporation completed a lead-zinc circuit at Cerro de Pasco as well as an electrolytic zinc refinery at La Oroya.

The restructuring of copper production, the expansion of iron mining, and the introduction of technical advances in all phases of the mining process made the decade of the 1960s successful for the foreign mining companies that operated in Peru. The output of the industry tripled from 1959 to 1970 through a process of relatively continuous though somewhat uneven growth. Fortuitously for the companies, the decade was characterized by rising metal prices that favored the expansion of production (see Table 5.7 and Appendix J). In this remarkable period of boom two years stand out. Nineteen-sixty, the year of the inauguration of Toquepala, was exceptional because output in the industry increased by 75 percent. In 1968, another notable year for growth, total production increased by more than 40 percent (see Table 2.2). The surge in output in 1968 was in part the result of the opening of Cobriza. In that year there was also a substantial increase in the production of gold because the United States Government ended its fixed-price purchasing of the metal. Following deregulation the price of gold rose (see Appendix C, Table C.2).

The revolution in mining technology and the restructuring of the labor process in the 1960s generated a significant rise in productivity. In the comparison of two periods, 1955 to 1959 and 1960 to 1964, we can observe that productivity and output increased by more than 50 percent (see Tables 5.4 and 2.2), while the labor force increased by only 23 percent (see Table 5.8).

TABLE 5.7 Index of World Market Metals Prices[a], **1945-1980**

		(1963 = 100)	
Year	Index	Year	Index
1945	45.8	1963	100.0
1946	57.7	1964	108.2
1947	75.8	1965	118.2
1948	85.1	1966	138.2
1949	75.2	1967	137.4
1950	78.5	1968	149.8
1951	98.0	1969	165.4
1952	104.4	1970	168.3
1953	94.1	1971	143.7
1954	93.3	1972	148.1
1955	110.4	1973	215.3
1956	115.3	1974	291.7
1957	93.8	1975	242.3
1958	86.2	1976	256.0
1959	95.0	1977	262.4
1960	97.7	1978	283.4
1961	93.1	1979	436.6
1962	94.8	1980	598.2

SOURCES: Computed by the author from data presented in Appendix C, Table C.2.

[a]The price index is weighted to reflect the composition of output of the Peruvian mining industry.

TABLE 5.8 **Total Number of Workers Employed in the Peruvian Mining Industry[a], 1945-1975**

Year	(1945 = 100) Total Employment	Index of Total Employment
1945	22,304	100.0
1946	21,392	95.9
1947	22,275	99.8
1948	24,760	111.0
1949	27,927	125.0
1950	24,696	110.7
1951	26,203	117.4
1952	26,524	118.8
1953	27,180	121.8
1954	29,199	130.9
1955	30,311	135.7
1956	31,545	141.4
1957	31,597	141.6
1958	27,316	122.4
1959	30,167	135.2
1960	35,597	159.5
1961	53,422	158.8
1962	34,069	152.8
1963	39,625	177.6
1964	41,165	184.5
1965	n.a.	n.a.
1966	40,551	181.7
1967	48,548	217.8
1968	50,441	226.1
1969	51,665	231.6
1970	54,066	242.3
1971	53,576	240.1
1972	53,859	241.4
1973	50,285	225.4
1974	68,847	308.5[b]
1975	53,993	242.1

SOURCES: Computed by the author from data presented in Ministerio de Energía y Minas, *Anuario Minero del Perú*, 1966-1972; Ministerio de Energía y

(continued)

Restructuring the Labor Force

The transformation of Peruvian mining from underground to open-pit methods coupled with the modernization of the shaft mines and the processing plants altered the labor requirements for the industry. Underground mining requires workers experienced in the crafts of ore identification and extraction, as well as others skilled in the construction of the elaborate tunnels and supports that make it possible to exploit mineral veins. These traditional mining skills were rendered obsolete by non-selective mining techniques. Open-pit operations required workers who could operate large-scale equipment, not workers skilled at identifying and following an ore body. Therefore, Marcona and Southern Peru did not seek workers with prior experience in the mines. Nonetheless, historical problems associated with labor transiency and militancy sensitized the companies to the need for a stable work force, preferably one that would not be combative in its relations with management.

Traditionally in the mining industry technicians and supervisory personnel were classified as *empleados* and unskilled workers as *obreros*. This division involved separate union organizations. The *empleados'* union of the Cerro de Pasco Corporation, founded in

---

Minas, *Anuario de la Minera del Perú*, 1973-1975; Ministerio de Fomento, *Anuario de la Industria Minera en el Perú*, 1945-1949; Ministerio de Fomento y Obras Públicas, *Anuario de la Industria Minera en el Perú*, 1950-1965; *Anuario Minero-Comercial*, 1970; and "Declaraciones Anuales Consolidadas de Concesionarios, Empresas y Empresarios Mineros" (Lima: Archivos, División de Estadística, Dirección General de Minería, Ministerio de Energía y Minas, 1945-1975).

[a]Includes *obreros* (unskilled or blue collar workers) and *empleados* (skilled workers, technicians, and supervisory personnel). Administrative personnel and office staff have been excluded from the *empleado* category.

[b]According to official data employment rose by approximately 35 percent from 1973 to 1974. In 1975 employment declined almost to the level that it had been in 1973. The data indicate that the increase occurred among *obreros* who worked in the mines. This rapid rise and fall in the level of employment is unusual and I can find no convincing explanation of this drastic fluctuation. Therefore, for the purpose of calculating productivity I use average employment figures for 1971 through 1975. This gives a figure for average employment in the industry of 56,112 for the years 1971 to 1975 which indicates a slight rise in the size of the labor force from the late 1960s.

n.a. - not available

1947 as the Federación de Empleados de la Cerro de Pasco Corporation, resembled a professional association. Unlike the trade union of *obreros,* the Federación de Empleados was decidedly pro-management.[31] Marcona and Southern Peru aspired to reproduce the harmonious relationship that Cerro had forged with its Federación de Empleados by altering the traditional classification of workers in the industry.[32] Prior to the 1960s *empleados* comprised an average of 7 percent of the labor force. After the expansion of open-pit mining an average of 17 percent of the workers in the industry were *empleados,* with the highest proportion in the open-pit mines (see Table 5.9).

The decreasing differentiation between the skills and work of *empleados* and *obreros* is reflected in remunerations of the two categories of workers, as well as in job classifications. Starting in the 1950s wages of *obreros* rose faster than salaries of *empleados,* reducing the income differential. From 1950 through 1958 *obreros'* average wages increased 140 percent, when the average remuneration of *empleados* increased by 115 percent. From 1959 through 1970 *obreros'* average wages rose by 415 percent, and *empleados'* salaries by 350 percent (see Table 5.10).

The strategy of reducing differentiation in the labor force as a means of subduing labor militancy came back to haunt the companies. Throughout the nineteen-sixties and seventies the single trade union representing *obreros* and *empleados* at Toquepala, the Sindicato de Trabajadores de Toquepala y Anexos, was the most militant union in the mining sector, if not in all of Peru. It waged a series of long strikes against Southern Peru to achieve wages, benefits, and working conditions commensurate with those of copper miners in the United States.[33] The single union at Toquepala promoted unity and militancy among its labor force. In addition, the location of the mines, the political climate, and the leadership of the union all contributed to the combativeness of the workers of Southern Peru.

For historical and ecological reasons that have received little attention from scholars, the social structure in the mineral zones in the south of Peru differed markedly from those of the central highlands. Because the valleys and *punas* in the south are drier and less fertile than those of central Peru the population in the regions surrounding the open-pit mines traditionally was less numerous, poorer, and more migratory than the population of the heartland of Peruvian mining. Historical data on the backgrounds of the workers of Southern Peru and Marcona is limited. However, evidence

TABLE 5.9 Number of *Empleados* in the Peruvian Mining Industry, 1945-1975

Year	Number of *Empleados*	*Empleados* as % of Labor Force
1945	1,127	5
1946	1,356	6
1947	2,123	7
1948	1,573	6
1949	1,571	6
1950	1,325	5
1951	1,590	6
1952	1,928	7
1953	1,845	7
1954	2,118	7
1955	2,046	8
1956	2,165	7
1957	2,347	7
1958	2,266	8
1959	2,577	9
1960	2,897	8
1961	2,845	8
1962	2,724	8
1963	4,151	10
1964	4,347	11
1965	n.a.	n.a.
1966	6,626	18
1967	7,842	16
1968	8,123	16
1969	8,515	16
1970	8,878	16
1971	9,200	17
1972	9,982	19
1973	8,531	17
1974	11,561	17
1975	11,604	21

SOURCES: The same as for Table 5.8.   n.a. - not available

TABLE 5.10 Remuneration of *Obreros* and *Empleados* in the Peruvian Mining Industry[a], 1945-1975

Year	Wages/ Obreros S/.	Index (1945 = 100)	Salaries/ Empleados S/.	Index (1945 = 100)
1945	1,403	100	7,535	100
1946	1,616	115	7,982	106
1947	2,123	151	8,889	118
1948	2,426	173	9,668	128
1949	3,056	218	13,547	180
1950	4,003	285	15,365	204
1951	4,951	353	18,826	250
1952	5,263	375	19,098	253
1953	6,379	455	21,788	289
1954	7,344	523	27,560	366
1955	7,973	568	27,556	366
1956	8,652	617	26,338	350
1957	9,200	656	27,263	362
1958	9,578	683	33,075	439
1959	11,255	802	45,402	603
1960	12,871	917	51,967	690
1961	14,295	1,019	50,972	676
1962	16,855	1,201	61,153	812
1963	19,041	1,357	68,690	912
1964	20,481	1,460	77,836	1,033
1965	n.a.	n.a.	n.a.	n.a.
1966	36,415	2,596	109,103	1,448
1967	36,625	2,610	113,602	1,508
1968	44,999	3,207	166,363	2,208
1969	50,717	3,615	184,128	2,444
1970	57,829	4,122	203,072	2,695
1971	67,558	4,815	221,263	2,936
1972	82,172	5,857	229,675	3,048
1973	107,111	7,639	330,628	4,388
1974	103,993	7,412	276,794	3,527
1975	168,081	11,980	355,280	4,715

(continued)

suggests that the majority of workers recruited by these companies came from Lima or from provincial cities and towns. While in all probability they had peasant backgrounds, they did not migrate to the mines directly from their villages.[34] This suggests that in general their ties to their original communities were weaker than those of miners in the central highlands. As a consequence return migration to their villages might be less frequent.

Even for workers of Southern Peru and Marcona who were of more recent peasant origin, the isolation of the open-pit mines made it difficult to sustain regular contact with their communities. This deterred their regular return to their villages to participate in productive as well as social activities. In this manner the geographic location of the open-pit mines contributed to the permanence of their labor force. In addition, by the nineteen-sixties the dissolution of traditional social relations in the highlands of Peru had eroded the self-sufficiency of the majority of peasant families. Waves of migration from the countryside to cities and mines was steady and permanent. As a result many migrants maintained little contact with their communities and their return was infrequent. This, too, fostered the increasing stability of the labor force in the mines.

As the workers in La Southern and Marcona severed their ties to their communities and remained at the mines for extended periods they and their families struggled to subsist primarily on wages earned in the mines. Their future contained few prospects other than wage labor. This promoted a working class consciousness. In addition, because many of the workers in the open-pit operations migrated from urban or industrial environments they brought to the

---

SOURCES: Computed by the author from data presented in Ministerio de Energía y Minas, *Anuario Minero del Perú*, 1966-1972; Ministerio de Energía y Minas, *Anuario de la Minería del Perú*, 1973-1975; Ministerio de Fomento, *Anuario de la Industria Minera en el Perú*, 1945-1949; Ministerio de Fomento y Obras Públicas, *Anuario de la Industria Minera en el Perú*, 1950-1965; *Anuario Minero-Comercial*, 1970; and "Declaraciones Anuales Consolidadas de Concesionarios, Empresas y Empresarios Mineros" (Lima: Archivos, División de Estadística, Dirección General de Minería, Ministerio de Energía y Minas, 1945-1975).

[a]Average annual wages paid to *obreros* and average annual salaries paid to *empleados* in *soles*.

n.a. - not available

mines their trade union experiences, or at least a familiarity with workers' organizations and struggles.

The relative permanence of the work force, its geographic isolation, and prior experience with trade unionism all contributed to the militancy of the workers in the open-pit mines. Perhaps of more importance, however, were contemporaneous examples of peasant movements in the central and southern highlands. Peasants' organizations led a series of struggles for land and social justice throughout the decade of the 1960s.[35] These created a climate congenial to militant trade unionism. Finally, the leadership of the miners' unions crystallized workers' demands and frustrations into the militant union struggles that characterized the mining centers of southern Peru in the 1960s.

When the Cerro de Pasco Corporation introduced open-pit techniques in the late 1950s it attempted to modify the nature of its labor force. The Corporation recruited skilled workers to operate its mines and increasingly complex processing plants. Like Southern Peru and Marcona, Cerro endeavored to expand the proportion of *empleados* on its payroll. Consistent with this objective the Corporation fired 20 percent of its *obreros* between 1957 and 1960. In these years many of the *obreros* who remained with the company were obliged to accept lower job classifications.[36] These adjustments were resisted by the trade union that represented the *obreros* and the restructuring of the labor force was carried out in the midst of a series of long strikes against the company.[37]

Following this wave of dismissals the Corporation still faced the dilemma of how to increase the permanence and technical skills of its labor force. The proximity of the mines to the workers' traditional communities facilitated migration back and forth from the mines to the villages. Even though this migration was not as constant as it had been in previous decades, it continued to disrupt production. Throughout the 1950s and into the next decade many miners maintained their status as *communeros*, or members of traditional peasant communities. Some of these men continued to consider their work in the mines as something transitory, hoping to save enough money to return permanently to their communities to resume their household economy.[38]

The Corporation introduced a series of measures to discourage transiency. In 1960 the Corporation modernized and enlarged the División Ganadera by fencing in grazing lands that had been used by neighboring communities. After restricting access to these pastures, the company expanded its herds and the production of meat, dairy products, and wool. The output of the División Ganadera was used to increase the quantity of products that the Corporation provided to its workers at low prices. Company supply of basic consumption items promoted improvements in the standard of living of workers' families without an increase in money wages. Nevertheless, the Corporation was forced to increase money wages in response to workers' demands.

Other incentives to induce workers to remain in the mines included loans and retirement benefits for long-standing employees. To upgrade skills and increase productivity the Corporation inaugurated an active program of training courses for its personnel in the 1960s. All of the companies of the *gran minería* attempted to raise productivity, reduce militancy, and contain labor costs in the 1960s. At first it appeared that they were successful. However, fundamental problems soon began to emerge.

The Crisis Re-emerges: The 1970s

The mining industry in Peru grew throughout the 1960s. One indicator of the prosperity of the industry was growth in output. More significant for profitability, however, was the rise in productivity. From 1959 to 1969 per capita output for each working period, or *tarea*, increased by 84 percent (see Table 5.4). Most of the growth in productivity occurred at the beginning of the decade, as a result of the technological revolution implied by open-pit mining methods. In keeping with industry projections, changes in productivity occured unevenly and more slowly in the middle 1960s. Since this was characteristic of periods following major technical innovations, industrial analysts continued to make exuberant predictions about the future of the industry. Nevertheless, soon there were signs that caused alarm.

In the mid-1970s productivity declined significantly. Output per *tarea* in 1975 was only 73 percent of what it had been five years earlier. The drop in productivity was an indication of serious barriers to industrial growth and corporate profitability, more so than the concurrent decline in production. Most contemporary analysts attributed the recession in the industry to falling world market prices. However, close scrutiny reveals that fluctuations in Peruvian mining in the 1970s appear unrelated to price movements. When Peruvian production peaked in 1972, metals prices had declined by an average of 12 percent compared to 1970 (see Table 5.1). When prices almost doubled from 1972 to 1974, the output of the Peruvian industry declined.

By the mid-1970s, when unfavorable price movements were clearly not the explanation of poor performance, corporate analysts and ministerial spokesmen attributed difficulties to rising wages. Wages had been increasing dramatically since the 1950s. From 1950 to 1958 average wages rose by 150 percent. This implied a 45 percent rise in price-deflated wages. In the next decade money wages increased by 350 percent, and price-deflated wages by 100 percent. Price-deflated wages continued to rise in the early 1970s, although their rate of growth slowed slightly. From 1970 to 1975 price-deflated wages increased by 40 percent (see Tables 5.6 and 5.11).

This period of rising wages coincided with the increasing proletarianization of the labor force in the mining sector. As discussed in Chapter Four, through the 1940s it was common for miners and their families to receive foodstuffs and clothing from their rural communities. Consequently, wages earned in the mines were not the sole support of these workers' families. This suggests that the endurance of traditional society had contradictory effects. While it contributed to the persistent shortage and transience of labor, it also enabled companies to keep wages low. The companies' low-wage strategy was increasingly eliminated in the nineteen-fifties and sixties with the erosion of traditional social relations.

The number of years a man worked in the mines tended to increase in the 1960s.[39] Frequently this resulted in weaker ties between miners and their communities of origin. As a consequence, workers' families needed to purchase more of their necessities, to substitute for products that formerly were supplied by kin and communities. To maintain traditional levels of consumption, it was necessary for wages to rise to cover these purchases. Therefore, one aspect of union struggles in the mining industry in the 1960s was the demand for wages that would allow miners' families to purchase products that in the past they acquired outside of wage relations. Struggles between capital and labor tended to be more militant and protracted as wages came to be the sole support of the working class in the mining indsutry.

This suggests that in societies where capitalism and wage labor relations are maturing rapidly, such as Peru in the 1960s, rising wages (even when adjusted for price increases) might not necessarily indicate corresponding improvements in workers' standards of living. In part, or in its entirety, rising wages might reflect a

TABLE 5.11   Average Annual Price-Deflated Wages in the Peruvian Mining Industry[a], 1945-1975 (in Peruvian *soles*)

Year	(1945 = 100) Wages	Index
1945	10,358	100
1946	11,160	108
1947	11,129	107
1948	9,431	91
1949	10,613	103
1950	11,706	113
1951	13,379	129
1952	13,540	131
1953	14,674	142
1954	16,531	160
1955	16,455	159
1956	16,779	162
1957	16,680	161
1958	16,902	163
1959	18,429	178
1960	19,225	186
1961	19,481	188
1962	21,630	209
1963	24,242	234
1964	24,146	233
1965	n.a.	n.a.
1966	34,370	332
1967	32,102	310
1968	35,483	343
1969	37,620	363
1970	40,216	388
1971	43,316	418
1972	47,101	455
1973	56,964	550
1974	44,103	426
1975	56,668	547

(continued)

process of social transformation whereby workers must purchase products that were previously acquired outside of market relations. For this reason, price adjusted wages are not identified as "real wages."[40] In common usage an analysis of "real wages" reveals changes in the standard of living. However, in periods of rapid proletarianization in underdeveloped countries an analysis of the relationship between the money wage and the cost of living index is but one part of an analysis of changes in the standard of living. The other part of that analysis is more complex and difficult to quantify, because it involves the changing composition of the basket of products that workers and their families consume, and the classification of these products according to their value and price (see Chapter One).

Unfortunately, lack of data prevents the quantification of the complex relationship between commodities purchased in markets, those supplied without a money exchange, and those where price diverges from value. However, from 1959 to 1975 when price-deflated wages in the industry doubled it is probably the case that the standard of living of miners' families improved. Our theoretical analysis suggests, though, that the improvements were not of the same magnitude as the increase in price-deflated wages.

In the nineteen-sixties and early seventies workers in the industry won concessions from capital in the form of higher wages primarily because of their trade union militancy. If rising wages had

---

SOURCES: Computed by the author from data presented in Ministerio de Energía y Minas, *Anuario Minero del Perú*, 1966-1972; Ministerio de Energía y Minas, *Anuario de la Minería del Perú*, 1973-1975; Ministerio de Fomento, *Anuario de la Industria Minera en el Perú*, 1945-1949; Ministerio de Fomento y Obras Públicas, *Anuario de la Industria Minera en el Perú*, 1950-1965; *Anuario Minero-Comercial*, 1970; "Declaraciones Anuales Consolidadas de Concesionarios, Empresas y Empresarios Mineros" (Lima: Archivos, División de Estadística, Dirección General de Minería, Ministerio de Energía y Minas, 1945-1975; and Ministerio de Trabajo, Dirección General de Estadísticas, *Industria de la Construcción*, 1945-1976, p.12.

[a]Price-deflated wages are money wages paid to *obreros* and *empleados* divided by a cost of living index. I use the cost of living index for Lima, the only continual cost of living index that is available from 1945-1975. Although consumer prices in Lima differ from those in highland departments I assume a similarity in the rate and direction of price changes.

n.a. - not available

been counterbalanced by growing productivity this process would not have restrained the expansion of the industry. However, as shown, productivity declined dramatically in the early 1970s. Consequently, labor costs per unit of output increased. This pressure on profitability was compounded by a persistently rising wage cost to capital. From 1959 to 1969, productivity rose by 85 percent but the wage cost to capital increased by almost 120 percent (see Tables 5.4 and 5.5). With relative and absolute labor costs rising faster than productivity, wage costs per unit of output increased.[41] This laid the groundwork for the crisis that emerged in the 1970s.

In the early seventies economic indicators signaled gathering difficulties for the mining sector. Output stagnated, productivity declined drastically in the middle of the decade, and the wage cost to capital rose. Taken together these indicators suggested sharply rising costs of production. In response to the crisis many smaller firms in the sector discontinued operations and locked out their workers. These redundancies generated more labor strife and trade union militancy. The larger firms revived some of the options that they had been considering periodically during the past decade—including the possibility of selling their assets to the state.

For the companies there was a momentary respite from the growing crisis. The rising trend in the wage cost to capital was abruptly reversed from 1973 to 1975. Although wages rose, a surge in metal prices offset this. From 1973 to 1975 the wage cost to capital was on average half of what it had been in the preceding three years (see Table 5.5). Also, the industry was on the threshold of another quantitative change, with the Southern Peru Copper Corporation about to inaugurate Cuajone, its second large open-pit mine. Amassing the US$ 800 million to finance Cuajone and the physical development of the mine took a decade. In the middle seventies industrial analysts predicted that Cuajone would alter the mode of operation in the industry just as Toquepala had done twenty years earlier.

The crisis of the seventies and the massive investment in Cuajone established the economic and political context for government policy in the mining sector. Past Peruvian governments had intervened in the industry to promote conditions favorable to large investments. The military government of President Juan Velasco Alvarado, which came to power in 1968, was also interventionist, but conditions had changed. Consequently, intervention by the state assumed a new form—direct participation in the sphere of production.

CHAPTER SIX

Nationalizations and Their Aftermath

The Grand Alliance and State Power

The Cerro de Pasco Corporation's investments in Peru at the turn of the twentieth century had momentous and far-reaching consequences. Not only did they transform the mining industry and hasten social change in the regions surrounding the mines, they contributed to major alterations in the nature of the Peruvian state. As Cerro, W. R. Grace and Company, the International Petroleum Company, and other foreign firms established production operations in Peru they forged alliances with the Peruvian elite. Together the two groups, the Peruvian oligarchy and foreign capital, dominated the state. For the first three decades of the century the Peruvian elite was dominated by landowners from the northern coast and the highlands whose control over labor rested on traditional social relations of debt-peonage in its infinite varieties, including *enganche*. This grand alliance was not without tension, in part because the foreign companies essentially were capitalist firms, constrained by social conditions in Peru to undertake production with various forms of forced labor. However, as long as both the precapitalist oligarchy and foreign capital produced primarily for the international market they were mutually interested in ensuring that the state fostered optimal conditions for exporting.[1]

With the expansion of free wage labor, particularly in the 1930s, the Peruvian partners of this alliance became more diversified. Sharecropping or *yanaconaje,* once the dominant form of labor on the sugar estates of the northern coast, slowly disappeared. The transformation of labor systems began first on the plantations owned by foreign capital and gradually spread to Peruvian-owned estates. The emergence of a local agrarian bourgeoisie did not disrupt the grand alliance between the landed oligarchy and foreign capital because the principal objective of the entente remained the promotion of exports. Foreign and Peruvian exporters sought to ensure the continuation of an open export economy, in particular the advantageous exchange rate, tariff, and credit policies. The oligarchy and foreign firms did little to facilitate

161

the expansion of the internal market because the level of economic demand within Peru did not condition the success of their enterprises. Nevertheless, the dissolution of traditional social relations and the extension of free wage labor contributed to the development of the internal market. The Peruvian bourgeoisie, growing with the expansion of the wage labor force, responded to the increased demand for manufactured products such as shoes, textiles, clothing, and processed foods and beverages by expanding production. As the industrial bourgeoisie grew in number and strength, so did its conflicts with the grand alliance of Peruvian and foreign exporters that dominated the state. The relatively weak industrial bourgeoisie sought a state that would play a more active role in generating an internal market in labor power and commodities. It also demanded increased access to credit for the expanding manufacturing sector. Conflicts between the industrial bourgeoisie and the alliance of exporters are revealed in part in struggles over the forms and functions of the state. Since the 1920s associations of industrialists have made repeated attempts to pressure governments to foster their interests, particularly to protect the home market.[2] At times industrialists were moderately successful at persuading the legislature to adopt what might be called pro-industrial policies. However, for decades the gains were limited, as frequently ignored in practice as they were rescinded in law.

National politics in Peru from the 1930s to the 1960s is an apparently bewildering complex of changing electoral alliances, successful and unsuccessful coups, annulled elections, and drastic policy reversals. These events become more comprehensible when they are analyzed in the context of a struggle to dominate the state. For example, the industrial bourgeoisie frequently allied with APRA in order to secure its candidates an electoral base and to influence policy.[3] In the 1940s increasingly favorable industrial policies demonstrate the growing strength of owners of manufacturing enterprises. Nevertheless, in general the state continued to reflect the priorities of the expanded alliance of the precapitalist oligarchy, the agrarian bourgeoisie, and foreign capital.

As one aspect of a multifaceted response to the declining profitability of export production in the 1950s (of both mining and agriculture), foreign capital began to take advantage of the expanding internal market. North American and European firms increasingly relocated investments from export sectors to manufacturing.[4] The Cerro de Pasco Corporation and W. R. Grace and Company, among the oldest U.S. partners in the grand alliance, led the development of the manufacturing sector. The reorientation of local and foreign investment is reflected in the sectoral redistribution of real Gross Domestic Product (GDP). From 1956 to 1968 the manufacturing sector's share of GDP rose from 15 to 20 percent, while agriculture's share declined from 31 to 15 percent.[5] Foreign capital as a whole no longer was interested exclusively in preserving favorable conditions for exporting because these conditions frequently were prejudicial to production for the domestic market. Overseas investors increasingly were concerned that the Peruvian government create a propitious climate for manufacturing. With the economic base of the Peruvian partners of the alliance shrinking relative to the manufacturing sector, and foreign capital reorienting its investments, the strength of the traditional alliance progressively was undermined.

The increasing strength of the industrial bourgeoisie and the gradual shift in the balance of power away from the traditional elites was a complex and gradual process. In the 1960s tension in the social fabric reflected the increasing competition between industrialists and landowners. This struggle was played out in many arenas: the national legislature, the cabinet of President Fernando Belaúnde Terry, and the national banking system.[6] In the financial sphere manufacturers competed with agriculturalists for scarce credit.[7] An economic crisis in 1967-1969, which took the form of a severe strain on the balance of payments, brought this contest to a head. Resolution of the crisis required drastic policies, but the traditional remedies to correct the trade balance—exchange rate devaluation and deflationary monetary and fiscal policy— implied dire consequences for the emerging industrial bourgeoisie.

Fortunately for the industrial bourgeoisie its economic project was consistent with the developmentalist ideology emerging within the Peruvian Armed Forces.[8] The ranking officers in the Army came to believe that Peru's traditional elite, the precapitalist oligarchy and the agrarian bourgeoisie, was directly responsible for the country's backwardness. These officers took as their mission the modernization of Peruvian society, which implied the elimination of precapitalist social relations and the power of the traditionally dominant classes.

The Contradictory Revolution, 1968-1975

The military coup of 1968, which brought to power the Armed Forces under the leadership of President Juan Velasco Alvarado, marked the culmination of Peru's bourgeois revolution. The military conceptualized its project in terms of the modernization of Peru. This implied expansion of exports, growth in the internal market, and the elimination of traditional or backward systems of production. The army intended to accomplish its objectives via a strong, interventionist state that dictated economic policy and played a direct role in the economy.

The sectors that presented the most obvious barriers to this project, agriculture and finance, were among the first to be transformed. These sectors historically were intertwined as a significant portion of Peruvian bank credit traditionally facilitated the expansion of sugar and cotton production. In 1968 several banks were nationalized, including the Peruvian subsidiaries of Chase Manhattan. This proved an effective method of encouraging the banking system to reformulate its lending policies. The short-run crisis (1967-1969) for national industrial capital was relieved by a shift in the pattern of lending of Peruvian banks. In 1967-1968, about 26 percent of credit went to industry; in 1969-1970, 33 percent; and in 1971-1973, 38 percent.[9] Through a relatively far-reaching agrarian reform the government broke the power of the traditional landed elite. The objective of the reform was the modernization and capitalization of the sector, rather than distributing land to the tiller. While the effects of the reform were contradictory, reflecting complex institutional forms and varied implementation, there is a consensus that the reform radically reduced the incidence and importance of traditional social relations.[10]

Many of the policies of the Velasco government were controversial, none more so than those involving foreign capital. As one of its first measures, the new government nationalized the International Petroleum Company (IPC), a subsidiary of Standard Oil of New Jersey. The oilfields of IPC had been exploited since the beginning of the twentieth century and were virtually dry. Remarkable about the expropriation of IPC is not its direct economic effects, since there is agreement that the fields were worth little, but the importance given to it. The expropriation became a symbolic act. President Velasco heralded the move as a strike against imperialism and the U.S. government retaliated in kind by threatening to invoke the Hickenlooper Amendment which would impose an embargo on credits to Peru from U.S. banks and multilateral lending agencies. With the debate over IPC full blown, the government proceeded to nationalize the International Telephone and Telegraph Company (ITT), sugar estates of W. R. Grace and Co., and the *haciendas* of the Cerro de Pasco Corporation (the División Ganadera) these last under the provisions of the agrarian reform.

In its first years the government appeared anti-imperialist. Harsh denunciations of foreign economic intervention accompanied each nationalization and threatened others. Velasco's favorite slogan was that Peru was "neither communist nor capitalist." Opponents of the regime, within Peru and in Washington, ignored the first part of this refrain and became obsessed with the second. Most observers, sympathetic or otherwise to the objectives of the military government, agreed that the regime was anti-capitalist and anti-imperialist.[11]   The government described the process as "revolutionary" and this characterization became so widely accepted that this period in Peru is still called "the Peruvian Revolution."[12]

It gradually became evident, however, that all was not as it seemed.[13] As early as 1970 it became apparent that the government intended to compensate the "expropriated" foreign companies. One after another individual firms negotiated with the Velasco government and most emerged contented with the compensation they received. The Chase Manhattan Bank is a case in point. When the government nationalized the Banco Continental, Chase Manhattan received US$ 6.3 million for its shares. This provoked an outcry in Peru since Chase had purchased these shares six years earlier for US$ 1.7 million.[14] Eventually all of the nationalized companies were compensated, in some cases beyond the expectations of their directors. In February, 1974, the Greene Agreement between the governments of Peru and the U.S. resolved all outstanding claims for compensation. In general the companies were satisfied with their indemnification.[15]

Behind the anti-imperialist rhetoric were concrete indications that the government never intended to isolate Peru from foreign, particularly U.S., capital. Throughout these tense years, filled with expropriations and accusations of imperialist plunder on the one hand and threats of economic and political reprisals on the other, the Government of Peru was negotiating the terms of a massive investment in the mining sector with the American Smelting and

Refining Company. Despite the government's revolutionary image foreign capital flowed into Peru. From 1970 to 1971 there was a reduction in net direct foreign investment, as companies cautiously evaluated the government's intentions and the results of the early nationalizations. However, by 1972 direct foreign investment revived and increased annually until 1975, the year Velasco was replaced as president. Although the governments that preceded Velasco's were viewed as favorable to foreign capital, net direct foreign investment in Peru was much greater during the Velasco period than before. From 1960 to 1967 net direct foreign investment was US$ 84 million; from 1968 to 1975 (an equal number of years) it totalled US$ 400 million. Even when one takes inflation into account, direct foreign investment was more important in the second period than the first: absolutely, as a proportion of total domestic investment, and in relation to GDP.[16]

The Velasco regime was not opposed, in principle, to foreign capital. On the contrary, it facilitated foreign investment throughout the economy and endeavored to attract massive overseas investments in the construction of large scale infrastructure: paricularly mining and petroleum production, and irrigation projects. Most of the firms that were nationalized had been key to the export-oriented economy controlled by the grand alliance. These firms were seen by the military reformers as part of the economic foundation of the alliance that dominated Peru until 1968. To fulfill their mission the officers eliminated the old power bloc which they perceived as unproductive and unwilling to participate in the modernization of Peru. From the perspective of Velasco, his cohorts, and supporters, Peru was underdeveloped because historically it had been plundered by the grand alliance. The remedy was expropriation. Rather than sever relations with foreign capital the Peruvian military envisioned a new alliance with imperialism whereby the government would dictate "the rules of the game." The new rules included regulation of the conditions and location of foreign investments. In addition, through state policy the government sought to alter the relationship between overseas and domestic capital. By regulating foreign firms, subsidizing local ones, and intervening directly in the economy, the state intended to enable Peruvian entrepreneurs to compete more successfully with foreign capital.[17]

This ambitious project, launched by the Armed Forces and carried out in cooperation with leading representatives of the industrial bourgeoisie, was a delicate task. Its goal was to alter the way in which foreign capital operated in Peru and to increase the competitiveness of local firms without stemming the inflow of overseas investments. In addition, it attempted to break the power of the agrarian bourgeoisie and the precapitalist oligarchy without threatening the capitalist class. These objectives, which were not essentially contradictory but at moments seemed to be so, gave the regime its initial revolutionary and anti-imperialist appearance.

The government of President Velasco embarked on a program to transform the social and economic structures of Peru. That this was a capitalist rather than an anti-capitalist project in no way altered the government's need to have popular support. In its clash with an oligarchy that saw Peru as its feifdom, the government called upon the anger and frustration of the masses to legitimate its decrees. In its struggle to establish a new relationship with foreign capital, which involved expropriating firms that were popularly believed to own and control most of Peru including most of its politicians, the military government relied on a legacy of nationalism and anti-imperialism to mobilize support.

The rhetoric of the government was posed in the framework of a nationalist struggle. Velasco and his ministers reminded workers and peasants of their historical oppression by foreign firms and their Peruvian allies in order to enlist allegiance to the developmentalist agenda. The appeal to popular support took this form because the success of the modernization effort, and the possibility that the industrial bourgeoisie might become increasingly competitive vis-a-vis foreign capital, depended in part on the ability to lower production costs. Workers in mining, industry, and agriculture were asked, then forced, to refrain from fighting for higher wages for the good of Peru. To suggest that such sacrifices were for the betterment of the bourgeoisie, more than of the country, was branded ultra-leftist.[18]

From the moment the military officers rushed President Belaúnde Terry to a waiting plane to be whisked to Miami in 1968, Peru's traditional elite was opposed to the new regime. Opposition turned to hysteria as the government nationalized banks, enacted an agrarian reform, and implacably set itself the goal of expropriating enterprises it perceived as unproductive. Industrial capitalists, a less powerful and less visible group, recognized the military officers as their allies and cooperated with the state. The Velasco government had only a short "honeymoon" with workers and peasants. The regime created a series of institutions, such as SINAMOS (Sistema Nacional de Apoyo a la Movilización Social), the Comunidades Industriales, and state-initiated trade unions to harmonize relations between owners and workers in each sector. These efforts initially were successful. But as price-deflated wages declined, working conditions deteriorated, and expectations expanded, some of these organizations withered away while others took on a militancy that haunted their creators.[19]

Appearances often belied reality in the transformative process of the Velasco period. These apparent contradictions fueled disagreements in activist, policymaking, and academic communities about the nature of the self-proclaimed Peruvian Revolution. The relationship between the Peruvian government and foreign capital became possibly the most contentious issue in the debate. The mining sector more than any other shows the complexities of the Peruvian Revolution. Two major U.S. firms were nationalized after 1968, Cerro de Pasco and Marcona, at the same time that a third, the Southern Peru Copper Corporation, was negotiating the terms of one of the largest investments in the history of the world copper industry. A scrutiny of the nationalizations and of their effects contributes to an understanding of the process of political and economic change in Peru.

Nationalizations

State ownership of a part of the industrial sector is the norm in most countries of Latin America, even in the 1980s after the World Bank and the International Monetary Fund fostered privatization. From the beginning of the twentieth century reformist and revolutionary governments in country after country nationalized the extractive sectors. The Mexican oil industry was nationalized by President Cárdenas in 1938; the Bolivian tin industry was nationalized during the revolution of 1952; Venezuelan oil was nationalized under the Social Democratic Presidency of Carlos Andrés Pérez in 1976; and the Chilean copper industry was progressively nationalized under Presidents Frei and Allende in 1969 and 1970. The Chilean take-over of Kennecott and Anaconda, large U.S. copper companies, was not interpreted by most politicians and scholars of Latin America as a revolutionary measure. These nationalizations were initiated by the Christian Democratic government of President Eduardo Frei, who was trumpeted as the savior of Chile by the U.S. Department of State, and supported by the conservative sectors of Chilean society. Frei himself characterized the nationalizations as Chile's "second independence."[20] While such pronouncements and the terms of compensation were unacceptable to the companies involved, they caused little concern in business and government circles in the United States.[21] In Brazil and Argentina many basic industries were created within the state sector and have never been privately owned. Peru was an anomaly in South America because until 1968 the state played little direct role in production. Regional norms virtually mandated Peruvian nationalization of its extractive industries. Outside pressure for nationalizations within the mining industry came from CIPEC, the Intergovernmental Council of Copper Exporting Countries, founded in 1967 by Chile, Zambia, the Congo, and Peru. This organization was modeled after the Organization of Petroleum Exporting Countries (OPEC), to coordinate price and production policies.

From the late 1960s to the middle 1970s the Peruvian mining industry was in crisis. The crisis was not readily apparent and passed unnoticed by some industry analysts. Although production was declining relative to the trend, some seasoned observers went so far as to hail the industry's uneven performance in this period as robust and expansionary. Such a conclusion rested on indicators of absolute changes in production. From 1968 to 1976 the volume of output rose slowly, although this tendency was complicated by years when production declined dramatically (see Table 2.1). However, a more careful diagnosis of the sector in these years would not rest on absolute changes in production. Declining productivity and rising wages, which put pressure on corporate profits, were indicators of an underlying crisis. Most companies in the sector responded to the profit squeeze by lowering wages and reducing investment. Some went further, and attempted to sell their assets in order to invest in more lucrative sectors. Among the latter was the Cerro de Pasco Corporation, no longer the largest, but still in many ways the flagship of the industry.

Profitability in the Cerro de Pasco Corporation had been declining for more than a decade.[22] From the 1950s Cerro reduced investment in its network of underground mines as the company restructured its productive base in order to decrease its reliance on underground mining (see Chapter Five). The Corporation concentrated on modernizing and expanding its smelting and refining facilities and purchased increasing quantities of custom ores, mined by other companies. In the 1960s, besides large-scale experimentation with open-pit techniques, the Corporation set up numerous subsidiaries that produced inputs for mining and smelting and finished metal products for the internal market in Peru. By the late 1960s the Cerro de Pasco Corporation had controlling interests in virtually every company in the Peruvian metallurgical processing industry.[23]   However, despite this longstanding attempt at diversification, a large portion of Cerro's capital remained locked in outmoded mines and machinery. By 1968 the Cerro de Pasco Corporation stopped investing in its Peruvian subsidiary and illegally increased profit remittances to the United States.[24] Not only were the directors of the Corporation wary of the nationalist stance of the new government in Peru, they were seeking more profitable investment opportunities in Peru and elsewhere.[25]

When money wages rose rapidly in the industry in the 1960s, and underground mining became increasingly less competitive in the world market, the Cerro de Pasco Corporation was able partially to compensate for rising costs by containing wage increases. Chapter Five analyzes how the Corporation was able to complement wages through the production of foodstuffs in its División Ganadera. In 1969 Cerro's lands were nationalized as part of the agrarian reform and the División Ganadera was eliminated. This ended the company's ability to subsidize the consumption of workers and their families. The cost of living of the employees of the Corporation rose rapidly, contributing to long and militant strikes in 1970 and 1971. Data in Table 6.1 demonstrate that 1970-1973 marked a peak in strike activity in the industry. The longest and most militant strikes occurred in the Cerro de Pasco Corporation and among the strikers' demands was the nationalization of the company.

By the early 1970s Cerro's economic prospects were not encouraging. The Corporation was engaged in prolonged struggles with its work force, its properties were deteriorating, and it lived under the constant threat of nationalization. In 1971 the Corporation offered to sell its mining operations to the Peruvian state. Negotiations broke down several times and the transfer was not effected until January, 1974. The Cerro de Pasco complex, under the new name CENTROMIN, became the property of the Peruvian state. The Government of Peru offered to pay US$ 58 million for the assets, which did not include Cerro's partial ownership of the Southern Peru Copper Corporation nor its stock in other Peruvian firms. Cerro, however, demanded a higher compensation. Within the terms of the Greene Agreement Cerro received the US$ 67 million it claimed. However, the agreement recognized Peru's counter-claim of US$ 38.5 million for illegal profit repatriation.

Finally, Cerro received US\$ 28.5 million net for its entire mining and processing complex in the central highlands of Peru.[26]

The nationalization of the Cerro de Pasco Corporation reveals one aspect of the military government's strategy vis-a-vis foreign capital. Cerro was not investing in its archaic mining complex and there was scant likelihood that it or any other private firm would capitalize these assets in the future. Production based on this network of underground mines had little prospect of profitability. Nevertheless, increasing export production was key to the government's economic project and necessitated the continued operation of the anachronistic mining complex in the central highlands. Rather than permitting Cerro to decapitalize its assets further, as the International Petroleum Company had done for decades, the government assumed an active role in the economy. It incorporated into the state sector a firm that it perceived to be critical for the development of capitalism in Peru, yet one that was no longer of interest to private capital.[27]

Rather than a blow against imperialism the nationalization of the Cerro de Pasco Corporation represented one aspect of the restructuring of foreign capital in Peru. While the purchase of Cerro took the form of a nationalization, and its transfer to the state was accompanied by strong anti-imperialist rhetoric, the process involved no threat to the larger interests of U.S. capital. The rhetoric of nationalization was for internal consumption, to bolster the government's popular support. Simultaneous with the negotiations to purchase Cerro, the government concluded an agreement with a consortium of the largest mining companies in the world, which included Cerro, to initiate a massive mining venture in southern Peru.

The nationalization of the Marcona Mining Company bore similarities to the process involving Cerro. Unlike Cerro, in the late 1960s and early 1970s Marcona introduced major technical innovations in the processing of iron ore. Despite this, production stagnated. The output of iron ore increased by only 8 percent from 1968 to 1974. This slow growth, combined with relatively low world market prices, put pressure on Marcona's profits. As a result, the company reoriented its investment policy, expanding its transport fleet as well as mining operations outside of Peru. In 1974 Marcona offered to sell all of its Peruvian operations to the state. But, to the accompaniment of the usual anti-imperialist pronouncements, the government publicly decried the offer as unacceptable. In the middle of the next year Marcona was

TABLE 6.1   Strike Activity in the Peruvian Mining Industry, 1966-1974

Year	Number of Strikes	Number of Man-Hours Lost Affected (in thousands)	Number of Workers
1966	26	1,437	26,965
1967	32	n.a.	n.a.
1968	21	353	9,426
1969	26	1,898	20,794
1970	71	3,975	61,447
1971	96	6,542	71,168
1972	40	991	15,856
1973	90	3,832	61,401
1974	66	1,878	28,403

SOURCES: Servicio de Empleo y Recursos Humanos (SERH), 1967; Ministerio de Trabajo, *Las Huelgas en el Perú* (Lima: 1970); Instituto Nacional de Planificación, *Informe Socio-Económico* (Lima: 1974, 1975, 1976), pp. 70-71; and Sociedad de Minería, Departamento de Estudios Económicos y Estadísticas, Archives.

nationalized (and was called HIERRO-PERU) and the government announced that it would not grant compensation.

The economic crisis that coincided with the military coup of 1968 was temporarily resolved by increased foreign and local investment in the private sector and by growing public indebtedness to foreign banks and multilateral organizations to expand and capitalize the state sector.   As the economic crisis re-emerged in 1975 it became increasingly obvious that foreign capital had not been cast aside.   In this context Velasco's revolutionary and anti-imperialist image became tarnished as well as inappropriate to the new situation.

In 1975 the military reshuffled its leadership and General Velasco was replaced by General Francisco Morales Bermúdez. The new president quickly tempered official rhetoric, bringing the government's image in line with economic and political realities.

Soon after the coup it became clear that the pattern already established between the government and nationalized firms would be repeated yet again. The Marcona Mining Company estimated the value of its assets in Peru between US$ 70 and US$ 80 million. The government agreed to compensate Marcona a total of US$ 61 million through a combination of cash, marketing contracts, and shipping agreements.[28]

The relationship between the Government of Peru and the third large U.S. company in the *gran minería*, the Southern Peru Copper Corporation (SPCC), was markedly different. In 1968, SPCC was in the process of arranging a financial package of about US$ 800 million to develop the Cuajone copper complex which would increase Peruvian copper production by an estimated 50 percent. Instead of threats of expropriation President Velasco and his Minister of Energy and Mines, General Fernández Maldonado, sought to assure the stockholders and financiers of SPCC that the government would cooperate in every way to facilitate the development of Cuajone.

In the middle 1960s there was a major scandal in Peru concerning SPCC's first venture. It was discovered that the contract between the government and SPCC for the development of Toquepala, signed in 1954, granted privileges and exemptions to SPCC beyond those legislated in the Mining Code of 1950. In response to a growing consensus that the terms of the contract were grossly prejudicial to Peru, the Peruvian Congress recommended that Toquepala no longer be considered a marginal enterprise. The Congress directed the executive to alter the tax structure for the company and a new contract was signed in 1968. Some analysts suggested that the new structure was still unnecessarily favorable to La Southern.[29]

The next year Southern and the Velasco regime signed an agreement governing the exploitation of Cuajone. The accord came under the terms of the old Mining Code of 1950, infamous for its pro-company provisions. Just after this contract was signed the government passed a new mining code, but Southern avoided the more stringent legislation.[30] In 1974 and 1976 Southern and Government of Peru signed further accords to assure the consortium of mining companies and banks that their investment in Cuajone would be safe from governmental interference. In 1977 Cuajone came on line, producing 40 percent of Peru's copper.

The relationship between the Government of Peru and U.S. mining companies during the period known as the Peruvian

Revolution can be understood by removing the veil of appearances and official rhetoric. From 1968 to 1975 the Peruvian government assumed an active and quite modern role in restructuring capital in the economy, much like many Social Democratic governments of Western Europe. Firms that officials of the government decided were crucial to Peru's economic development, but that were not investing and expanding enough to satisfy official expectations, were purchased—nationalized with compensation. In those basic industries where production was not sufficiently profitable to attract private investment the government created state enterprises and organized production to promote the expansion of capitalism. Financial risks and losses were assumed by the state and production maintained to sustain national economic growth. The nationalizations of the Cerro de Pasco Corporation and the Marcona Mining Company were characteristic of this process. However, the government's relations with the Southern Peru Copper Corporation were completely different. Southern Peru was prepared to invest in its operations in Peru so the government reciprocated by providing conditions that were favorable to the investment.

The pattern that emerges between the Government of Peru and foreign capital in the mining industry was representative of the period of the Peruvian Revolution. The Velasco regime was not fundamentally anti-imperialist. Rather it sought to establish a new alliance with imperialism which would be characterized by a larger role for the Peruvian industrial bourgeoisie and for the state. The Velasco project envisioned that the state would develop economic plans that identified priority sectors and seek foreign capital to participate in the fulfillment of these projections. Only in those branches of the economy unable to attract private capital would the state participate directly in production.[31] This was a capitalist, not a socialist, project.

The military government had an active mining policy that went further than defining the terms of foreign investment. It included a plan to develop Peru's mining and refining capacity, a marketing strategy, and the repossession of deposits that were not exploited. In 1970, as part of the mining legislation enacted by the administration of President Velasco, the government created Minero-Perú, a state mining company. The mandate of the company was to seek foreign financing to develop new mineral deposits and to expand Peru's refining capacity. In the heyday of the Velasco period the government envisioned the massive expansion of mining production. On radio and television, in official speeches and newspapers, the names of the mines that were key to Peru's development and that promised to make all Peruvians rich were repeated like an incantation, Cerro Verde Santa Rosa, Tintaya, Michiquillay, Antamina, Bambas, Quellaveco. Minero-Perú sought loans and investments to develop the riches that were going to transform Peru into the fabled Potosí of the colonial period.

Minero-Perú began the construction of state-owned copper refineries at Ilo and Cerro Verde, and a zinc refinery at Cajamarquilla to increase Peru's capacity to export fully processed minerals. Historically little refining was done in Peru. The Peruvian government maintained that through the export of unrefined metals foreign firms camouflaged the ore content of their products in order to evade Peruvian taxes. In addition, U.S. companies traditionally took advantage of under-utilized refining capacity in the U.S. Southern Peru's copper ores were processed at the company's smelter at Ilo, then transported to the U.S. for refining by the American Refining and Smelting Corporation (ASARCO). Initially ASARCO established Southern Peru (SPCC) to supply its U.S. refineries with semi-processed or blister copper. This tradition created tension between the military government and foreign mining companies.

Prior to 1968 mineral sales were entirely within the purview of the mining companies and specialized marketing firms; the state played no role in commercialization. By manipulating transfer prices and underreporting exports companies were able to evade Peruvian taxes and regulations concerning profit remittances and foreign exchange.[32] In 1973 the government created Minero-Perú Commerical (MINPECO), a state marketing agency, to control commercialization. Cuajone was the only mine in Peru exempted from selling its mineral products to MINPECO for international sales.

The Velasco government's strategy for the sector was ambitious. Unfortunately most of the vision never became a reality. Of the long list of deposits that the government planned to exploit only Tintaya and Cerro Verde were developed and output from these mines was far below the initial projections. The second stage of the expansion of the Ilo copper refinery was postponed, and the Cerro Verde and Cajamarquilla projects were vastly scaled down. Minero-Perú Comercial survived but was relegated to a marginal role under the Presidency of Belaúnde Terry, when participation became voluntary instead of compulsory. In the nineteen-eighties most mining companies marketed their products much as they did before the creation of the state agency. Even Cuajone, the hope of the private sector, never reached its anticipated scale of production. Between 1977, when Cuajone came on line, and 1985 the industry grew slowly and erratically (see Table 6.2).

One of the explanations of the failure of the mining strategy of the Velasco era is that the government contracted foreign loans to develop the sector but the implementation of the projects proved far costlier than originally anticipated. As a result many projects were initiated but almost none were completed. Consequently, the state was burdened with large debt payments but did not have the projected growth in export earnings to finance that debt. This dilemma was complicated by the discovery that the initial economic calculations for developing the projects were based on exaggerated estimations of the mineral grade in many of the deposits and on optimistic price projections that never became a reality.

Fernando Belaúnde Terry became President again in 1980. For the mining sector this meant a return to the policies of the nineteen-fifties and early sixties. Private capitalists were encouraged to participate in state enterprises. That they chose not to do so indicates the unprofitable nature of most of these operations. Taxes on profits and on exports were lowered across the board and state policy on refining and marketing lost its former militancy, and all but disappeared. In 1982 refined metals still accounted for less than half of Peru's mineral exports (see Appendix L.3) despite the Velasco government's commitment to the development of refining capacity within Peru. The Belaúnde Administration's credo of privatization and the inviolability of the marketplace was reflected in changes in the structure of property ownership in the industry. In the period 1979-1984 state participation declined from its peak in 1976. In this gradual restructuring of capital local firms were unable to take advantage of the policies favoring privatization. In 1976 local firms owned 18 percent of the value of the assets in the industry. In the period 1979-1984 local capital's share fell to 13 percent. It was foreign capital that prospered: 55 percent of the assets in the mining sector was owned by foreign capital in 1976; in the 1979-1884 period this increased to 62 percent (see Table 6.3).

The governments of Presidents Morales Bermúdez and Belaúnde Terry attempted to revitalize Peru's traditional socio-economic structures and class alliances and eradicate the reforms of the Velasco era. Belaúnde's administration even endeavored to

TABLE 6.2   Indexes of the Volume of Production in the Peruvian Mining Industry[a], 1977-1985

Year	$(1945 = 100)$ Output
1977	779.8
1978	786.9
1979	809.9
1980	776.8
1981	769.9
1982	825.0
1983	805.8
1984	843.0
1985	931.7
	$(1977 = 100)$
1977	100.0
1978	106.9
1979	110.0
1980	105.5
1981	104.6
1982	112.1
1983	109.4
1984	114.5
1985	126.6

SOURCES: Computed by the author from data presented in Ministerio de Energía y Minas, *Anuario de la Minera del Perú 1977-1985* (Lima), Table 1.

[a]Volume of production measured in constant prices. Data are consistent with the data for 1945-1977 presented in Chapters Two and Five.

TABLE 6.3   Structure of Property Ownership in the Peruvian Mining Industry, 1968-1984

Forms of Property	1968	(percentage) 1976	1979-84
State	18.4	27.8	25.0
Foreign/Private	81.6	54.7	62.0
Private/Peruvian	n.d.	17.5	13.0

SOURCES: Manuel Cisneros Orna and Oswaldo Carpio Villegas, *Realidad Minera* (Lima) 1984, No. 1, Table 5, p. 13.

n.d. - no data

reverse aspects of the agrarian reform. However, foreign firms in the mining industry did not agitate for a return to the past. While they welcomed the new tax structure, regulations facilitating profit remittances, and the freedom to market their products, foreign capital as a whole was fortified by the transformations accomplished by the military reformers. U.S. firms no longer were tied to antiquated mines and machinery that proved burdensome in competitive struggles within the industry. Instead, foreign capital was free, even encouraged by the Peruvian state, to invest in those aspects of production that potentially were more profitable.

Patterns of Growth in the Nineteen-Seventies and Eighties

Following the period of stagnation in the middle 1970s the mining industry began to expand. After the Cuajone mine came on line in 1977, Peruvian mine output reached a new plateau. Average annual production was 32 percent higher from 1977 through 1985 than it had been from 1968 through 1976 (see Tables 2.2 and 6.2). The pattern of growth that began to appear in the 1950s re-emerged. Expansion in mineral production was not associated with changes in world prices; rather, it accompanied the development of major open-pit deposits.

In 1980 and 1981 industry analysts warned of a coming recession in mineral production. These predictions were based on a short term decline in output, particularly of iron, lead, and zinc; and low world prices for non-ferrous metals. The forecasts proved excessively pessimistic for output recovered for all of Peru's major mineral products with the exception of iron. Iron ore production remained very low following the nationalization of Marcona. From 1977 to 1985 gold and silver production expanded very rapidly while copper, lead, and zinc production rose slowly and unevenly (see Appendixes L.1 and L.2).

The new production plateau achieved in 1977 masked a contradictory trend, however. A periodization of the process of growth in the industry since 1950 reveals that average annual growth rates have been declining. From the passage of the Mining Code of 1950, to 1959 (just prior to the inauguration of Toquepala), production grew at an average annual rate of 8.1 percent. In the next period, 1960 to 1976 (prior to the inauguration of Cuajone), the growth rate was 3.4 percent. From 1977 to 1985 mineral output grew at an average annual rate of 2.3 percent. This secular decline in mining production contributed to Peru's long-term economic crisis.

Readjustments in the Relationship Between Capital and Labor

The late 1970s and first half of the 1980s was a period of economic crisis in Peru. An unmanageable foreign debt, fiscal imbalances, and inflation triggered intervention by the International Monetary Fund (IMF). The IMF prescribed a structural adjustment policy, supposedly to correct economic imbalances, as the primary condition for renegotiating Peru's debt.[33] To comply with the IMF the Belaúnde administration eliminated price controls, as well as subsidies for food, transport, and energy. This triggered hyper-inflation, theoretically one of the problems that the policy was designed to resolve. By 1985 consumer prices were more than 50 times higher than in 1979 (see Appendix L.5). Money wages rose, but far less than prices. Throughout the economy price-deflated wages plummeted and the standard of living of the working class declined drastically.

In the mining sector average price-deflated wages paid to permanent workers fell by more than 25 percent from 1980 to 1985 (see Table 6.4). This reversed the trend of rising price-deflated wages that characterized the industry in the 1970s. However, wages did not decline equally throughout the industry. Table 6.4 shows that in the *gran minería* average wages and salaries of permanent workers fell by 34 percent. This was in contrast to the *mediana minería*, where price-deflated wages rose. The large companies, both foreign and state owned, were far more successful in containing wage demands than the smaller firms.

The decline in money wages and in the standard of living of the working class reflected major readjustments in the relations between capital and labor in the industry as well as in the wider economy. The success of the Velasco government in breaking the power of precapitalist landowners resulted in unanticipated social changes in the countryside. Many rural families and communities lost access to land and increasing numbers of peasants sought permanent wage labor. The dissolution of the peasantry neither began nor culminated in the 1960s and 1970s. However, the Peruvian revolution ushered in a qualitative leap in this process. At the same time the economic growth of this period increased the demand for workers throughout the economy. A majority of the peasant men and women who migrated to the mines, cities, and agricultural cooperatives, in the early 1970s found jobs. However, economic difficulties intensified in the late 1970s and early 1980s and companies responded by lowering production and reducing the size of their labor force. The capitalist sector no longer was expanding and able to absorb large numbers of new workers. As a result recently proletarianized peasants were without work as well as without land. One symptom of the economic crisis was rising unemployment and ever larger numbers of people moving into the cities to seek work. There were few jobs and migrants could find a livelihood only in the burgeoning "informal" sector.

Rising unemployment in the late 1970s and 1980s contributed to a decline in the power of trade unions, particularly in the mining sector. Common in this period were *marchas de protesta*, marches from the mines to Lima to dramatize the plight of the labor force. In these years the closing of mines resulted in massive layoffs and the elimination of job stability. There was also a dramatic deterioration in working conditions. In this environment the miners' trade unions generally were unsuccessful in bargaining for wage increases that kept pace with inflation.

TABLE 6.4 Indexes of Average Annual Price-Deflated Wages of Permanent Workers in the Peruvian Mining Industry[a] [b], 1980-1985 (in Peruvian *Soles*)

Year	Industry Wide	(1980 = 100) Gran Minería	Mediana Minería
1980	100	100	100
1981	101	94	114
1982	113	101	120
1983	87	74	101
1984	80	69	105
1985	76	66	103

SOURCES: Computed by the author from data presented in Ministerio de Energía y Minas, *Anuario de la Minería del Perú 1977-1985* (Lima) ,Tables 142-153.

[a]Price-deflated wages are money wages paid to *obreros* and *empleados* divided by the cost of living index. I use the cost of living index for Lima, the only continual index available (see Appendix L.5).

[b]Data on payment to contract laborers are not available. Since contract workers received lower pay than permanent workers, inclusion of this category of workers would lower average pay. See discussion of contract workers below. The relative fall in living standards of *obreros* and *empleados* represents another inequality in the distribution of the decline in price-deflated wages. For the sector as a whole price-deflated wages paid to *obreros* fell far more than those of *empleados*. Again there is a marked difference between the *gran* and the *mediana minería*. For *obreros* price-deflated wages fell more in the large firms than in the smaller firms. In the case of *empleados*, price-deflated salaries also fell in the *gran minería*, but rose in the *mediana minería* (see Table 6.5). With the exception of *empleados* employed in the *mediana minería*, there was a generalized and decisive immiserization of the working class in the mining industry in the first half of the nineteen-eighties.

TABLE 6.5 Indexes of Average Annual Price-Deflated Wages to *Obreros* and Salaries to *Empleados* in the Peruvian Mining Industry[a][b], 1980-1985

| | (in Peruvian *soles*) (1980 = 100) | | | |
| | Obreros[c] | | Empleados | |
Year	Gran	Mediana	Gran	Mediana
1980	100	100	100	100
1981	94	118	94	95
1982	102	121	99	107
1983	66	92	81	106
1984	58	93	82	111
1985	55	84	78	117

SOURCES: Computed by the author from data presented in Ministerio de Energía y Minas, *Anuario de la Minería del Perú 1977-1985* (Lima), Tables 142-153.

[a] Price-deflated wages and salaries are divided by a cost of living index. I use the cost of living index for Lima, the only continual index available (see Appendix L.5).

[b] The difference in remuneration between the *gran* and the *mediana minería* is so great that it arouses suspicion about the accuracy of the data. Although it is the official data of the Ministerio de Energía y Minas, I suggest that the data might possibly be faulty. Nevertheless, it can be used with confidence to indicate the trend in the differential in wages between the *gran* and the *mediana minería* in this period; a trend that has been noted in other sources.

[c] Data on payment to contract laborers not available. Since contract workers received lower pay than permanent workers, inclusion of this category of workers would lower average pay. See discussion of contract laborers below.

High unemployment and large numbers of men looking for permanent work in the mines provided the pre-conditions for readjustments in the labor force in the industry. Through the 1950s mining companies suffered from shortages of labor, while in the 1970s and 1980s companies enjoyed the advantages of a surfeit of workers. Instead of devising methods of bonding workers to the companies, such as *enganche*, companies expanded the use of contract workers in lieu of permanent laborers. Under the contract system workers were hired for a set time period, usually several months. Often the length of contracts would be just short of the period when workers legally became covered by job stability and workers' benefits. Because companies were not required to submit information to the Ministerio de Energía y Minas on their contract workers, there are few reliable data on this "hidden" portion of the labor force. It is estimated that between 20 and 30 percent of the workers in the mines in the middle 1980s were contract laborers, and that their pay was about half that of the stable workers with whom they labored.[34]

The importance of contract labor is reflected in the attitude that trade unions adopted towards these workers. With the initial proliferation of contract workers in the late 1970s and early 1980s trade unions made no attempt to organize contract workers. Their strategy centered on denouncing companies for undercutting the union and evading union pay, protective legislation, and benefits. However, by the middle of the 1980s, with increasing numbers of contract workers in the labor force, trade unions began to organize these workers into the union.[35]

Because contract laborers were not included in data on the labor force the validity of official statistics on the size of the labor force and payment to labor is thrown into question. For this reason it is meaningless to calculate productivity in the industry in the late 1970s and the 1980s, since this calculation is based on the number of *tareas* or tasks performed or, in the absence of this, on the number of workers in the labor force.

Major adjustments in the relationship between labor and capital in the 1980s enabled the industry to recover from the earlier crisis. Job stability, benefits, and occupational safety standards that had been won through decades of struggles were denied to contract workers. Also, the long-term trend of rising price-deflated wages was abruptly reversed and price-deflated wages declined drastically in the 1980s.

Table 6.6   Total Interest Paid by All Firms in the Peruvian Mining Industry, 1977-1984

Year	(millions of US$) Payments
1977	115.8
1978	136.9
1979	113.1
1980	212.0
1981	294.0
1982	417.0
1983	571.3
1984	662.9

SOURCES: Computed by the author from data presented in Ministerio de Energía y Minas, *Anuario de la Minería del Perú 1977-1985* (Lima), Tables 142-147.

The Legacy of Indebtedness

The Velasco government left as one of its legacies a large foreign debt. Most of the debt was contracted for productive purposes, to expand the level of exports. The government envisioned turning the vast deserts of the Peruvian coast into fertile agricultural lands and the massive low grade mineral deposits into productive mines. Unfortunately, for the military visionaries and for future generations of Peruvians, most of these borrowed funds were invested in projects that never were completed. The huge harvests of cotton, sugar, and sorghum never became a reality, nor the mines that were to make Peru the world's leading copper producer. The state was burdened with mounting interest payments but lacked the increased exports necessary to finance them. The administration of President Belaúnde maintained this tradition of indebtedness.[36]

Increasing indebtedness took its toll in the mining sector. In the 1970-1974 period the sector as a whole owed an average of US$ 17 million per annum in interest payments; from 1975-1979 this figure rose to US$ 88 million per year; and from 1980-1984 the sector owed an average of US$ 431 million per year.[37]   Payments balloned in the early 1980s, rising steadily from US$ 115.8 million in 1977 to US$ 662.9 million in 1984 (see Table 6.6).[38] The burden of interest payments was not distributed evenly throughout the sector. Southern Peru's debt burden declined in the 1980s while that of the state-owned companies, Minero-Perú and Tintaya, rose rapidly (see Appendix L.6).

In hindsight it appears that the nationalizations in the mining industry were not successful. CENTROMIN and HIERRO-PERU burdened the state with large deteriorating industrial complexes that governments since Velasco's have been struggling to revitalize. While output by CENTROMIN began to increase in the 1980s, as a consequence of the renovation and expansion of Cobriza, it was at the expense of increasing indebtedness. The debt contracted by the mining sector, coupled with loans for oil imports, agricultural infrastructure, and defense, became a crushing financial burden for the Peruvian state.

Copper prices remained low for more than a decade, from 1977 to 1986. Commodity analysts predicted that copper prices might never recover because of the substitution of plastics and fiber optics for copper in industrial uses.[39] This prognosis made copper exporting countries reassess their economic strategies, which continued to depend on copper production. However, in late 1987 copper prices began to soar. At the beginning of the year high grade cathode copper was quoted on the London Metal Exchange (LME) at US$ 62 per pound. In December of that same year copper prices closed on the LME at US$ 130. Despite the doubling of prices, companies in Peru and Chile declared that they would not alter their production quotas.[40] This corroborates the conclusion that in the era of large-scale open-pit mining operations price changes bear little relation to cyclical fluctuations in mineral production.

Debate over the methods of exploiting mineral wealth has dominated Peruvian politics for the past five hundred years. Since the nineteen-forties one side in this debate has called for the establishment of a favorable investment climate to attract foreign capital to develop Peru's mineral resources. An opposing position advocates state control over the production and commercialization of minerals. After the nationalizations of the 1970s, the forms of ownership in the Peruvian mining industry reflected an unfortunate compromise between these two strategies. Foreign firms controlled the profitable ventures, while state ownership was relegated to those marginal operations that no longer attracted private capital. This may have been advantageous for private, particularly foreign, capital. However, it was considerably less so for the Peruvian state. And so the debate continued unabated.

APPENDIX A

Sources for the Statistical Data, Construction of Time Series, and Statistical Methods

List of Tables

The hypothesis that is tested in this study is that factors external to the Peruvian economy such as the world demand for metals and international metals prices were not significant determinants of growth, stagnation, and crisis in the Peruvian mining industry in the twentieth century. Instead, I propose that internal factors such as wages, the availability of labor, and productivity conditioned the expansion and contraction of the sector. For the purposes of analysis this distinction between external and internal factors must be made an empirical distinction. This is done in several complementary ways. For reasons explained below, the statistical analysis is divided into two periods, 1900-1945 and 1945-1977. First, in each period, the simple relationship between changes in world production and changes in Peruvian production is estimated. This allows me to measure the correlation between the two and to statistically measure the extent to which Peruvian production moves with world production. Changes in levels of production rather than the correlation in the levels themselves are used because of the strong upward trend in both Peruvian and world production. When two time series have strong trends, relating levels can give high correlation measures (R^2) even though the series may in fact be unrelated or only weakly so. Correlating changes in levels of production provides a summary of the relationship between Peruvian and world production for a period as a whole, not for particular years or selected sub-periods. In order to consider shorter time periods other measures are used.

First, I construct indexes of real (constant price) output for both Peruvian and world production, and year-to-year movements in these indexes is compared. But particularly in the 1900-1945 period, a simple inspection of these two indexes is not very illuminating. Since Peruvian production begins in 1900 from a base near zero, its absolute changes, as both indexes grow over time, are larger than for the index of world production. This largely reflects the greater ability to increase output a given proportion when production is low, and the addition of another mine in Peru could, say, double production. This problem of comparison of the indexes is related to the fact that a mature mining industry will exhibit a different trend from a newly-initiated one. In order to deal with this problem, I also provide tables and figures on the percentage rate of change in Peruvian and world production. This measure, called the first relative central difference, avoids the misleading impression one gets by merely comparing changes in levels of production (the indexes of output themselves). However, comparing percentage changes does not completely compensate for the difficulty mentioned above, that in the earlier period (1900-1945) the Peruvian industry began from a very low base. When Peruvian production increases at a faster rate than world production in the early years, this may represent nothing more than the advantages unique to a young industry, or what neoclassical economists call economies of scale. Such advantages, usually associated with high initial costs of fixed capital with regard to individual producers and infrastructural costs for the industry as a whole, are notoriously difficult to quantify, and are not the subject of this study. I seek to indirectly separate these out by a third technique of comparison, trend analysis. In this case, the variations in Peruvian and world production are measured relatively to predicted trend values for each. This commonly-employed statistical technique allows me to judge for each time series whether production is high or low compared to the long-run performance of that time series.

This technique has its limitations. The most relevant for purposes of comparing production in the Peruvian industry to production in the world industry is that by eliminating the trend from each time series, one implicitly assumes that Peruvian and world production interact cyclically and are independent in secular trend. In practice, the possible distortion in interpretation created by taking out the trend in each time series is not very great. In the period 1900-1945 the Peruvian trend in production is much higher than the world trend, but this is largely explained by the tiny base from which Peruvian production began in 1900. In the later period, 1945-1977, the trends in Peruvian production and world production are not significantly different. Thus, the differences in Peruvian and world production are cyclical in this period, and these are actually the variations which trend analysis is designed to clarify. Each of the measures of comparison provides a particular view of the relationship between the Peruvian industry and the world industry. Each has its drawbacks or distortions and each its usefulness. In the statistical analysis in this book the purpose is to use each to separate external and internal factors, while recognizing the limitation of any single measure.

In considering external and internal factors, in certain periods I refer to the role of world market prices. While these are explicitly treated separately, they are, in fact, subsumed within the comparison of world output and Peruvian output. In calculating world production, I aggregate the different metals by using constant prices. However, changes in this index reflect responses by the world industry to changes in conditions of profitability, a major aspect of which is market prices for the metals. In general, one would expect increases in world output to be associated with increases in prices, but this need not be the case, and is not the case in all years. In a period in which world mineral product rises and Peruvian production does not, the movement in prices, whether up or down, cannot itself explain the difference between Peruvian and world performance, since the movement in prices is a common influence on both. This is not to say that price changes are irrelevant, but points out that the key indicator for comparison is production, in Peru and the world. The index of world prices, therefore, provides supplementary and complementary information to the analysis, but does not by itself account for differences in year-to-year performance. In order to make the price index most useful to this study, it has been calculated on the basis of Peruvian quantity weights, so that the movement in the index reflects the relative importance of each metal in Peruvian production. As a consequence, it is not the relevant index for measuring the impact of world prices on world production.

One of the contributions of this study is its presentation of consistent time series for production, employment, productivity, money and price-deflated wages, and the wage cost to capital for the Peruvian metal mining industry for the years 1900-1985. The official publications of the successive Peruvian ministeries charged with oversight of the mining industry present extensive data on the mining industry beginning in the second decade of the twentieth century. However, after working with these data I found it obvious that they contained many problems and inconsistencies, and while the data were useful as a point of departure, it was necessary to construct more reliable time series.

Since my major concern is with variations in production over time, it was first necessary to construct a consistent time series for the volume of metal mining output. This proved difficult because the data on the volume of output that appear in official Peruvian publications are not consistent from year-to-year. There is a lack of standardization of the measure of the volume of output, in particular in regard to the level of processing at which ore content is measured. Theoretically what is always measured is recoverable ore content, but in practice the inconsistencies introduce wide variations into the data on total output.

In order to eliminate these inconsistencies, in this study in so far as possible the volume of output of the metal mining industry is measured in the most refined state to which the metals were processed in Peru. This technically represents the volume of production of the metal mining and metallurgy sector.

Data on the volume of output for the industry as a whole are presented in this study in the form of the value of production in constant prices. This is a measure of physical production. Weights cannot be used because the metals are of different qualities. This measure, the value of production in constant prices, is presented in the official Peruvian statistics since 1950 as the value of production in constant 1963 *soles*. Before 1950 these statistics are unavailable in the official sources. Therefore, I have constructed a corresponding time series for production from 1903-1949 by multiplying the volume of production (in weight) for the five major metals mined in Peru at that time, by the implied (1963) price (see Table A.1).[1] I chose to use constant (1963) prices to be consistent with the official statistics and to facilitate comparisons between this study and other analyses of Peruvian mining. In order to test whether the use of 1963 prices introduces a bias into the data I also constructed a production index using average prices for the 1903-1977 period, and discovered that the differences in the two series are not great.[2]

Since the original sources from which the official production figures for the 1903-1945 period were derived have been destroyed, I was not able to verify these data. However, the original sources for published official statistics on the volume of production for the 1945-1977 period are available. I used these data to test the reliability of my time series on production from 1945-1977, which was derived in the first instance from published data. I selected random years and recalculated the data presented in the "Declaraciones Anuales Consolidadas de Concesionarios, Empresas y Empresarios Mineros," lengthy questionnaires submitted annually by each mining company to the Ministerio de Energía y Minas (1966 to the present), and to its predecessors, the Ministerio de Fomento y Obras Públicas (1950-1965) and the Ministerio de Fomento (1945-1949). I determined that once adjustments are made for the variation in how and when mining output is measured, and this is rendered consistent, the data presented in the official sources are essentially accurate. However, I discovered that official production data for the 1970s are unreliable. The most obvious problem is that the official data from the Ministerio de Energía y Minas (MEM), given in the value of production in constant 1963 *soles*, indicate that the volume of production almost doubles between 1972 and 1973, and increases

TABLE A.1   Implied 1963 Prices for Measuring the
Value of Production in Constant 1963 *Soles* in the
Peruvian Mining Industry

Metal		Price
Copper	S/.	15,493 per metric ton
Iron	S/.	169 per metric ton
Lead	S/.	4,309 per metric ton
Zinc	S/.	3,809 per metric ton
Gold	S/.	29 per gram
Silver	S/.	1,025 per kilogram

SOURCES: Ministerio de Fomento y Obras Públicas, *Anuario de la Industria Minera en el Perú* (Lima 1964).

even more in 1974 (see Table A.2)[3]. This is impossible since the volume of production [in weight] of each metal, except gold and zinc, falls between 1972 and 1973; and the increase in gold and zinc production is small (see Table A.3 for the volume of production [in weight] of Peru's major metallic mineral products from 1969 to 1977).

Because of the unreliability of the official index of the value of production in constant *soles* for the 1970s, I constructed another index based on the volume of production [in weight] for each metal, as given by the Ministerio de Energía y Minas and the Sociedad Nacional de Minería y Petróleo, multiplied this by the implied 1963 price of each metal, and added these weighted prices.[4] Official MEM data on the value of production in constant prices was published through 1975.   In order to obtain production data for 1976 through 1985 I multiplied the volume of production (in weight) of each metal by the implied prices. The index of the value of Peruvian production in constant *soles* as used in this study is one that I have constructed.

TABLE A.2   Official and Constructed Indexes of the Volume of Production (Measured in Constant 1963 Prices) in the Peruvian Mining Industry, 1969-1976

Year	Official Data	Constructed Data
1969	590.1	590.1
1970	620.2	630.4
1971	513.0	611.6
1972	574.2	662.5
1973	1056.5	632.6
1974	1191.9	633.6
1975	846.3	547.7
1976	n.a.	779.8

SOURCES: Ministerio de Energía y Minas, *Anuario de la Minería del Perú* (Lima: 1969-1975); Sociedad Nacional de Minería y Petróleo, *Perú Minero-Comercial* (Lima: 1976-1980).

The time series on world mining production is constructed in such a way as to make it comparable to the data on the Peruvian industry. World production figures are calculated on the basis of only those metals that were produced in Peru in corresponding years. The volume of production in weight of each metal is multiplied by its implied 1963 price. These weighted prices are added together to give a time series of the value of production in constant (1963) prices.

Because of the constraints imposed by the sources, labor productivity is calculated in two ways. From 1905-1945 productivity is measured by dividing the value of production in constant prices by the total number of people employed in the metal mining industry. From 1945 to 1975 more detailed data are available from the "Declaraciones Anuales Consolidadas de Concesionarios, Empresas y Empresarios Mineros" making it possible to measure productivity more precisely. In the latter period productivity is measured by dividing the value of production in constant prices by the number of *tareas* performed.[5] This is a measure of the average volume of output produced by one worker in an eight-hour day. While this measure of productivity is more

TABLE A.3   Volume of Production of Peru's Major
Metallic Mineral Products, 1969-1977

Year	Copper M.T.	Lead M.T.	Zinc M.T.	Silver Kg.	Gold Grams	Iron M.T.
1969	198,803	154,543	300,303	1,116,194	4,094,488	5,937,853
1970	220,225	156,770	299,136	1,239,023	3,349,145	6,249,358
1971	207,346	165,814	318,073	1,242,642	2,604,989	5,616,689
1972	219,216	184,381	376,129	1,255,664	3,965,528	6,085,626
1973	202,686	183,413	390,576	1,163,642	2,949,116	5,852,000
1974	211,593	165,798	378,029	1,084,907	3,112,787	6,219,000
1975	165,813	154,168	364,915	1,058,350	3,135,203	5,067,255
1976	228,407	174,707	456,069	1,202,492	3,764,503	3,190,869
1977	338,110	170,744	405,250	1,235,757	3,247,000	4,107,078

SOURCES: The same as for Table A.2.

M.T. - metric tons.

reliable than the measure that I was obliged to use for the 1905-1945 period, it too has its problems. It is obviously highly affected by any errors that may be present in the data on the value of production in constant prices, as well as by discrepancies in recording and reporting the number of *tareas* performed annually on a company-by-company basis.

The data on the number of people employed present similar problems as the data on productivity. From 1905 to 1945 employment in the metal mining industry is calculated by subtracting the number of persons employed in the petroleum sector from total employment in the mining industry. From 1945, information from the "Declaraciones Anuales Consolidadas de Concesionarios, Empresas y Empresarios Mineros" makes it possible not only to determine more precisely the number of people employed in the metal mining and metallurgical sector, but to analyze differentiation within the working class. The data specify the number of *obreros* and the number of *empleados* employed annually.[6]

Data that permit the calculation of wages in the metal mining industry as a whole are not available prior to 1924. While data exist that would permit the calculation of average wages in the metal mining sector from 1924 to 1945, they appear highly inconsistent and unreliable.[7] Therefore, I do not analyze wage changes and their effects from 1903 to 1945. Data from the "Declaraciones Anuales Consolidadas de Concesionarios, Empresas y Empresarios Mineros," make it possible to be more precise in the determination of average money wages and salaries in the metal mining and metallurgy sector. For each company in the sector the "Declaraciones" provide the total wages paid to *obreros* and total salaries paid to *empleados*. To calculate average remuneration the total wage and salary bills are divided by the number of *obreros* and *empleados* employed by each company.

Another contribution of this study is its empirical analysis of the two aspects of the wage: the wage as it represents labor costs to capitalists, on the one hand, and the wage as it represents the standard of living of workers, on the other. In order to analyze the impact of changes in the level of the wage on labor costs I calculate the difference between changes in the prices of the product (in this case the metals) and changes in the level of the wage. This allows me to analyze the wage cost to capital. Other problems present themselves in calculating the wage as it represents the standard of living of the workers, or the price-deflated wage. This is because the only continuous cost of living index that exists for Peru is based on the cost of living in Lima, which varies from costs at the mines for the same items. Although indexes of the cost of living exist for some cities in the highlands, these are scattered and cover relatively few years, mostly the 1970s and 1980s. Because I am concerned with the mining industry as a whole, throughout Peru since the 1940s, I use the cost of living for Lima to approximate the price-deflated wages of the miners.

Because the post-1945 data are based on different sources and generally are more reliable than the data for the earlier years, the data pre- and post-1945 are not strictly comparable. Therefore, I have divided the statistical analysis of the industry in the twentieth century into two periods: 1900-1945 and 1945-1977. By doing this I am able to present and analyze time series on the metal mining and metallurgy industry that are as consistent as possible. However, despite efforts to clean the data, many inconsistencies and problems surely remain. Although this suggests that the data still contain some inaccuracies for individual years, I do not believe that this has a great effect on the tendencies that emerge over time. I am concerned with trends in the development of the metal mining industry, not with particular annual fluctuations. Therefore, I believe that for my purpose the time series that I present are valid and valuable. Where the data for one year appear surprising, or impossible, I try to explain these aberrations.

The data were collected from the following official published sources:

Boletín de la Sociedad Nacional de Minería
Boletín del Cuerpo de Ingenieros de Minas (1903-1922)
Boletín Oficial de Minas y Petróleo (1924-1932)
La Industria Minera en el Perú (1932-1939)
Anuario de la La Industria Minera en el Perú (1940-1965)
Anuario Minero del Perú (1966-1972)
Anuario de la Minería del Perú (1973-1985)

These data were supplemented and complemented by data published in Pablo Macera, *Estadísticas históricas del Perú: sector minero (precios)* (Lima: Centro Peruano de Historia Económica, 1972), and Pablo Macera and Horacio Pinto, *Estadísticas históricas del Perú: sector minero (volumen y valor)* (Lima: Centro Peruano de Historia Económica, 1972); and unpublished data in the "Declaraciones Anuales Consolidadas de Concesionarios, Empresas y Empresarios Mineros," Archives, División de Estadística, Dirección General de Minería, Ministerio de Energía y Minas (Lima), 1945-1975.

APPENDIX B

Volume of Metal Production in the Peruvian Mining Industry and in the World Mining Industry

List of Tables

TABLE B.1   Copper Ore Production in the Peruvian
Mining Industry and in the World Mining Industry,
1900-1978[a]

Year	(Thousands of metric tons) World Production	Peruvian Production	Peruvian Production as % of World Production
1900	500	9.4[b]	1.9
1905	694	12.2	1.8
1910	891	27.4	3.1
1915	1092	34.7	3.2
1920	942	33.0	3.5
1925	1395	36.9	2.6
1930	1510	48.2	3.2
1935	1385	29.6	2.1
1940	2250	44.0	2.0
1945	2000	31.9	1.6
1950	2270	30.2	1.3
1955	2730	43.4	1.6
1960	3840	209.2	5.4
1965	5100	198.6	3.9
1970	6460	205.9	3.2
1975	7317	165.8	2.3
1978	7855	366.5	4.7

SOURCES: *The Statistical Yearbook* (New York: The United Nations, Department of Economic and Social Affairs, 1948, 1952, 1955, 1959, 1965, 1974, 1976, 1978); *Mineral's Yearbook: 1971 Area Reports: International, vol. III* (Washington, D.C.: Bureau of the Mines, U.S. Department of the Interior, 1973); *Metal Statistics: 1965-1975*, 63rd ed. (Frankfurt Am Main: Metallgesellschaft AG, 1976); Pablo Macera and Honorio Pinto, *Estadísticas históricas del Perú: sector minero II (volumen y valor)* (Lima: Centro Peruano de Historia Económica, 1972); and *Boletín del cuerpo de ingenieros de minas* (Lima: 1902, 1903).

[a]The data on world production of the metals that are given in tables B.1-B.6 do not exactly correspond to the data on world metal production in Appendix F. This is because the data on world production in these tables are primarily taken
(continued)

from *The Statistical Yearbook*, where production data are given country-by-country. This allows me to calculate what portion of the metals is produced in the advanced capitalist countries, and what portion is produced in the underdeveloped countries.

[b]This is production in 1901, the first year for which official data on metal production are available in Peru.

TABLE B.2   Lead Ore Production in the Peruvian Mining Industry and in the World Mining Industry, 1900-1978

| | (Thousands of metric tons) | | |
Year	World Production	Peruvian Production	Peruvian Production as % of World Production
1900	873	1.3[a]	> 1
1905	969	1.5	> 1
1910	1,127	1.9	> 1
1915	1,147	2.7	> 1
1920	888	0.5	> 1
1925	1,510	4.4	> 1
1930	1,625	19.8	1.2
1935	13,372	8.5	2.1
1940	1,700	50.4	3.0
1945	1,150	53.7	4.7
1950	1,570	64.9	4.1
1955	1,930	118.8	6.2
1960	1,940	165.9	8.6
1965	2,730	154.3	5.7
1970	3,410	156.8	4.6
1975	3,576	154.2	4.3
1978	3,613	170.5	4.7

SOURCES: The same as for Table B.1.

[a]Data are for 1901.

TABLE B.3 **Zinc Ore Production in the Peruvian Mining Industry and in the World Mining Industry, 1925-1978**

| Year | (Thousands of metric tons) | | |
	World Production	Peruvian Production	Peruvian Production as % of World Production
1925[a]	1135	1.9	>1
1930	1458	11.3	>1
1935	1452	4.7	>1
1940	1935	17.7	>1
1945	1475[b]	61.2	4.1
1950	2050	78.9	3.8
1955	2640	166.1	6.3
1960	2960	277.6	9.4
1965	4350	254.5	5.9
1970	5530	320.7	5.8
1975	6090	364.9	6.0
1978	6411	402.6	6.3

SOURCES: The same as for Table B.1.

[a]Zinc was experimentally mined in Peru in 1924. The commercial mining of zinc began in Peru in the late 1930s.

[b]This figure represents world zinc production in 1946. Data on world zinc production are not available for 1945.

TABLE B.4   Iron Ore Production in the Peruvian Mining Industry and in the World Mining Industry, 1955-1977

| | (Thousands of metric tons) | | |
Year	World Production	Peruvian Production	Peruvian Production as % of World Production
1955	174,500	1,059	>1
1960	230,900	2,818	1.2
1965	325,800	4,459	1.4
1970	424,100	7,928	1.9
1975	522,500	7,753	1.5
1977	482,800	4,107	>1

SOURCES: *The Statistical Yearbook* (New York: The United Nations, Department of Economic and Social Affaris, 1948, 1952, 1955, 1959, 1965, 1974, 1976, 1978); *Mineral's Yearbook: 1971 Area Reports: International, vol. III* (Washington, D.C.: Bureau of the Mines, U.S. Department of the Interior, 1973); *Mineral's Yearbook: 1968* (Washington, D.C.: Bureau of the Mines, U.S. Department of the Interior, 1964), p.7.

TABLE B.5   Silver Production in the Peruvian Mining Industry and in the World Mining Industry, 1900-1974

Year	World Production	(Metric tons) Peruvian Production	Peruvian Production as % of World Production
1900	5400	170.8[a]	3.2
1905	4911	191.4	3.9
1910	6896	258.6	3.8
1915	5763	294.4	5.1
1920	5358	277.4	5.2
1925	7517	645.3	8.6
1930	7800	478.7	6.1
1935	6700	548.3	8.2
1940	8400	602.4	7.2
1945	4500	404.3	8.8
1950	5500	415.8	7.6
1955	6100	713.8	11.7
1960	7000	942.7	13.5
1965	7949	1134.0	14.3
1970	9574	1239.0	12.9
1974	9377	1084.0	11.6

SOURCES: The same as for Table B.1.

[a]Data are for 1901.

TABLE B.6 Gold Production in the Peruvian Mining Industry and in the World Mining Industry, 1900-1974

Year	(Kilograms) World Production	Peruvian Production[a]
1900	386,335	1,073.3[b]
1905	575,045	776.6
1910	688,841	707.9
1915	706,615	1,590.6
1920	508,089	1,951.7
1925	591,774	3,420.4
1930	604,000	2,766.0
1935	776,000	3,451.0
1940	1,140,000	8,748.0
1945	659,000	5,370.0
1950	752,100	4,602.0
1955	840,000	5,311.0
1960	1,047,000	4,472.0
1965	1,282,000	3,272.0
1970	1,288,000	2,954.0
1974	1,027,000	2,327.0

SOURCE: The same as for Table B.1; and Robert H. Ridgway, *Summarized Data of Gold Production* (Washington, D.C.: U.S. Department of Commerce, Bureau of Mines Economic Paper No. 6, 1929), p. 6.

[a]Peruvian gold production is less than 1 percent of world gold production in every year.

[b]Data are for 1901.

APPENDIX C

Value of Mining Production and World Market Prices

List of Tables

TABLE C.1 Indexes of the Value of Production in the World Mining Industry[a] and the Peruvian Mining Industry, 1903-1945

	(1903 = 100)	
Year	World Industry[b]	Peruvian Industry[c]
1903	100	100
1904	107	94
1905	121	129
1906	140	180
1907	144	220
1908	129	152
1909	135	150
1910	138	199
1911	139	203
1912	161	275
1913	152	262
1914	132	228
1915	159	299
1916	230	525
1917	244	570
1918	226	474
1919	163	427
1920	153	359
1921	98	339
1922	125	405
1923	164	513
1924	173	498
1925	224	589
1926	229	734
1927	212	613
1928	224	721
1929	266	791
1930	192	578
1931	141	322
1932	113	258
1933	143	386

(continued)

TABLE C.1 (cont.)

Year	(1903 = 100) World Industry[b]	Peruvian Industry[c]
1934	204	496
1935	231	782
1936	263	829
1937	344	1,024
1938	305	1,133
1939	330	1,358
1940	355	1,678
1941	373	1,692
1942	375	1,714
1943	334	1,687
1944	306	1,700
1945	271	1,723

SOURCES: *Statistische Zusammenstellungen Über Aluminium, Blei, Kupfer, Nickel, Quecksilber, Silber, Zinc und Zinn* (Franfurt Am Main: Metallgesellschaft, 1907, 1913, 1931); Robert H. Ridgway, *Summarized Data of Gold Production* (Washington, D.C.: U.S. Department of Commerce, Bureau of Mines Economic Paper No. 6, 1929), p. 6; Pablo Macera and Honorio Pinto, *Estadísticas históricas del Perú: sector minero II (precios)*; and *Estadísticas históricas del Perú: sector minero II (volumen y valor)* (Lima: Centro Peruano de Historia Económica, 1972).

[a]Includes the value of production only of those metals produced in Peru for the respective years; i.e., from 1903-1945 it includes gold, silver, copper, and lead; zinc is included from 1925, and iron from 1953.

[b]In current U.S. dollars.

[c]Value in current *soles*, showing the domestic revenue received by producers in Peru. Thus, the series is not an index of foreign exchange earned, but is relevant for comparison to domestic costs of production.

TABLE C.2 World Market Prices 1900-1980

Year	Gold[a]	Silver[b]	Copper[c]	Lead[d]	Zinc[e]	Iron[f]
1900	20.67	0.62	16.19	4.37	4.39	. .
01	20.67	0.60	16.11	4.33	4.07	. .
02	10.67	0.53	11.63	4.07	4.84	. .
03	20.67	0.54	13.24	4.24	5.19	. .
04	20.67	0.58	12.82	4.31	4.93	. .
1905	20.67	0.60	15.59	4.71	5.73	. .
06	20.67	0.67	19.28	5.66	6.05	. .
07	20.67	0.65	20.00	5.33	5.81	. .
08	20.67	0.53	13.21	4.20	4.58	. .
09	20.67	0.52	12.98	4.27	5.35	. .
1910	20.67	0.54	12.74	4.45	5.37	. .
11	20.67	0.53	12.38	4.42	5.61	. .
12	20.67	0.60	16.34	4.47	6.80	. .
13	20.67	0.57	15.27	4.37	5.50	. .
14	20.67	0.54	13.60	3.86	5.06	. .
1915	20.67	0.49	17.28	4.67	13.05	. .
16	20.67	0.65	27.20	6.86	12.63	. .
17	20.67	0.81	27.18	8.79	8.81	. .
18	20.67	0.96	24.63	7.41	7.89	. .
19	20.67	1.11	18.69	5.76	6.99	. .
1920	20.67	1.00	17.46	7.96	7.67	. .
21	20.67	0.62	12.50	4.55	4.66	. .
22	20.67	0.67	13.38	5.74	5.72	. .
23	20.67	0.64	14.42	7.27	6.61	. .
24	20.67	0.66	13.02	8.10	6.34	. .
1925	20.67	0.69	14.04	9.02	7.62	. .
26	20.67	0.62	13.80	8.42	7.34	. .
27	20.67	0.56	12.92	6.76	6.24	. .
28	20.67	0.58	14.57	6.31	6.03	. .
29	20.67	0.53	18.11	6.83	6.51	. .
1930	20.67	0.38	12.98	5.52	4.56	. .
31	20.67	0.29	8.12	4.24	3.64	. .
32	20.67	0.28	5.56	3.18	2.88	. .
33	24.27	0.34	7.03	3.87	4.03	. .
34	35.00	0.47	8.43	3.86	4.16	. .

(continued)

TABLE C.2 (cont.)

Year	Gold[a]	Silver[b]	Copper[c]	Lead[d]	Zinc[e]	Iron[f]
1935	35.00	0.64	8.65	4.07	4.33	. .
36	35.00	0.45	9.47	4.71	4.90	. .
37	35.00	0.44	13.17	6.01	6.52	. .
38	35.00	0.43	10.00	4.74	4.61	. .
39	35.00	0.39	10.97	5.05	5.11	. .
1940	35.00	0.34	11.30	5.18	6.34	. .
41	35.00	0.34	11.80	5.79	7.47	. .
42	35.00	0.38	11.78	6.48	8.25	. .
43	35.00	0.44	11.78	6.50	8.25	. .
44	35.00	0.43	11.78	6.50	8.25	. .
1945	35.00	0.51	11.78	6.50	8.25	. .
46	35.00	0.80	14.80	8.11	8.73	. .
47	35.00	0.72	20.96	14.67	10.50	. .
48	35.00	0.74	22.27	18.04	13.59	. .
49	35.00	0.72	19.20	15.36	12.14	. .
1950	35.00	0.74	22.27	18.04	13.59	. .
51	35.00	0.89	26.07	17.50	17.89	. .
52	35.00	0.85	31.74	16.47	16.21	. .
53	35.00	0.85	30.84	13.49	10.86	6.76
54	35.00	0.85	29.89	14.05	10.68	6.91
1955	35.00	0.89	39.12	15.14	12.23	7.11
56	35.00	0.91	40.43	16.01	13.49	7.47
57	35.00	0.91	27.16	14.69	11.40	8.31
58	35.00	0.89	24.12	12.11	10.31	8.59
59	35.00	0.91	28.89	12.21	11.45	8.69
1960	35.00	0.91	29.89	11.95	12.94	8.73
61	35.00	0.92	27.92	10.87	11.54	8.99
62	35.00	1.08	28.51	9.63	11.63	8.84
63	35.00	1.28	28.41	11.14	12.30*	9.22
64	35.00	1.29	30.99	13.60	13.87	9.52
1965	35.00	1.29	35.60	16.00	14.80	9.53
66	35.00	1.29	49.51	15.12	14.80	9.49
67	35.00	1.55	47.19	14.00	14.14	9.92
68	40.06	2.14	50.29	13.21	13.80	10.21
69	41.51	1.79	61.93	14.90	14.90	10.34

(continued)

Table C.2 (cont.)

Year	Gold[a]	Silver[b]	Copper[c]	Lead[d]	Zinc[e]	Iron[f]
1970	36.41	1.77	62.75	15.62	15.62	10.80
71	41.25	1.55	47.87	13.80	16.43	11.55
72	58.44	1.68	46.52	15.03	18.05	12.20
73	97.58	2.56	78.76	16.29	20.96	12.84
74	159.62	4.72	90.51	22.53	36.95	16.34
1975	161.17	4.42	53.25	21.52	38.96	21.41
76	124.94	4.35	60.89	23.10	37.01	24.28
77	147.98	4.62	56.70	30.70	34.39	26.27
78	193.55	5.41	59.20	33.65	31.00	28.86
79	307.50	11.09	86.90	52.64	37.30	32.64
1980[g]	608.05	21.37	98.40	42.82	47.50	. .

SOURCES: *Metal Statistics* (Frankfurt Am Main: Metallgesellschaft, 1907-1977); and unpublished statistics from the U.S. Bureau of Mines.

[a]Gold: New York $ per Troy ounce.
[b]Silver: New York $ per Troy ounce.
[c]Copper: Electrolitic New York ¢ per pound.
[d]Lead: New York (Nominal) ¢ per pound.
[e]Zinc: San Luis ¢ per pound.
[f]Iron: average value at mine, $ per long ton. Price of iron listed from 1954, the first year that iron was mined commercially in Peru.
[g]1980: first 9 months only.
*As of 1963 zinc prices quoted in special high grade.

APPENDIX D

Statistical Correlation Between Changes in the Peruvian Mining Industry and Changes in the World Mining Industry, 1900-1945

Correlation Between Changes in Output in the Peruvian and the World Mining Industries

Figure D.1 presents the year-to-year proportional changes in metal production for 1903-1945, measured as follows:

If Q is production and t stands for a particular year,

$$\frac{Q_t - Q_{t-1}}{1/2(Q_t + Q_{t-1})} \times 100$$

In Figure D.1 Peruvian changes are indicated by the dashed line and world changes by the solid line. This measure, called the first relative central difference, avoids the misleading impression one gets by merely comparing changes in levels of production (the indexes of output). However, comparing percentage changes does not completely compensate for the difficulty that in the period 1900-1945 the Peruvian industry began from a very low base. When Peruvian production increases at a faster rate than world production in the early years, this may represent nothing more than the advantages unique to a young industry, or what neoclassical economists call economies of scale. Such advantages, usually associated with high initial costs of fixed capital with regard to individual producers and infrastructural costs for the industry as a whole, are notoriously difficult to quantify, and are not the subject of this work. I seek to indirectly separate these out by trend analysis.

The percentage changes in Peruvian and world metal production can be tested for the degree of statistical correlation. A simple linear regression, with Peruvian changes specified as the dependent variable, gives the following coefficients:

$$\dot{Q}_p = 1.010 + 0.989\dot{Q}_w \qquad R_2 = 0.325 \qquad F = 19.3$$

$$(t = 4.4) \qquad N = 42$$

Given the number of observations, 42, the estimated relationship is statistically significant. While the relationship is significant, only 33 percent of the variation in Peruvian production is associated with variations in world production. One way to show this graphically is Figure D.2, where for each year, the percentage change in world production is subtracted from the percentage change in Peruvian production. Thus, by a glance at Figure D.2, one can pick out the years when Peruvian and world production diverged the most. Taking the period as a whole, two-thirds of the variation in Peruvian production do not conform to the variations in the weighted average changes of all producers. This is *prima facie* evidence for the impact of internal factors.

Correlation between Changes in Output in the Peruvian Mining Industry and Changes in World Market Prices

The effect of world prices on Peruvian production is estimated by specifying changes in Peruvian production as the dependent variable, and changes in an index of relevant world prices as the independent variable. This is reported below, first using changes in the two variables for the same years, then by lagging world price changes one year.

$$\dot{Q}_p(t) = 1.852 + 0.260\dot{P}_w(t) \qquad R^2 = .277 \qquad F = 15.3$$

$$(t = 3.9) \qquad N = 42$$

$$\dot{Q}_p(t) = 1.990 + 0.220\dot{P}_w(t-1) \qquad R^2 = .201 \qquad F = 9.8$$

$$(t = 3.1) \qquad N = 41$$

Both regressions show statistically significant results, though the non-lagged specification performs better. However, only 28 percent of the variation in Peruvian production is explained by changes in world market prices. The remainder of the variation is explained by variables not included in the regressions.

213

FIGURE D.1 Annual Percentage Changes in Peruvian and World Metal Production, 1903-1945

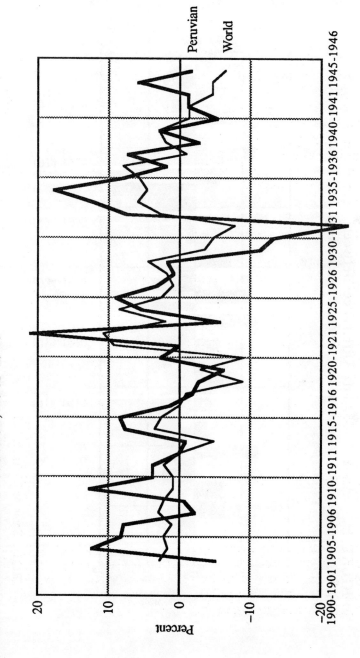

SOURCES: The same as for Table B.6.

214

FIGURE D.2 Annual Absolute Difference Between Percentage Change in Peruvian Metal Production and Percentage Change in World Metal Production, 1903-1945

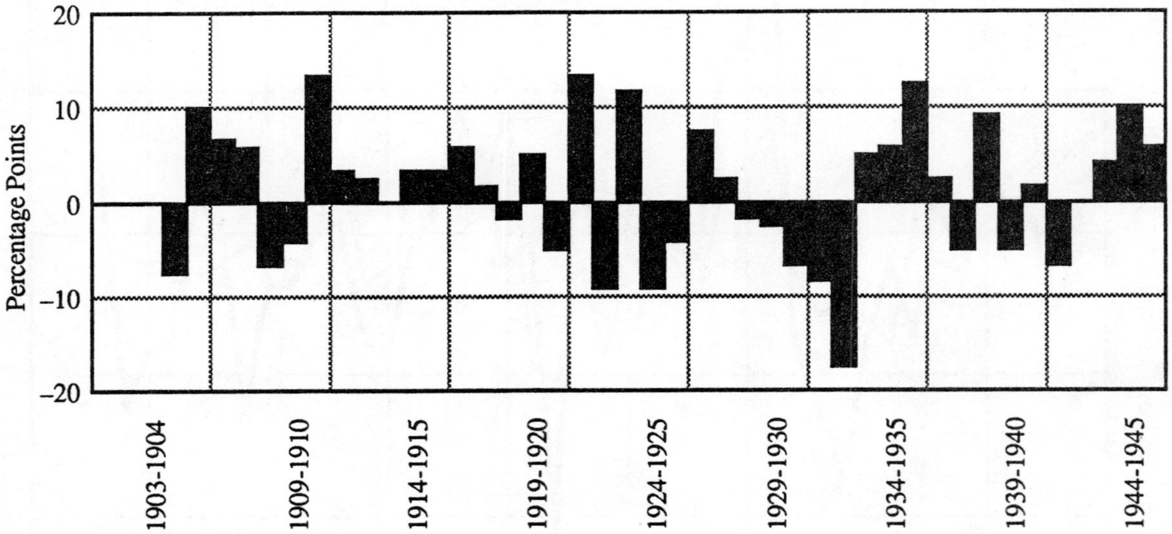

SOURCES: Same as for Table B.6.

APPENDIX E

Statistical Correlation Between Changes in the Peruvian Mining Industry and Changes in the World Mining Industry, 1945-1977

Correlation Between Changes in Output in the Peruvian and the World Mining Industries

Figure E.1 presents the year-to-year proportional changes in metal production for 1945-1977, measured as follows:

If Q is production and t stands for a particular year,

$$\frac{Q_t - Q_{t-1}}{1/2(Q_t + Q_{t-1})} \times 100$$

In Figure E.1 Peruvian changes are indicated by the dashed line and world changes by the solid line. A comparison between Figures D.1 and E.1 shows that the differences between changes in world and Peruvian production are considerably greater in the 1945-1977 period than in the 1900-1945 period.

In applying the same statistical tests to the later period as I did to the former period, I determined that all relationships are non-significant in the 1945-1977 period. With regard to changes in world production and Peruvian production, the correlation is less than 1 percent, as reported below:

$$\dot{Q}_p = 2.693 + 0.141\dot{Q}_w \qquad R^2 = 0.004 \qquad F = 0.2$$

$$(t = 0.3) \qquad N = 29$$

The relationship between changes in Peruvian output and in world output is not significant. The hypothesis that the two variables are only randomly related cannot be rejected.

The absence of a significant relationship can be noted in Figure E.2, where I subtract changes in world production from changes in

Peruvian production, as a way of showing the deviations of Peruvian production from world output.

Correlation Between Changes in Output in the Peruvian Mining Industry and Changes in World Market Prices

The effect of world prices on Peruvian production is estimated by specifying changes in Peruvian production as the dependent variable, and changes in an index of relevant world prices as the independent variable. This is reported below, first using changes in the two variables for the same years, then by lagging world price changes one year.

When the explanatory value of changes in world prices is tested, not only is the relationship non-significant, but the coefficient of changes in world prices is not of the predicted sign, both using a non-lagged and a lagged specification.

$$\dot{Q}_p(t) = 2.517 - 0.034\dot{P}_w(t) \qquad R^2 = 0.002 \qquad F = 0.1$$

$$(t = 0.3) \qquad N = 32$$

$$\dot{Q}_p(t) = 3.094 - 0.087\dot{P}_w(t-1) \qquad R^2 = 0.015 \qquad F = 0.4$$

$$(t = 0.7) \qquad N = 31$$

That is, taken alone, changes in world prices are not significantly related to changes in Peruvian output.

217

FIGURE E.1   Annual Percentage Changes in Peruvian and World Metal Production, 1945-1976

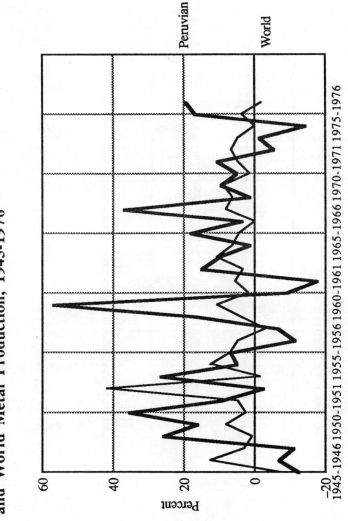

SOURCES: The same as for Table 2.2.

218

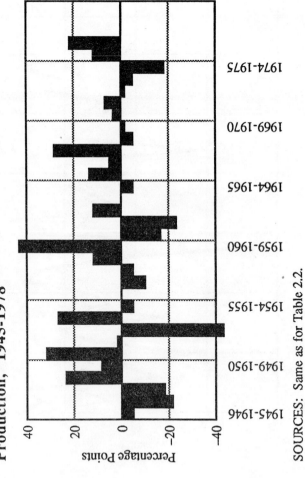

FIGURE E.2 Annual Absolute Difference Between Percentage Change in Peruvian Metal Production and Percentage Change in World Metal Production, 1945-1978

SOURCES: Same as for Table 2.2.

APPENDIX F

Statistical Correlation Between Changes in Peruvian and World Metal Production, 1945-1977

List of Tables

TABLE F.1 Percentage Change in Peruvian and World Copper Production, 1945-1975

Year	Peruvian	World
1945-46	–23.1	–14.9
1946-47	–8.2	20.6
1947-48	–21.1	4.3
1948-49	56.7	–2.4
1949-50	20.7	11.4
1950-51	6.3	5.4
1951-52	–14.4	3.8
1952-53	10.8	1.3
1953-54	19.4	1.8
1954-55	4.0	9.1
1955-56	8.9	11.5
1956-57	20.7	2.4
1957-58	–5.3	–5.8
1958-59	–2.7	10.2
1959-60	264.4	14.9
1960-61	7.3	3.6
1961-62	–16.3	3.7
1962-63	8.9	1.5
1963-64	–2.1	3.5
1964-65	2.2	3.6
1965-66	10.9	5.1
1966-67	–6.5	8.9
1967-68	10.8	7.4
1968-69	–5.9	1.2
1969-70	5.7	9.0
1970-71	–7.5	6.6
1971-72	4.4	1.9
1972-73	–14.5	–4.4
1973-74	21.7	7.3
1974-75	59.1	1.6

(continued)

Test of relationship between Peruvian and world copper production:

y = percentage change in Peruvian production
x_1 = percentage change in world production
x_2 = time trend variable

$$y = 4.163 + 0.085x_1 - 10.277x_2$$
$$\quad\quad\quad (0.034) \quad\quad (5.609)$$

$$t = 2.5 \quad\quad t = 1.83 \quad \text{sign} @ \quad \frac{x_1}{0.01} \quad \frac{x_2}{0.05}$$

$R^2 = 0.181$
$SEE = 37.2$

SOURCES: The same as for Table 2.2 and Appendix C, Table C. 2.

TABLE F.2   Percentage Change in Peruvian Copper
Production and Copper Prices, 1945-1977

Year	Peruvian Production	Price Change
1945-46	−23.1	25.8
1946-47	−8.2	41.6
1947-48	−21.1	6.3
1948-49	56.7	−13.8
1949-50	20.7	11.1
1950-51	6.3	22.2
1951-52	−14.4	21.7
1952-53	10.8	−2.8
1953-54	19.4	−3.1
1954-55	4.0	30.9
1955-56	8.9	3.3
1956-57	20.7	−32.8
1957-58	−5.3	−11.2
1958-59	−2.7	19.8
1959-60	264.4	3.5
1960-61	7.3	−6.6
1961-62	−16.3	2.1
1962-63	8.9	−0.4
1963-64	−2.1	9.1
1964-65	2.2	14.9
1965-66	10.9	39.1
1966-67	−3.6	−4.7
1967-68	10.3	6.6
1968-69	−6.5	23.1
1969-70	10.8	1.3
1970-71	−5.9	−23.7
1971-72	5.7	−2.8
1972-73	−7.5	69.3
1973-74	4.4	14.9
1974-75	−14.5	−41.2
1975-76	21.7	14.3
1976-77	59.1	−6.9

(continued)

Test of relationship between production and prices:

y = percentage change in Peruvian production
x_1 = percentage change in world price
x_2 = time trend variable

$$y = 6.988 - 0.029x_1 - 1.039x_2$$
$$(.077) \qquad (.569)$$

$$t = 0.4 \qquad t = 1.83 \quad \text{sign} @ \quad \frac{x_1}{\text{NS}} \quad \frac{x_2}{0.05}$$

$R^2 = 0.109$
$\text{SEE} = 450.3$

SOURCES: The same as for Table 2.2 and Appendix C, Table C. 2.

TABLE F.3 Percentage Change in Peruvian and World Lead Production, 1945-1977

Year	Peruvian	World
1945-46	−17.0	−2.6
1946-47	22.8	18.1
1947-48	−11.1	6.6
1948-49	33.3	6.9
1949-50	−3.1	9.4
1950-51	25.8	2.8
1951-52	6.4	8.1
1952-53	19.3	5.1
1953-54	9.1	5.5
1954-55	12.0	4.8
1955-56	1.7	3.1
1956-57	10.6	4.0
1957-58	−8.1	−1.2
1958-59	−3.2	−0.3
1959-60	8.3	3.2
1960-61	4.5	2.0
1961-62	−2.9	4.4
1962-63	12.0	0.7
1963-64	1.4	0.9
1964-65	2.0	6.7
1965-66	5.2	5.8
1966-67	−1.2	0.1
1967-68	−3.1	3.5
1968-69	0.0	8.6
1969-70	1.3	4.8
1970-71	5.7	0.5
1971-72	10.9	1.8
1972-73	−0.5	2.2
1973-74	−9.3	−0.4
1974-75	−7.2	0.3
1975-76	4.5	−2.5
1976-77	5.0	4.8

(continued)

Test of relationship between Peruvian and world lead production:

y = percentage change in Peruvian production
x = percentage change in world production

$y = 0.111 + 1.118x$

$R^2 = 0.181$
$N = 32$

SOURCES: The same as for Table 2.2 and Appendix C, Table C. 2.

TABLE F.4   Percentage Change in Peruvian Lead Production and Lead Prices, 1945-1977

Year	Peruvian Production	Price Change
1945-46	−17.0	24.8
1946-47	22.8	80.9
1947-48	−11.1	23.0
1948-49	33.3	−14.0
1949-50	−3.1	−13.4
1950-51	25.8	31.6
1951-52	6.4	−5.9
1952-53	19.3	−18.1
1953-54	9.1	4.2
1954-55	12.0	7.8
1955-56	1.7	5.7
1956-57	10.6	−8.2
1957-58	−8.1	−17.6
1958-59	−3.2	0.8
1956-60	8.3	−2.1
1960-61	4.5	−9.0
1961-62	−2.9	−11.4
1962-63	12.0	15.7
1963-64	1.4	22.1
1964-65	2.0	17.6
1965-66	5.2	−5.5
1966-67	−1.2	−7.4
1967-68	−3.1	−5.6
1968-69	0.0	12.8
1969-70	1.3	4.8
1970-71	5.7	−11.7
1971-72	10.9	8.9
1972-73	−0.5	8.4
1973-74	−9.3	38.3
1974-75	−7.2	−4.5
1975-76	4.5	7.3
1976-77	5.0	32.9

(continued)

Test of relationship between production and prices:

y = percentage change in Peruvian production
x = percentage change in world price

$y = 3.930 + 0.044x$

$R^2 = 0.007$

SOURCES: The same as for Table 2.2 and Appendix C, Table C. 2.

228

TABLE F.5 Percentage Change in Peruvian and World
Zinc Production, 1945-1977

Year	Peruvian	World
1945-46	−3.6	−1.2
1946-47	−3.5	15.2
1947-48	1.8	6.9
1948-49	20.4	3.5
1949-50	18.5	12.8
1950-51	15.5	8.8
1951-52	14.6	11.2
1952-53	24.5	2.6
1953-54	2.4	0.2
1954-55	15.4	8.1
1955-56	2.0	6.0
1956-57	−11.1	1.7
1957-58	−9.6	−2.5
1958-59	8.1	0.9
1959-60	18.0	6.3
1960-61	8.9	2.4
1961-62	7.6	3.4
1962-63	6.0	1.8
1963-64	21.5	10.6
1964-65	7.2	7.2
1965-66	11.8	5.3
1966-67	7.4	6.4
1967-68	−4.6	4.0
1968-69	3.1	7.3
1969-70	−0.3	2.4
1971-72	6.3	0.9
1972-73	18.2	2.9
1973-74	4.0	4.0
1974-75	−3.3	0.0
1975-76	4.9	1.5
1976-77	1.6	5.8

(continued)

Test of relationship between Peruvian and world zinc production:

y = percentage change in Peruvian production
x = percentage change in world production

$y = 2.541 + 0.862x$

$R^2 = 0.145$

SOURCES: The same as for Table 2.2 and Appendix C, Table C. 2.

TABLE F.6 Percentage Change in Peruvian Zinc Production and Zinc Prices, 1945-1977

Year	Peruvian Production	Price Change
1945-46	−3.6	5.8
1946-47	−3.5	20.3
1947-48	1.8	29.4
1948-49	20.4	−10.7
1949-50	18.5	11.0
1950-51	15.5	32.7
1951-52	14.6	−9.4
1952-53	24.5	−33.0
1953-54	2.4	0.0
1954-55	15.4	12.6
1955-56	2.0	10.3
1956-57	−11.1	−15.5
1957-58	−9.6	−9.6
1958-59	8.1	11.1
1959-60	18.0	13.0
1960-61	8.9	−10.8
1961-62	7.6	0.8
1962-63	6.0	5.8
1963-64	21.5	12.8
1964-65	7.2	6.7
1965-66	11.8	0.0
1966-67	7.4	−4.5
1967-68	−4.6	−2.4
1968-69	3.1	8.0
1969-70	−0.3	4.8
1970-71	6.3	5.2
1971-72	18.2	9.9
1972-73	4.0	16.1
1973-74	−3.3	76.3
1974-75	−3.4	5.4
1975-76	4.9	−5.0
1976-77	1.6	−7.1

(continued)

Test of relationship between production and prices:

y = percentage change in Peruvian production
x = percentage change in world price

$$y = 6.973 - 0.068x$$

$$R^2 = 0.068$$

SOURCES: The same as for Table 2.2 and Appendix C, Table C. 2.

APPENDIX G

Value of Production of the Major Metals as a Percentage of the Value of Total Production in the Peruvian Metal Mining Industry* 1903-1945

Year	Copper %	Silver %	Gold %	Lead %	Zinc %
		(Current *Soles*)			
1903	39	47	12	2	. .
1904	44	46	7	4	. .
1905	46	45	7	2	. .
1906	45	44	8	3	. .
1907	60	32	4	4	. .
1908	55	35	7	3	. .
1909	59	35	4	2	. .
1910	62	33	4	2	. .
1911	57	37	4	2	. .
1912	55	37	6	2	. .
1913	56	35	6	2	. .
1914	55	36	8	2	. .
1915	67	25	6	2	. .
1916	74	21	4	1	. .
1917	72	23	3	1	. .
1918	68	28	4	. .	. .
1919	55	40	5	. .	. .
1920	53	40	6	. .	. .
1921	51	39	10	. .	. .
1922	49	43	8	. .	. .
1923	48	43	9	. .	. .
1924	39	50	10	1	. .
1925	39	50	8	2	1
1926	40	42	5	6	7
1927	48	37	7	3	5

(continued)

233

Year	Copper %	Silver %	Gold %	Lead %	Zinc %
		(Current *Soles*)			
1928	49	35	8	7	2
1929	55	29	3	8	5
1930	55	23	7	10	5
1931	60	23	15	2	. .
1932	39	28	30	3	. .
1933	41	32	26	1	. .
1934	32	35	25	6	3
1935	22	48	17	11	3
1936	27	35	21	12	5
1937	32	25	23	18	3
1938	26	29	29	24	3
1939	27	24	31	15	3
1940	31	20	28	16	4
1941	28	16	31	19	7
1942	28	18	28	19	7
1943	27	21	22	21	10
1944	26	22	19	21	10
1945	25	21	19	22	14

SOURCES: *Boletín del Cuerpo de Ingenieros de Minas del Perú* (1903-1922); *Boletín Oficial de Minas y Petróleo* (1924-1932); Jorge Hohagan, *La Industria Minera en el Perú* (1932-1939); Jorge Hohagen, *Anuario de la Industria Minera en el Perú* (1940-1945); Pablo Macera, *Estadísticas históricas del Perú : sector minero (precios)* (Lima: Centro Peruano de Historia Económica, 1972); Pablo Macera and Horacio Pinto, *Estadísticas históricas del Perú : sector minero II (volumen y valor)* (Lima: Centro Peruano de Historia Económica, 1972).

* Total production in the Peruvian Metal Mining Industry is the aggregate of the five metals included in this table.

APPENDIX H

Labor Productivity in the Peruvian Mining Industry, 1945-1975

Year	Output per *obrero* in constant *soles* (x1000)	Index of Output per *obrero* in constant *soles* (1945 = 100)	Output per *tarea* in constant *soles*	Index of Output per *tarea* in constant *soles* (1945 = 100)
1945	100,578	100.0	304.33	100.0
46	92,836	92.3	286.52	94.1
47	82,736	82.3	244.16	80.2
48	65,428	65.1	203.06	66.7
49	72,327	72.9	229.69	75.5
1950	96,522	96.0	275.94	90.7
51	130,241	129.5	404.50	132.9
52	138,913	138.1	393.28	129.2
53	130,175	129.4	352.61	115.9
54	158,073	157.2	297.26	130.5
1955	163,179	162.2	395.61	130.0
56	165,460	164.5	439.73	144.5
57	144,773	143.9	372.04	122.2
58	155,091	154.2	454.55	149.4
59	164,959	164.0	517.48	170.0
1960	242,860	241.5	761.34	250.2
61	215,026	213.8	755.00	248.1
62	184,127	183.1	626.99	206.1
63	185,938	184.9	504.66	165.8
64	195,274	194.2	679.29	223.2
1965	n.a.	n.a.	n.a.	n.a.
66	256,931	255.5	786.15	258.3
67	214,543	213.3	659.15	216.6
68	295,367	293.7	890.35	292.6
69	290,436	288.8	949.70	312.1
1970	296,348	294.6	976.16	320.8
71	292,771	291.1	968.89	318.4
72	287,271	285.6	957.36	314.6
73	288,253	286.6	841.37	276.5
74	210,431	209.2	805.04	264.5
75	245,828	244.4	716.71	235.5

(continued)

236

SOURCES: Ministerio de Energía y Minas, *Anuario Minero del Perú*, 1966-1972; Ministerio de Energía y Minas, *Anuario de la Minería del Perú*, 1973-1975; Ministerio de Fomento, *Anuario de la Industria Minera en el Perú*, 1945-1949; Ministerio de Fomento y Obras Públicas, *Anuario de la Industria Minera en el Perú*, 1950-65; *Anuario Minero-Comercial*, 1977; "Declaraciones Anuales Consolidadas de Concesionarios, Empresas y Empresarios Mineros" (Lima: Archivos, Division de Estadística, Dirección General de Minería, Ministerio de Energía y Minas, 1945-1975).

APPENDIX I

Indexes of Average Price-Deflated Wages and Salaries and Money Wages* and Salaries in the Peruvian Mining Industry 1924-1945

Year	(1924 = 100) Price-deflated wages and salaries	Money wages and salaries
1924	100	100
1925	87	93
1926	103	110
1927	114	118
1928	112	109
1929	111	105
1930	131	118
1931	146	124
1932	224	181
1933	221	174
1934	166	133
1935	181	147
1936	134	114
1937	147	134
1938	143	131
1939	137	125
1940	116	114
1941	89	94
1942	121	143
1943	93	120
1944	93	138
1945	112	184

SOURCES: *Boletín del Cuerpo de Ingenieros de Minas* (1903-1922); *Boletín Oficial de Minas y Petroleo* (1924-1932); Jorge Hohagen, *La Industria Minera en el Perú* (1932-1939); Jorge Hohagen, *Anuario de la Industria Minera en el Perú* (1940-1945); Pablo Macera, *Estadisticas historicas del Perú: sector minero (precios)* (Lima: Centro Peruano de Historia Economica, 1972); Pablo Macera and Horacio Pinto, *Estadísticas historicas del Perú; sector minero II (volumen y valor)* (Lima: Centro Peruano de Historia Económica, 1972).

*Price-deflated wages are money wages deflated by the cost of living.

APPENDIX J

Price Changes in the World Metals Market* 1903-1980

Year	Price Changes
1903-1904	0.0
1904-1905	14.0
1905-1906	8.2
1906-1907	1.3
1907-1908	−33.8
1908-1909	−1.4
1909-1910	0.2
1910-1911	−2.1
1911-1912	20.3
1912-1913	−5.8
1913-1914	−10.0
1914-1915	16.0
1915-1916	40.2
1916-1917	6.7
1917-1918	−5.2
1918-1919	−15.7
1919-1920	−2.7
1920-1921	−39.0
1921-1922	9.0
1922-1923	7.1
1923-1924	−3.0
1924-1925	7.2
1925-1926	−4.4
1926-1927	−10.9
1927-1928	5.1
1928-1929	13.0
1929-1930	−31.3

(continued)

Year	Price Changes
1930-1931	−35.5
1931-1932	−26.7
1932-1933	23.5
1933-1934	17.5
1934-1935	10.3
1935-1936	−1.1
1936-1937	23.2
1937-1938	−22.1
1938-1939	5.2
1939-1940	3.4
1940-1941	6.5
1941-1942	4.9
1942-1943	2.3
1943-1944	−0.4
1944-1945	2.9
1945-1946	23.0
1946-1947	27.1
1947-1948	11.6
1948-1949	−12.4
1949-1950	4.3
1950-1951	22.1
1951-1952	5.9
1952-1953	−10.0
1953-1954	−0.9
1954-1955	16.8
1955-1956	4.3
1956-1957	−20.6
1957-1958	−8.4
1958-1959	9.7
1959-1960	2.8

(continued)

Year	Price Changes
1960-1961	−3.8
1961-1962	1.8
1962-1963	5.3
1963-1964	7.9
1964-1965	8.8
1965-1966	15.6
1966-1967	−0.6
1967-1968	8.6
1968-1969	9.9
1969-1970	1.7
1970-1971	−15.8
1971-1972	3.0
1972-1973	37.0
1973-1974	30.1
1974-1975	−18.5
1975-1976	5.5
1976-1977	2.5
1977-1978	7.7
1978-1979	42.6
1979-1980	31.2

SOURCES: *Metal Statistics* (Frankfurt Am Main: Metallgesellschaft, 1907-1977); and unpublished statistics from the U.S. Bureau of Mines.

*This index of price changes is weighted to reflect the composition of output in Peru.

APPENDIX K

Index of the Wage Cost to Capital in the Peruvian Mining Industry, 1945-1975

	(in U.S. Dollars)	
Year		Index
1945		100
1946		94
1947		92
1948		65
1949		48
1950		67
1951		68
1952		67
1953		81
1954		83
1955		76
1956		77
1957		103
1958		99
1959		94
1960		109
1961		121
1962		140
1963		158
1964		159
1965		n.a.
1966		225
1967		202
1968		194
1969		198
1970		219
1971		294
1972		333
1973		303
1974		202
1975		367

(continued)

SOURCES: Ministerio de Energía y Minas, *Anuario Minero del Perú*, 1966-72; Ministerio de Energía y Minas, *Anuario de la Minería del Perú*, 1973-75; Ministerio de Fomento, *Anuario de la Industria Minera en el Perú*, 1945-49; Ministerio de Fomento y Obras Públicas, *Anuario de la Industria Minera en el Perú*, 1950-65; *Anuario Minero-Commercial*, 1977; "Declaraciones Anuales Consolidadas de Concesionarios, Empresas y Empresarios Mineros" (Lima: Archivos, División de Estadística, Dirección General de Mineria, Ministerio de Energia y Minas, 1945-1975); Banco Central de Reserva del Perú, *Memoria*, 1972; Banco Central de Reserva del Perú, *Boletín*, various issues.

n.a. - not available

APPENDIX L

Data on the Peruvian Mining Industry, 1977-1985

List of Tables

Table L.1 Peruvian Metal Production, 1977-1985

Year	Copper[a]	Lead[b]	Zinc[c]	Silver[d]	Gold[e]	Iron[f]
1977	308.9	174.2	398.0	1,211	3,652	4,106.9
1978	360.6	167.8	377.2	1,284	3,680	3,275.5
1979	369.2	161.5	391.7	1,320	4,539	3,629.5
1980	336.1	174.1	418.9	1,236	4,719	3,783.3
1981	322.9	204.7	410.1	1,178	6,084	4,009.0
1982	353.8	197.6	460.1	1,305	4,188	3,841.7
1983	318.8	207.4	491.7	1,570	5,242	2,902.2
1984	354.0	193.7	465.9	1,651	5,829	2,739.6
1985	91.3	201.5	523.4	1,802	6,621	3,421.2

SOURCE: Ministerio de Energía y Minas, *Anuario de la Minería del Perú,* 1977-1985 (Lima), Table 1.

[a]Copper: thousands of metric tons
[b]Lead: thousands of metric tons
[c]Zinc: thousands of metric tons
[d]Silver: metric tons
[e]Gold: kilograms
[f]Iron: thousands of metric tons

TABLE L.2 Indexes of Peruvian Metal Production 1977-1985

Year	Copper	Lead	(1977 = 100) Zinc	Silver	Gold	Iron
1977	100	100	100	100	100	100
1978	117	96	95	106	101	80
1979	120	93	98	109	124	88
1980	109	100	105	102	129	92
1981	105	118	103	97	167	98
1982	115	113	116	108	115	94
1983	103	119	124	130	144	71
1984	115	111	117	136	160	67
1985	127	116	132	149	181	83

SOURCE: Ministerio de Energía y Minas, *Anuario de la Minería del Perú, 1977-1985* (Lima), Table 1.

TABLE L.3 Level of Processing of Peruvian Mineral Exports, 1982

	Percent
Copper	
refined	63
blister	27
concentrates	10
Silver	
refined	45
blister	1
concentrates	54
Lead	
refined	43
concentrates and minerals	57
Zinc	
refined	35
concentrates and minerals	65

SOURCE: Manuel Cisneros Orna and Oswaldo Carpio Villegas, *Realidad Minera* (Lima: 1984), Table 7, p. 17.

TABLE L.4   World Metals Prices, 1977-1987

Year	Copper[a]	Lead[b]	Zinc[c]	Silver[d]	Gold[c]	Iron[c]
1977	59.4	28.0	26.8	4.62	147.98	n.a.
1978	61.9	29.8	26.9	5.43	193.55	n.a.
1979	90.1	54.6	33.7	11.09	307.50	21.60
1980	99.3	41.3	34.5	20.63	612.56	25.40
1981	79.0	32.3	39.0	10.52	459.64	26.28
1982	65.6	24.7	33.8	7.94	375.91	28.39
1983	70.3	19.3	34.6	11.44	424.00	23.16
1984	62.6	20.1	40.5	8.14	360.66	20.25
1985	63.2	17.7	34.3	6.14	317.66	20.25
1986	62.3	18.4	34.2	5.47	368.24	18.32
1987	80.9	n.a.	n.a.	n.a.	440.00	n.a.
Jan.	61.04					
Feb.	62.57					
Mar.	66.45					
Apr.	68.29					
May	68.94					
Jun.	71.27					
Jul.	76.83					
Aug.	79.63					
Sep.	82.11					
Oct.	89.16					
Nov.	114.35					
Dec.	129.96					

SOURCES: U.S. Bureau of Mines (Washington, D.C.), unpublished data.

[a]London Metals Exchange (LME)
[b]Handy & Herman, $ per Troy ounce
[c]U.S. Bureau of Mines
[d]Pellet Feed, Peru, $ per dry long ton, unit 1% iron

TABLE L.5 Consumer Price Index, Lima, 1979-1985

Year	(1980 = 100) Index
1979	62.8
1980	100.0
1981	175.4
1982	288.4
1983	609.0
1984	1280.2
1985	3372.0

SOURCES: *International Financial Statistics* (Washington, D.C.: International Monetary Fund, December 1986), volume XXXIX, No. 12, p. 394; and *Bulletin of Labour Statistics: 1986* (Geneva: International Labour Organization, 1986), p. 114.

TABLE L.6 Interest Paid by Firms in the *Gran Minería* (Millions of U.S. Dollars), 1980-1984

	1980	1981	1982	1983	1984
Centromin	77.2	113.2	125.9	101.1	68.6
Southern Peru	34.6	28.2	20.9	35.1	25.6
Hierro Peru	2.5	0.85	3.2	−2.9	−5.6
Minero Peru	51.3	82.3	117.9	246.4	256.1
Tintaya	n.a.	n.a.	11.9	51.6	182.1
Total *Gran Minería*	165.6	224.6	279.8	431.4	526.9

SOURCE: *Anuario de la Minería del Perú: 1977-1985* (Lima: Ministerio de Energía y Minas), Tables 142-147.

NOTES

Introduction

1. For analyses of the Peruvian mining industry in the colonial period see John Fisher, *Minas y mineros en el Perú colonial, 1776-1824* (Lima: Instituto de Estudios Peruanos, 1977), and "Silver Production in the Viceroyalty of Peru, 1776-1824," *Hispanic American Historical Review*, 55:1 (February 1975) pp. 25-44. A large research project on mining in the Andes from the colonial period to the present recently was completed. While the results of the research are not yet published the research proposal itself is interesting. See C. Sempat Assadourian, Heraclio Bonilla, Antonio Mitre and Tristan Platt, *Minería y espacio económico en los andes, siglos XVI-XX* (Lima: Instituto de Estudios Peruanos, 1980).

2. Throughout the colonial period the silver mines of Potosí were within the Viceroyalty of Peru. With independence this portion of the former Viceroyalty was incorporated into the Republic of Bolivia.

3. In this book "the Peruvian mining industry" refers to the mining and processing of the six major metals produced in Peru: copper, lead, zinc, iron, silver and gold. In Peru this sector is referred to as metal mining (*minería metálica*) or mining and metallurgy (*minero-metalúrgica*).

4. For a detailed and well documented presentation of this position see Rosemary Thorp and Geoffrey Bertram, *Peru 1890-1977: Growth and Policy in an Open Economy* (London: The Macmillan Press Ltd., 1978). This excellent work is the standard source on Peruvian economic history for the twentieth century. Kruijt and Vellinga present the classic dependency argument. They state that "the enclave [the Peruvian mining industry] has been integrated into the world economy as an appendix of the economy of the metropole and its development depends on the dynamics of supply and demand in the world metal market." Dirk Kruijt and Menno Vellinga, "The Political Economy of Mining Enclaves in Peru," presented at the conference *The State and Multinational Companies in Latin America*, Institute of Latin American Studies, University of Glasgow (January 1976) p. 12.

5. Thorp and Bertram, *Peru 1890-1977*; William Bollinger, "The Rise of United States Influence in the Peruvian Economy, 1867-1921," (revised manuscript of M.A. thesis, University of California, Los Angeles, 1972) pp. 151-233; Dirk Kruijt and Menno Vellinga, *Labor Relations and Multinational Corporations: The Cerro de Pasco Corporation in Peru (1902-1974)* (Assen, The Netherlands: Van Gorcum, 1979); José Flores Marín, *Minería colonial y coyuntura mundial, 1913-1919* (Lima: Centro Peruano de Historia Económica, 1974); Honorio Pinto Herrera, *Un sector exportador dependiente: la minería metálica en el Perú 1945-1970* (Lima: Universidad Nacional Mayor de San Marcos, 1973); and Claes Brundenius, "The Anatomy of Imperialism: The Case

of the Multinational Corporation in Peru," *Journal of Peace Research*, 9 (1972) pp. 189-207.

6. See, Dirk Kruijt and Menno Vellinga, *Labor Relations and Multinational Corporations*; I. G. Bertram, "Development Problems in an Export Economy: A Study of Domestic Capitalists, Foreign Firms and Government in Peru, 1919-1930," Ph.D. dissertation, University of Oxford, 1974; and William Bollinger, "The Rise of United States Influence."

7. The North American firm known in Peru in 1901 as the Cerro de Pasco Mining Company has gone through a series of minor name changes which reflect the changing composition of its product as well as corporate restructuring. For an account of this see Adrian DeWind, Jr., "Peasants Become Miners: The Evolution of Industrial Mining Systems in Peru," Ph.D. dissertation, Columbia University, 1977, pp. 116-117. To avoid confusion I refer to this company as the Cerro de Pasco Corporation, the name by which it was known during most of its years in Peru.

8. "It has almost become part of the new orthodoxy that the framework for [analyzing economic growth in Peru] is to be found by studying the historical significance of Peru's place in the world economy." Thorp and Bertram, *Peru 1890-1977*, p. 10.

9. Structuralist economic theory forms the broad framework for this study. In particular, the debates on the nature of the transition to capitalism influenced my analysis of the barriers to capitalist development and economic growth. See Rodney Hilton, ed., *The Transition from Feudalism to Capitalism* (London: New Left Books, 1976); and Robert Brenner, "Agrarian Class Structure and Economic Development in Pre-Industrial Europe," *Past and Present*, 70 (February 1976). This article, along with the debate that it stimulated in *Past and Present* is published in T. H. Aston and C. H. E. Philpin, eds., *The Brenner Debate: Agrarian Class Structure and Economic Development in Pre-Industrial Europe* (Cambridge: Cambridge University Press, 1985). See also Robert Brenner, "The Origins of Capitalist Development: a Critique of Neo-Smithian Marxism," *New Left Review*, 104 (July-August 1977); John Weeks, *Capital and Exploitation* (Princeton: Princeton University Press, 1981); John Weeks, *Limits to Capitalist Development: The Industrialization of Preu, 1950-1980* (Boulder: Westview Press, 1985); and John Weeks, "Epochs of Capitalism and the Progressiveness of Capital's Expansion," *Science & Society*, XLIX:4 (Winter 1985-1986) pp. 414-436.

10. For analyses of the formation of the mining proletariat see DeWind, "Peasants Become Miners, " and "From Presants to Miners: The Background to Strikes in the Mines of Peru, " *Science & Society*, 29:1 (Spring 1975) pp. 44-72; Heraclio Bonilla, *El minero de los andes: Una aproximacíon a su estudio* (Lima: Institutio de Estudios Peruanos, 1974); and Alberto Flores Galindo, *Los mineros de la Cerro de Pasco, 1900-1930* (Lima: Pontífica Universidad Católica del Perú, 1974). For projected research on the development of the internal market and the structure of production, see Assadourian et. al., *Minería y espacio económico*. For the relationship between foreign companies, local firms and the state, see David G. Becker, *The New Bourgeoisie and the Limits of Dependency:*

Mining, Class and Power in "Revolutionary" Peru (Princeton: Princeton University Press, 1983).

11. For an excellent analysis of the transformation of the class structure and of the development of capitalism in the central highlands see Florencia E. Mallon, *The Defense of Community in Peru's Central Highlands: Peasant Struggle and Capitalist Transition, 1860-1940* (Princeton: Princeton University Press, 1983). Other interesting studies of the regions surrounding the mines include Julian Laite, *Industrial Development and Migrant Labour* (Manchester: Manchester University Press, 1981); Normal Long and Bryan R. Roberts, eds., *Peasant Cooperation and Capitalist Expansion in Central Peru* (Austin: University of Texas Press, 1978); Juan Martínez Alier, *Los huacchilleros del Perú* (Lima: Institutio de Estudios Peruanos, 1973); Norman Long and Bryan Roberts, eds., *Miners, Peasants and Entrepreneurs: Regional Development in the Central Highlands of Peru,* (Cambridge: Cambridge University Press, 1984); and Richard N. Adams, *A Community in the Andes: Problems and Progress in Muquiyauyo* (Seattle: University of Washington Press, 1959).

12. This debate began in the early 1970s with André Gunder Frank's exposition of dependency theory. See André Gunder Frank, *Capitalism and Underdevelopment in Latin America* (New York: Modern Reader, 1969). Throughout the Third World dependency theory became the prevalent explanation for underdevelopment and remains so to this day. Many authors have questioned the validity of the theory. See in particular John Weeks and Elizabeth Dore, "International Exchange and the Causes of Backwardness," and Samir Amin, "Reply to Weeks and Dore," *Latin American Perspectives*, 4:2 (Spring 1979) pp. 62-90; John Weeks and Elizabeth Dore, "Reply to Samir Amin," *Latin American Perspectives*, 4:3 (Summer 1979) pp. 114-116; Carlos Sempat Assadourian, "Modos de producción, capitalismo y subdesarrollo en América Latina," in Assadourian et al., *Modos de producción en América Latina* (Córdoba, Argentina: Cuadernos de Pasado y Presente/40, 1973); Brenner, "The Origins of Capitalist Development"; Bill Warren, *Imperialism: Pioneer of Capitalism* (London: New Left Books, 1980); and Weeks, *Limits to Capitalist Development*. For a summary of this debate see Magnus Blomstrom and Bjorn Hettne, eds., *Development Theory in Transition: The Dependency Debate and Beyond* (London: Zed Books Ltd., 1984).

13. For an analysis of how productivity is measured see Chapters Four and Five.

14. It should be noted that the process described here is not the process of increasing relative surplus value. Surplus value can be raised relatively only at the level of capital as a whole, and results in the progressive reduction in the value of labor power. See Weeks, *Limits to Capitalist Development*, pp. 67-75.

15. Briefly, wages represent the value of labor power, or the abstract labor time embodied in the collection of commodities that workers customarily consume. Under capitalism there is a tendency for increases in productivity in the production of the commodities that workers consume to result in a decline in their value. Therefore, there is a tendency for the exchange value of labor power

to decline given a constant standard of living of the working class. This point is developed in more detail in Chapter Four.

16. For analyses of the transformation of the class structure within the mining regions, see Mallon, *The Defense of Community*; Long and Roberts, eds., *Miners, Peasants and Entrepreneurs* and *Peasant Cooperation and Capitalist Expansion*; and Laite, *Industrial Development and Migrant Labour*. For the transformation of the class structure in Peruvian society at large, see Elizabeth Dore and John Weeks, "The Intensification of the Assault Against the Working Class in 'Revolutionary' Peru," *Latin American Perspectives* 3:2 (Spring 1976) pp. 55-83; William Bollinger, "The Bourgeois Revolution in Peru: A Conception of Peruvian History," *Latin American Perspectives* 4:3 (Summer 1977) pp. 18-56; Elizabeth Dore, "Un ensayo de interpretación del desarrollo del capitalismo en el Perú," *Revista Latinoamericana de Historia Económica y Social* (HISLA) (1986) VII. For analyses of technical changes in the mining industry see DeWind, "Peasants Become Miners"; Stanley Kerry Hamilton, "Factors Influencing Investment and Production in the Peruvian Mining Industry 1940-1965," Ph.D. dissertation, The University of Wisconsin, 1967; and W.F.C. Purser, *Metal-Mining in Peru, Past and Present* (New York: Praeger Publishers, 1971).

Chapter One

1. The first, third, and fourth sections of this chapter are a revised version of John Weeks and Elizabeth Dore, "International Exchange and the Causes of Backwardness," *Latin American Perspectives*, 4:2 (Spring 1979), pp. 62-90.

2. The terms "backward" and "advanced" in reference to countries are commonly used in the Marxist literature. A backward country is one where pre-capitalist social relations of production remain important, although not necessarily predominant. An advanced country is one where capitalism is highly developed, and where the economy is overwhelmingly characterized by capitalist social relations of production.

3. The use of the term "surplus extraction" is one indication of the lack of rigor of dependency theory. Dependency theorists tend not to specify in what form the surplus is produced and appropriated. Therefore, when I use the terms "surplus" and "surplus extraction" I do so in order to respresent the arguments of dependency theorists. Otherwise I employ the more specific terms "surplus product" and "surplus value."

4. This represents the more orthodox Marxist tradition. The work of Robert Brenner has been influential in the recent debates on the nature of historical transformation. See T. H. Aston and C. H. E. Philpin, eds., *The Brenner Debate: Agrarian Class Structure and Economic Development in Pre-Industrial Europe* (Cambridge: Cambridge University Press, 1985); and Robert Brenner, "The Origins of Capitalist Development: a Critique of Neo-Smithian Marxism," *New Left Review*, 104 (July-August 1977). Much of the literature on Peru is in this tradition. See, in particular, Florencia E. Mallon, *The Defense of Community in Peru's Central Highlands: Peasant Struggle and*

Capitalist Transition, 1860-1940 (Princeton: Princeton University Press, 1983);
Norman Long and Bryan R. Roberts, *Miners, Peasants and Entrepreneurs:
Regional Development in the Central Highlands of Peru* (Cambridge:
Cambridge University Press, 1984); William Bollinger, "The Bourgeois
Revolution in Peru: A Conception of Peruvian History," *Latin American
Perspectives*, 4:3 (Summer 1977), pp. 18-56; Rodrigo Montoya Rojas, *Al
propósito del carácter predominantemente capitalista de la economía peruana
actual* (Lima: Ediciones Teoría y Realidad, 1970); José María Caballero,
Economía agraria de la sierra peruana antes de la reforma agraria de 1969 (Lima:
Instituto de Estudios Peruanos, 1981); and Elizabeth Dore, "Un ensayo de
interpretación del desarrollo del capitalismo en el Perú," *Revista Latinoamericana
de Historia Económica y Social* (HISLA), 7 (1986) pp. 131-142.

5. John Weeks, "Epochs of Capitalism and the Progressiveness of
Capital's Expansion," *Science & Society*, 49: 4 (Winter 1985-86) pp. 414-436.

6. This is the most prevalent explanation for underdevelopment, leaving
neo-classical economic theory aside. It is interesting, however, to note that now
even some neo-classical economists subscribe to dependency theory.

7. "...[T]he metropolis expropriates economic surplus from its satellites
and appropriates it for its own development. The satellites remain
underdeveloped for the lack of access to *their own surplus* and as a consequence
of the same polarization and exploitation contradictions which the metropolis
introduces and maintains in the satellite's domestic economic structure.... One
and the same historical process of the expansion and development of capitalism
throughout the world has simultaneously generated--and continues to generate--
both economic development and structural underdevelopment." Andre Gunder
Frank, *Capitalism and Underdevelopment in Latin America* (New York: Modern
Reader, 1969) p. 9.

8. "...[W]hatever may have been the fractional increase of Western
Europe's national income derived from its overseas operations, they multiplied
the economic surplus at its disposal. What is more: the increment of the
economic surplus appeared immediately in a concentrated form and came largely
into the hands of capitalists who could use it for investment purposes. The
intensity of the boost to Western Europe's development resulting from the
'exogenous' contribution to its capital accumulation can hardly be exaggerated."
Paul A. Baran, *The Political Economy of Growth* (New York: Modern Reader,
1968), pp. 142-143.

9. See the discussion below of the writings of Ruy Mauro Marini.

10. Frank states that the use of money in Mexico in the sixteenth century
indicates that the Mexican economy was capitalist at that time. See Frank,
Capitalism and Underdevelopment in Latin America, p. 9. Paul Sweezy and
Immanuel Wallerstein argue that trade leads inevitably (and relatively rapidly) to
the development of capitalism. See Paul Sweezy, "The Debate on the Transition
to Capitalism," in Rodney Hilton, ed., *The Transition from Feudalism to
Capitalism* (London: New Left Books, 1976); and Immanuel Wallerstein, "The
Rise and Future Demise of the World Capitalist System: Concepts for
Comparative Analysis," *Comparative Studies in Society and History*, 16

(January 1974); and "From Feudalism to Capitalism: Transition or Transitions?", *Social Forces* 55 (December 1976).

11. The term "mode of production" has aroused considerable debate among Marxists. By mode of production I mean the economic, social, political, and ideological structures which determine how material life in a particular society is produced and reproduced. A mode of production is defined by the relationships among classes in the process of production. These relationships determine how production occurs and how a class of non-producers appropriates a surplus product or surplus labor from a class of direct producers. These relationships are "the social relations of production." See Susan Himmelweit, "Mode of Production," in T. Bottomore, ed., *A Dictionary of Marxist Thought* (Oxford: Basil Blackwell, 1983), pp. 335-337.

12. The term "forces of production" includes machinery, raw materials, natural resources, and labor power. The "development of the forces of production" signifies the advances in machinery, technology, and the skills and organization of the working class.

13. Paul A. Baran and Paul M. Sweezy, *Monopoly Capital* (New York: Monthly Review Press, 1966).

14. *Ibid.*

15. "What has prevented the *full* development of capitalism in Latin America and the Caribbean under imperialist domination?.... [T]here is a continual effort by foreign monopoly capital firms to block potential competition from new firms that might rival their position within the underdeveloped economies.... The national capitalist class remains small and unable to develop without protection because of the impact of a transplanted capitalist system dominated by foreign monopoly capital...." James L. Dietz, "Imperialism and Underdevelopment: A Theoretical Perspective and a Case Study of Puerto Rico," *Review of Radical Political Economics*, 11:4 (Winter 1979), p. 23.

16. *Ibid.*

17. This analysis of monopoly is developed in John Weeks, *Capital and Exploitation* (Princeton: Princeton University Press, 1981), pp. 149-172.

18. Rosa Luxemburg, *The Accumulation of Capital* (New York: Monthly Review Press, 1968); and Rosa Luxemburg, "The Accumulation of Capital: An Anti-Critique," in Rosa Luxemburg and Nikolai Bukharin, *The Accumulation of Capital: An Anti-Critique and Imperialism and the Accumulation of Capital* (New York: Monthly Review Press, 1972).

19. V. I. Lenin, "On the So-Called Market Question," in his *Collected Works*, Vol. I (Moscow: Progress Publishers, 1972), pp. 75-125.

20. Nikolai I. Bukharin, "Imperialism and the Accumulation of Capital," in Luxemburg and Bukharin, *The Accumulation of Capital: An Anti-Critique* (New York: Monthly Review Press, 1968).

21. Ruy Mauro Marini, "Dialéctica de la dependencia," *Sociedad y Desarrollo* (January-March 1972).

22. By treating distribution as the division between wages and profits Marini presents a neo-Ricardian argument. Neo-Ricardian theory holds that

surplus value is distributed between the capitalist class and the working class in the form of wages and profits. Marxist writers argue that wages are capital advanced within the circuit of capital to purchase labor power.

23. Marini, "Dialéctica de la dependencia."

24. John Weeks, "A Note on Underconsumption and the Labor Theory of Value," *Science & Society,* 46:1 (Spring 1982).

25. Bukharin, *Imperialism and the Accumulation of Capital.*

26. Aghiri Emmanuel, *Unequal Exchange* (London: New Left Books, 1972).

27. There are several excellent critiques of Emmanuel's theory of unequal exchange. See Charles Bettelheim, "Theoretical Comments," in A. Emmanuel, *Unequal Exchange* (London: New Left Books, 1972); and Anwar Shaikh, "On the Laws of International Exchange," *Science & Society* 43:1 (Fall and Winter 1979).

28. Marx called this process the production of relative surplus value. See, Karl Marx, *Capital,* Parts V and VI (Moscow: Progress Publishers, 1971).

29. *Ibid.*

30. For an analysis of the pattern of U.S. foreign direct investment from the middle 1950s through the end of the 1970s see John Weeks, *Limits to Capitalist Development: The Industrialization of Peru, 1950-1980* (Boulder: Westview Press, 1985), pp. 33-53. From 1957 to 1960, approximately forty percent of U.S. foreign investment was located in what the *Survey of Current Business* defines as "under-developed countries." By 1967-1970 this share had fallen to thirty-three precent, and was about twenty-seven percent in 1975-1976. See *The Multinational Corporation, Studies on U.S. Foreign Investment,* Vol. I (Washington, D.C.: Government Printing Office, 1972); and U.S. Department of Commerce, *Survey of Current Business* (Washington, D.C.: U.S. Government Printing Office, 1977).

31. Samir Amin, "The End of a Debate" (Dakar: United Nations, African Institute for Economic Development and Planning, 1973), p. 9. This article is reprinted in Amin, *Imperialism and Unequal Development* (New York: Monthly Review Press, 1977).

32. "It is obvious that if the labor-hour in all countries creates the same value, while labor power in one of the countries has a lower value, that is, the wage is lower, the rate of surplus value is higher [in that country]." Amin, "The End of a Debate," p. 9.

33. Recently the argument that value is determined by price has become known as the "validation argument." For a clear presentation of this position see Simon Mohun, "Abstract Labor and its Value Form," *Science & Society* 48: 4 (Winter 1984-1985), pp. 401-431. We might say that Amin was an unintentional precursor of this school of thought.

34. This critique of the position that value is determined by price is based on an article by John Weeks. See Weeks, "Abstract Labor and its Relation to Commodity Production," (1986) (typescript).

35. There is a vast literature that demonstrates this point. See in particular Jaime Crispi, *El agro chileno después de 1973: Expansión capitalista*

y campesinización pauperizante (Santiago, Grupo de Investigaciones Agrarias, 1980); Elena Alvarez, *Política económica y agricultura en el Perú, 1969-1979* (Lima: Instituto de Estudios Peruanos, 1983); and José María Caballero, *Economía agraria de la sierra peruana antes de la reforma agraria de 1969* (Lima: Instituto de Estudios Peruanos, 1981).

36. R. Thorp and G. Bertram, *Peru 1890-1977: Growth and Policy in an Open Economy* (London: Macmillan, 1978), pp. 86-89; and Honorio Pinto Herrera, *Un sector exportador dependiente: la minería metalica en el Perú 1945-1970* (Lima: Universidad Nacional Mayor de San Marcos, 1973).

37. Thorp and Bertram, *Peru 1890-1977*, pp. 89-95.

38. Recently John Weeks has elaborated a theory of the limits to capitalist development in Peru. Weeks' theory is consistent with the arguments presented in this book. See John Weeks, *Limits to Capitalist Development*, pp. 55-78.

39. For the standard presentation of the neo-classical theory of the stages of growth see W. W. Rostow, *The Stages of Growth: A Non-Communist Manifesto* (Cambridge: Cambridge University Press, 1971).

40. Cristóbal Kay, *El Sistema Señorial Europeo y la Hacienda Latinoamericana* (Mexico: Serie Popular Era, 1980).

41. John Weeks, "Epochs of Capitalism," p. 418.

42. Lenin criticized Kautsky for defining imperialism as the relationship between developed and underdeveloped areas. For Lenin's presentation of his debate with Kautsky see V. I. Lenin, *Collected Works*, Vol. XXII (Moscow: Progress Publishers, 1972), pp. 268-269; also Tom Kemp, *Theories of Imperialism* (London: Dennis Dobson, 1967), Chapters V and VII.

43. Weeks, "Epochs of Capitalism," pp. 414-416.

44. One of the pioneering theorists of this position is Bill Warren. See Warren, "Imperialism and Capitalist Industrialization," *New Left Review*, 81 (September-October 1973), pp. 3-44; and *Imperialism: Pioneer of Capitalism*, ed. John Sender (London: New Left Books, 1980).

45. Frank, *Capitalism and Underdevelopment in Latin America*; Sweezy, "The Debate on the Transition to Capitalism"; and Wallerstein, "The Rise and Future Demise of the World Capitalist System: Concepts for Comparative Analysis" and "From Feudalism to Capitalism: Transition or Transitions?"

46. Weeks and Dore, "International Exchange and the Causes of Backwardness"; Mallon, *The Defense of Community*; Dore, "Un ensayo de interpretación del desarrollo del capitalismo en el Perú"; and Weeks, "Epochs of Capitalism and the Progressiveness of Capital's Expansion."

Chapter Two

1. See Appendix B for tables on Peruvian metal production as a percentage of world metal production.

2. In 1978 the world's leading copper producers listed according to rank were: 1) The United States of America; 2) The U.S.S.R.; 3) Chile; 4) Canada; 5) Zambia; 6) Zaire; and 7) Peru. *La minería en el Perú* (Lima: *Anuario Minero-Comercial*, 1980), p. E13.

3. Throughout this book the term "world mining industry" is used to indicate world production of the six major metals that are produced in Peru: copper, lead, zinc, iron, silver, and gold.

4. Changes in the levels of production rather than the correlation in the levels themselves is used because of the strong upward trend in both Peruvian and world production. When two time series have strong trends, relating levels can give high correlation measures (R^2) even though in reality the series may be unrelated or only weakly so. Correlating changes in levels of production provides a summary of the relationship between Peruvian and world production for a period as a whole, not for particular years or selected sub-periods. In order to consider shorter time periods other measures are used.

5. Since Peruvian production begins in 1900 from a base near zero its absolute changes as both indexes grow over time are larger than the changes in the index of world production. This largely reflects the greater ability to increase output a given proportion when production is low and the addition of another mine in Peru could, possibly, double production. The problem of comparison of the indexes is related to the fact that a mature mining industry will exhibit a different trend from a newly-initiated one. In order to deal with this problem I test the correlation between the percentage rate of change in Peruvian and world production. This correlation in presented in Appendix D.

6. Using trend analysis, the least-squares growth path of a variable is calculated. Then the observation for each year is divided by the predicted value for that year (i.e., the value that lies on the growth path). As with any statistical technique, trend analysis has its limitations. The most relevant for purposes of comparing production in the Peruvian industry to production in the world industry is that by eliminating the trend from each time series, one implicitly assumes that Peruvian and world production interact cyclically and are independent in secular trend. In practice, the possible distortion in interpretation created by taking out the trend in each time series is not very great. In the period 1900-1945 the Peruvian trend in production is much higher than the world trend, but this is largely explained by the tiny base from which Peruvian production began in 1900. In the later period, 1945-1977, the trends in Peruvian production and world production are not significantly different. Thus, the differences in Peruvian and world production are cyclical in this period, and these are actually the variations which trend analysis is designed to clarify.

7. Trend analysis indicates that the relative deviations from the trend were greater for the Peruvian industry than for the world industry. This may indicate nothing more than that Peruvian production had a much faster trend rate of growth, beginning as it did from a very low base in 1900, the initiation of the time series.

8. See Appendix D.

9. This interpretation can be stated in a weaker way. The annual proportional changes in world output represent by definition the weighted average for all producing countries. The correlation of world changes and Peruvian changes then measures the degree to which Peruvian production corresponds to the average production change among countries.

10. A more detailed discussion of this statistical test is presented in Appendix D.

11. While prices are explicitly treated separately, they are, in fact, subsumed within the comparison of world and Peruvian output. In the calculation of world production, the different metals are aggregated by using constant prices. However, changes in this index reflect responses by the world industry to changes in conditions of profitability, a major aspect of which is market prices for the metals. In general, one would expect increases in world output to be associated with increases in prices, but this need not be the case, and is not the case in all years. In a period in which world mineral production rises and Peruvian production does not, the movement in prices, whether up or down, cannot itself explain the difference between Peruvian and world performance, since the movement in prices is a common influence on both. This is not to say that price changes are irrelevant, but points out that the key indicator for comparison is production, in Peru and the world. The index of world prices, therefore, provides supplementary and complementary information to the analysis, but does not itself account for differences in year-to-year performance.

12. In order to make the price index most useful to this study, it has been calculated on the basis of Peruvian quantity weights, so that the movement in the index reflects the relative importance of each metal in Peruvian production. As a consequence, it is not the relevant index for measuring the impact of world prices on world production.

13. See Appendix D for a detailed discussion of this statistical test.

14. A more detailed discussion of each of the statistical methods employed to test the correlation between changes in the mining industry on a world scale and the performance of the Peruvian mining industry for the period 1945-1977 is presented in Appendix E.

15. In my specified relationships between world prices and Peruvian output, "other things" are not held equal, however, for I am using simple, not multiple, regressions. Were I to expand the regressions to include other variables acting on production, I could predict theoretically that price changes would be significant. However, the purpose of this chapter is not to construct a satisfying econometric model of the demand and supply for Peruvian metal production, but by use of simple statisitical tests to evaluate the relationship between world production and prices and the pattern of growth of Peruvian mining.

16. These statistical tests are presented in Appendix F.

17. For a discussion of the history of the Southern Peru Copper Corporation (SPCC) see Chapter Four.

Chapter Three

1. There is evidence that the mines of Potosí were exploited by the Incas before the Spanish conquest. The Viceroyalty of Peru in the sixteenth and seventeenth centuries encompassed the Spanish colonies of South America. At

that time Potosí fell within the jurisdiction of *Alto Perú*, an
approximately corresponds to Bolivia. In 1776 the Viceroyalt,
Plata was carved out of the Viceroyalty of Peru, and included
territory that today is Argentina, Bolivia, Uruguay, and Paraguay. Cc
in the last fifty years of Spanish colonial rule the administration
passed from Lima to Buenos Aires.

2. Karen Spalding, *De Indio a Campesino: Cambios en la Estru.
Social del Perú Colonial* (Lima: Instituto de Estudios Peruanos, 1974), pp.
123; and John Murra, "Current Research and Prospects in Andean Ethnohistory
Latin American Research Review, 5 (Spring 1970), pp. 3-36.

3. Peter Bakewell, "Mining in Colonial Spanish America," in Leslie
Bethell, ed., *The Cambridge History of Latin America: Colonial Latin America.*
Vol. II (Cambridge: Cambridge University Press, 1984), pp. 105-110; and
Rafael Varón, "Minería Colonial Peruana: Un Ejemplo de Integración al
Sistema Económico Mundial, Siglos XVI-XVII," *Revista de Museo Nacional de
Historia* (Lima: 1978), pp. 143-170.

4. Karen Spalding, *Huarochirí: An Andean Society Under Inca and
Spanish Rule* (Stanford: Stanford University Press, 1984), p. 130; and Jeffrey
A. Cole, *The Potosí Mita, 1573-1700* (Stanford: Stanford University Press,
1985), Chapters 1 and 2.

5. For an excellent and thought-provoking interpretation of the impetus
for the Toledo reforms and the *mita,* see Steve J. Stern, *Peru's Indian Peoples
and the Challenge of Spanish Conquest* (Madison: University of Wisconsin
Press, 1982), Chapters 3 and 4. Also Bakewell, "Mining in Colonial Spanish
America," pp. 105-151; and Cole, *The Potosí Mita, 1573-1700*, Chapters 1 and
2.

6. Cole, *The Potosí Mita*, p. 3.

7. *Ibid.*

8. *Ibid.*, p. 9.

9. Bakewell, "Mining in Colonial Spanish America," p. 145.

10. Cole, *The Potosí Mita*, Chapters 3-6.

11. For an excellent analysis and interpretation of the social relations of
mining systems in colonial Peru, see Enrique Tandeter, "Forced and Free Labour
in Late Colonial Potosí," *Past and Present,* 93 (November 1981), pp. 98-136.
Also Cole, *The Potosí Mita*, pp. 105-122.

12. Cole, *The Potosí Mita,* pp. 23-45.

13. *Ibid.*, pp. 105-122.

14. J. H. Parry, *The Spanish Seaborne Empire* (New York: Alfred A.
Knopf, 1970), pp. 312 ff; and Bakewell, "Mining in Colonial Spanish America,"
pp. 135 ff.

15. During the first two hundred years of Spanish rule mineowners were
required to give the Crown one-fifth of the silver they produced. This tax
became known as the *quinto real.* In 1736 the tax rate was reduced to one-tenth
of total production. Throughout the colonial period a considerable portion of the
silver produced and sold in the New World was not registered with the colonial
authorities. This was in order to evade the royal tax. Because historians'

calculations of the quantity of silver produced in the Spanish Empire are based largely on the volume of silver appropriated by the Crown, widespread evasion of the tax has thwarted historians' attempts to accurately measure silver production in the colonial period. See Bakewell, "Mining in Colonial Spanish America."

16. The discussion of increasing the exploitation of *mita* labor is based on Tandeter, "Forced and Free Labour in Late Colonial Potosí."

17. *Ibid.*, p. 102.

18. *Ibid.*, pp. 102-112.

19. *Ibid.*

20. Pedro Vicente Cañete y Dominguez, *Guía Histórica, Geográfica, Física, Política, Civil y Legal del Gobierno e Intendencia de la Provincia de Potosí, Año 1791* (La Paz: 1952), p. 107. Cited in Oscar Cornblitt, "Society and Mass Rebellion in Eighteenth Century Peru and Bolivia," in Raymond Carr, ed., *Latin American Affairs* (St. Anthony's Papers, No. 22, London, 1970), p. 26.

21. Parry, *The Spanish Seaborne Empire*, pp. 107 ff.

22. I am not suggesting that this is Tandeter's position. On the contrary, his work is crucial to understanding the nature of forced labor in the mines. See Tandeter, "Forced and Free Labour in Late Colonial Potosí."

23. The expulsion of a mass of direct producers from the land is the primary precondition for the development of free wage labor under capitalism.

24. John Fisher, *Minas y Mineros en el Perú Colonial, 1776-1824* (Lima: Instituto de Estudios Peruanos, 1977), pp. 19-48, 181-212.

25. *Ibid.*, pp. 213-233.

26. *Ibid.*, pp. 223-228.

27. *Ibid.*, pp. 181-212.

28. The *repartimiento de mercancías* required Indians and peasants to purchase products, some of which were imported from Europe. The *repartimiento* could be imposed only through the use of force because the "consumers" produced their own subsistence goods and had neither the needs, the desire, nor the means to purchase. Some Indians and peasants sought work in the mines to earn the cash that they were required to spend in the *repartimiento*. See Elizabeth Dore, "Un ensayo de interpretación del desarrollo del capitalismo en el Perú," *Revista Latinoamericana de Historia Económica y Social* (HISLA), 7 (1986), pp. 131-142; and Jürgen Golte, *Repartos y rebeliones, Túpac Amaru y las contradicciones de la econômia colonial* (Lima: Instituto de Estudios Peruanos, 1980).

29. *Mercurio Peruano* 9 (January 30, 1791), p. 68. Cited in Fisher, p. 181.

30. Fisher, *Minas y Mineros en el Perú Colonial*, p. 182.

31. Florencia E. Mallon, *The Defense of Community in Peru's Central Highlands: Peasant Struggle and Capitalist Transition, 1860-1940* (Princeton: Princeton University Press, 1983), pp. 42-79; and Heraclio Bonilla and Karen Spalding, eds., *La independencia en el Perú* (Lima: Instituto de Estudios Peruanos, 1972).

32. Mallon, *The Defense of Community*, pp. 42-79.

33. Heraclio Bonilla, *Guano y burguesía en el Perú* (Lima: Instituto de Estudios Peruanos, 1974); and William Bollinger, "The Bourgeois Revolution in Peru: A Conception of Peruvian History," *Latin American Perspectives*, 4:3 (Summer 1977), pp. 18-54.

34. Julian Laite, *Industrial Development and Migrant Labour* (Manchester: Manchester University Press, 1981), and Mallon, *The Defense of Community*, pp. 42-167.

35. Mallon, *The Defense of Community*, pp. 42-167.

36. Mallon, *The Defense of Community*, pp. 73 ff. The literal translation of *enganche* is "the hook."

37. For example, Costa Rica. See John Weeks, "An Interpretation of the Central American Crisis," *Latin American Research Review*, 21:3 (Fall 1986), pp. 31-53.

38. Rosemary Thorp and Geoffrey Bertram, *Peru 1890-1977: Growth and Policy in an Open Economy* (London: The Macmillan Press Ltd., 1978), pp. 24 ff; William Bollinger, "The Bourgeois Revolution in Peru"; and Adrian W. DeWind, Jr., "Peasants Become Miners: The Evolution of Industrial Mining Systems in Peru," Ph.D. dissertation, Columbia University, 1977, pp. 85-100.

39. Alejandro Garland, "Cerro de Pasco," *Boletín de la Sociedad Nacional de Minería* (Perú) (hereafter referred to as *BSNM*), 4 (Summer 1901), pp. 656-659.

40. Long and Roberts argue that *contrata* and *enganche* were the labor recruitment systems selected by mineowners who preferred to establish contractual relationships with labor recruiters rather than directly with workers. See Norman Long and Bryan R. Roberts, *Miners, Peasants and Enterpreneurs: Regional Development in the Central Highlands of Peru* (New York: Cambridge University Press, 1984), pp. 235 ff. For a discussion of this position see Elizabeth Dore, book review of Norman Long and Bryan R. Roberts, eds., *Miners, Peasants and Entrepreneurs*, in *Studies in Comparative International Development*, 20:4 (Winter 1985-86), pp. 116-119.

41. Mallon, *The Defense of Community*, pp. 125-167.

42. "El establecimiento mineral de Casapalca," *BSNM*, 2 (February 28, 1898), p. 60; and Elias Malpartida, "Memoria que presenta a la junta general de la Sociedad Nacional de Minería el vice presidente Sr. Alejandro Garland," *BSNM*, 2 (February 28, 1899), pp. 54-55.

43. Pedro Dávalos y Lisson, "Revista anual sobre la industria de plata y cobre de Cerro de Pasco, con la estadística de sus productos, gastos y utilidades," *BSNM*, 4 (March 31, 1901).

44. Titles Archive of the Cerro Corporation, files 1-133 (1901-1910), Cerro de Pasco, Peru; and I. G. Bertram, "Entry of the Cerro de Pasco Mining Company to Peru," Lima, 1974.

Chapter Four

1. Alejandro Garland, "Cerro de Pasco," *Boletín de la Sociedad Nacional de Minería (BSNM)*, 4 (Summer 1901), pp. 656-659.

2. From the early sixteenth century sugar was grown on haciendas on the northern coast, where much of the work was done by black slaves. Following the abolition of slavery in 1854 coastal landowners replaced slave labor with Chinese indentured workers who were brought to Peru through the mid-1870s to labor on the coastal estates. With the elimination of the "coolie" trade *hacendados* turned to *enganche* to recruit workers for their estates.

3. Peter F. Klarén, *Modernization, Dislocation and Aprismo: Origins of the Peruvian Aprista Party, 1870-1932* (Austin: University of Texas Press, 1973), Chapters 1, 3, and 4; and William Bollinger, "The Bourgeois Revolution in Peru: A Conception of Peruvian History," *Latin American Perspectives*, 4:3 (Summer 1977), pp. 18-56.

4. Alejandro Garland, "Cerro de Pasco," *BSNM*.

5. There is a large literature on the entry of the Cerro de Pasco Copper Company into Peru. See Charles H. McArver, Jr., "The Role of Private American Economic Interests in the Development of Cerro de Pasco, 1877-1901," thesis, University of North Carolina, 1970; William S. Bollinger, "The Rise of United States Influence in the Peruvian Economy, 1869-1921," thesis, University of California at Los Angeles, 1972; I. G. Bertram, "Development Problems in an Export Economy: A Study of Domestic Capitalists, Foreign Firms and Government in Peru: 1919-1930," Ph.D. dissertation, University of Oxford, 1974; and Adrian W. DeWind, Jr., "Peasants Become Miners: The Evolution of Industrial Mining Systems in Peru," Ph.D. dissertation, Columbia University, 1977.

6. The North American firm known in Peru in 1901 as the Cerro de Pasco Mining Company has gone through a series of minor name changes which reflect the changing nature of its product as well as corporate restructuring. For an account of these alterations in the name of the company see DeWind, "Peasants Become Miners," pp. 116-117. During most of its years in Peru the company was called The Cerro de Pasco Corporation. Therefore, for simplicity, in all subsequent references in this book the company will be called The Cerro de Pasco Corporation.

7. Titles Archive of the Cerro Corporation, files 1-113 (1901-1910) Cerro de Pasco, Peru; and I. G. Bertram, "Entry of the Cerro de Pasco Mining Company to Peru," Lima, 1974 (unpublished manuscript).

8. Bertram, "Entry of the Cerro de Pasco Mining Company."

9. Florencia E. Mallon, *The Defense of Community in Peru's Central Highlands: Peasant Struggle and Capitalist Transition, 1860-1940* (Princeton: Princeton University Press, 1983), p. 173; and McArver, "The Role of Private American Economic Interests."

10. Dirk Kruijt and Menno Vellinga, *Labor Relations and Multinational Corporations: The Cerro de Pasco Corporation in Peru (1902-1974)* (Assen, The Netherlands: Van Gorcum, 1979), pp. 40-50.

11. It is likely that the North American firms operating in Peru lobbied for passage of the new mining legislation.

12. Jorge Basadre, *Historia de la República del Perú, 1822-1933*, 17 vols. (Lima: Ediciones Universitarias, 1965), vol. 9, pp. 308-309; and Mario Samamé Boggio, *Minería Peruana* (Lima: by the Author, 1974), pp. 202-203. It is interesting to compare the Spanish and the British traditions concerning mineral rights. In Britain, until the coal industry was nationalized in 1938, the owners of land also owned the minerals found beneath the surface. Consequently, the concentration of landownership also implied concentration in the ownership of mineral rights. In a series of interesting articles Ben Fine argues that landed property was a barrier to the expansion of the British coal industry prior to 1938. See Fine, "Landed Property and the British Coal Industry Prior to World War I" (London: Birkbeck College, 1982), Discussion Paper no. 120, p. 8; and "Land, Capital and the British Coal Industry Prior to World War II," in Michael Ball, ed., *Land, Rent, Housing and Urban Planning* (London: Croom Helm, 1985).

13. Mallon, *The Defense of Community in Peru's Central Highlands*, pp. 171-172; and McArver, "The Role of Private American Economic Interests."

14. Mallon, *The Defense of Community in Peru's Central Highlands*, pp. 171-172.

15. The following discussion of increasing social differentiation in highland society is based on Mallon, *The Defense of Community in Peru's Central Highlands*, Chapters 4 and 5, pp. 125-213. The process of the increasing social differentiation of the peasantry is the primary theme of Mallon's pathbreaking study. She analyzes the growing commercialization of highland society, the struggle of peasants to resist efforts to privatize communal lands, and the intensification of the pressures on the peasantry to work for wages.

16. See Chapter Three for a more detailed discussion of *enganche*. For contemporary accounts of labor shortages in the mining industry and descriptions of *enganche* see "El estado actual de la industria minera de Morococha," *Boletín del Cuerpo de Ingenieros de Minas (BCIM)*, 25 (1905), pp. 62-66; Alberto Noriega, "El *enganche* en la minera del Perú," *Boletín de Minas, Industrias y Construcciones*, Vols. 2-3 (1911), pp. 41-53; *BCIM*, 41 (1906), p. 27; and *BCIM*, 83 (1917), p. 137. There are several excellent studies that analyze *enganche* in the mining industry. For example see Heraclio Bonilla, *El minero de los Andes* (Lima: Instituto de Estudios Peruanos, 1974) p. 23; Alberto Flores Galindo, *Los mineros de Cerro de Pasco* (Lima: Pontificia Universidad Católica del Perú, 1974), pp. 34-45; Wilfredo Kapsoli, *Los movimientos campesinos en Cerro de Pasco: 1880-1963* (Huancayo, Perú: Instituto de Estudios Andinos, 1975), pp. 54-81; and Mallon, *The Defense of Community in Peru's Central Highlands*, Chapters 4, 5, and 6.

17. Mallon, *The Defense of Community in Peru's Central Highlands*, p. 156.

18. "El estado actual de la industria minera de Morococha," *Boletín del Cuerpo de Ingenieros de Minas (BCIM)*, 25 (1905), pp. 62-66; Alberto Noriega, "El *enganche* en la minería del Perú," *Boletín de Minas, Industrias y*

Construcciones, 2-3, (1911), pp. 41-53; *BCIM*, 41 (1906), p. 27; and *BCIM*, 83 (1917), p. 137; Bonilla, *El minero de los Andes*; and Flores Galindo, *Los mineros de Cerro de Pasco*.

19. Mallon, *The Defense of Community in Peru's Central Highlands*, pp. 187-188.

20. *Ibid.*, p. 220.

21. Julian Laite, "Migration and Social Differentiation Amongst Mantaro Vally Peasants," in Norman Long and Bryan R. Roberts, *Miners, Peasants and Entrepreneurs: Regional Development in the Central Highlands of Peru* (Cambridge: Cambridge University Press, 1984), p. 115.

22. Mallon, *The Defense of Community in Peru's Central Highlands*, p. 206; and DeWind, "Peasants Become Miners," Chapter 3.

23. John Weeks, "Epochs of Capitalism and the Progressiveness of Capital's Expansion," *Science and Society* 49:4 (Winter 1985-86), pp. 414-436.

24. Karl Marx, *Capital*, Vol. I Part Eight (Harmondsworth, England: Penguin Books, 1976), pp. 873-930.

25. Weeks, "Epochs of Capitalism."

26. Karl Marx, "Appendix: Results of the Immediate Process of Production," *Capital*, Vol. I (Harmondsworth, England: Penguin Books, 1976), pp. 948-1084.

27. See Mallon's discussion of Eulogio E. Fernandini and other Peruvian mineowners in *The Defense of Community in Peru's Central Highlands*, pp. 182-187.

28. *The West Coast Leader* (Lima), November 22, 1922, p. 1; October 12, 1926, pp. 22-24; and August 7, 1928, p. 23.

29. *The West Coast Leader* (Lima), October 12, 1926, pp. 22-24.

30. Rosemary Thorp and Geoffrey Bertram, *Peru, 1890-1977: Growth and Policy in an Open Economy* (London: The Macmillan Press Ltd., 1978), pp. 154-155. For Thorp and Bertram's calculation of U.S. ownership in the Peruvian mining industry in 1929 see footnote 3, p. 380. The third company that Thorp and Bertram include in their calculation, The Vanadium Corporation, is not analyzed in this study. For excellent analyses of the Peruvian mining industry in the late 1920s see Thorp and Bertram, pp. 84-85, 154.

31. For a vivid description of the social, economic, and ecological impact of the Oroya complex see Mallon, *The Defense of Community in Peru's Central Highlands*, pp. 225-230; José J. Bravo, "Informe Sobre los Humos de La Oroya," *BCIM*, 108 (1926), pp. 1-208; and DeWind, "Peasants Become Miners," pp. 230-244.

32. Mallon, *The Defense of Community in Peru's Central Highlands*, Chapters 2, 4, and 5; and Richard N. Adams, *A Community in the Andes: Problems and Progress in Muquiyauyo* (Seattle: University of Washington Press, 1959), p. 135.

33. The analysis of peasant resistance to encroachments on their lands and traditional rights is central to the historical narrative so carefully presented by Florencia Mallon in *The Defense of Community in Peru's Central Highlands*. Other excellent treatments of this process in the Central highlands of Peru are

presented in Giorgio Alberti and Rodrigo Sánchez, *Poder y conflicto social en el valle del Mantaro* (Lima: Instituto de Estudios Peruanos, 1974); and Juan Martínez Alier, *Los Huacchilleros del Perú* (Lima: Instituto de Estudios Peruanos, 1973).

34. Mallon, *The Defense of Community in Peru's Central Highlands*, Chapters 5 and 7; Pilar Campaña and Rigoberto Rivera, "Highland *Puna* Communities and the Impact of the Mining Economy," in Long and Roberts, *Miners, Peasants and Entrepreneurs*, pp. 88-106; and Laite, "Migration and Social Differentiation," pp. 107-139.

35. Bonilla, *El minero de los Andes*; Flores Galindo, *Los mineros de Cerro de Pasco*; and Kapsoli, *Los movimientos campesinos en Cerro de Pasco: 1880-1963*.

36. Mallon, *The Defense of Community in Peru's Central Highlands*, Chapters 7 and 8.

37. *Ibid.*, pp. 222-234.

38. Long and Roberts, *Miners, Peasants and Entrepreneurs*, pp. 44-87; Campaña and Rivera, "Highland *Puna* Communities and the Impact of the Mining Economy," pp. 88-106; and Laite, "Migration and Social Differentiation," pp. 107-139.

39. Dora Mayer, *La Conducta de la Compañía Minera del Cerro de Pasco* (Lima: Asociación Pro-Indígena, 1914); and Moises Poblete Troncoso, *Condiciones de vida y de trabajo de la población indigena del Perú* (Geneva: Oficina International de Trabajo, 1938), pp. 139-148.

40. *The West Coast Leader* (Lima), August 7, 1928, p. 23.

41. DeWind, "Peasants Become Miners," Chapter 5.

42. Flores Galindo argues that this struggle was essentially a "pre-political" peasant movement rather than a proletarian conflict. He contends that the flooding of the mines and destruction of company property were not part of a trade union strategy developed by the leaders of the mineworkers. Rather, he says these actions reflected the frustration of peasants. See Flores Galindo, *Los mineros de la Cerro de Pasco*, p. 71.

43. Denis Sulmont, *Historia del movimiento obrero minero metalúrgico* (Lima: Federación Nacional de Trabajadores Mineros y Metalúrgicos del Perú, 1980), pp. 15-21.

44. This argument is drawn from Mallon, *The Defense of Community in Peru's Central Highlands*, Chapter 7.

45. Flores Galindo, *Los mineros de la Cerro de Pasco*, pp. 50-64; and Bonilla, *El minero de los Andes*, pp. 46-52.

46. See Long and Roberts, *Miners, Peasants and Entrepreneurs*, Table 4, p. 53.

47. Data indicate that wages increased during the depression, fell from 1934 through 1940 when the industry expanded, and rose in the 1940s, a time when mineral production declined. Because these changes seem unlikely I conclude that the data on wages prior to 1945 are inconsistent. Nevertheless, for those who might be interested, a time series on real and money wages from 1924 through 1945 is presented in Appendix I.

48. Julian Laite, "Processes of Industrial Change in Highland Peru," in Norman Long and Bryan R. Roberts, eds., *Peasant Cooperation and Capitalist Expansion in Central Peru* (Austin: University of Texas Press, 1978), pp. 72-98.

49. Laite, "Migration and Social Differentiation"; DeWind, "Peasants Become Miners"; Long and Roberts, *Miners, Peasants and Entrepreneurs*; pp. 169-197; Martinez Alier, *Los Huachilleros del Perú*; and Mallon, *The Defense of Community in Peru's Central Highlands*, pp. 205-213.

50. DeWind, "Peasants Become Miners," Chapter 5; and Mallon, *The Defense of Community in Peru's Central Highlands*, pp. 214-243.

Chapter Five

1. Rosemary Thorp and Geoffrey Bertram, *Peru 1890-1977: Growth and Policy in an Open Economy* (London: The Macmillan Press Ltd., 1978), pp. 160, 382-383.

2. Mario Samamé Boggio, *Minería Peruana: biografía y estratégia de una actividad decisiva* (Lima: By the author, 1974), p. 384.

3. According to Hamilton the cause of the crisis was the decline in the quantity and quality of copper ores. See Stanley Kerry Hamilton, "Factors Influencing Investment and Production in the Peruvian Mining Industry 1940-1965," Ph.D. dissertation, The University of Wisconsin, 1976, pp. 77-83.

4. Least-squares trend analysis highlights the cyclical deviations from a long-term trend. See Chapter Two.

5. Adrian W. DeWind, Jr., "Peasants Become Miners: The Evolution of Industrial Mining Systems in Peru," Ph.D. dissertation, Columbia University, 1977, p. 52.

6. The only major increase in productivity in this period followed the lockout in the Cerro de Pasco Corporation in 1930. This increase in productivity was a result of lengthening the working day and intensifying the pace of work. It was not accomplished through technical change. See Chapter Four.

7. Víctor Villanueva, *El APRA en busca del poder* (Lima: Editorial Horizonte, 1975); and Víctor Villanueva, *La sublevación aprista de 1948; la tragedia de un pueblo y un partido* (Lima: Editorial Milla Batres, 1973).

8. Julian Laite, *Industrial Development and Migrant Labour* (Manchester: Manchester University Press, 1981), Chapter 4.

9. Dirk Kruijt and Menno Vellinga, *Labor Relations and Multinational Corporations: The Cerro de Pasco Corporation in Peru (1902-1974)* (Assen, Netherlands: Van Gorcum, 1979), p. 66.

10. Laite, *Industrial Development*, Chapter 4.

11. Denis Sulmont, *El movimiento obrero en el Perú / 1900-1956* (Lima: Editorial Pontificia Universidad Católica del Perú, 1975), p. 24.

12. "Cincuenta Años de Minería 1903-1953," *Anuario de la Industria Minera: 1953* (Lima), p. 325.

13. Cerro de Pasco Copper Corporation, *Annual Report: 1946*, translated and reprinted in Ministerio de Fomento y Obras Públicas, *Anuario de la Industria Minera del Perú en 1946* (Lima: 1947), pp. 121-122, selection translated by the author.

14. Orris Herfindahl, *Copper Costs and Prices: 1879-1957* (Baltimore: The Johns Hopkins University Press, 1971), p. 207.

15. Herfindahl, *Copper Costs and Prices*, pp. 211-212.

16. William Bollinger, "The Bourgeois Revolution in Peru: A Conception of Peruvian History," *Latin American Perspectives*, 4 (Summer 1977), pp. 18-56.

17. Stanley Kerry Hamilton, "Factors Influencing Investment and Production in the Peruvian Mining Industry 1940-1965," Ph.D. dissertation, The University of Wisconsin, 1967, p. 36.

18. *Reglamentos del código de minería* (Lima: Ministerio de Fomento y Obras Públicas, 1951).

19. Hamilton, "Factors Influencing Investment and Production," p. 41.

20. The depletion allowance equalled 15 percent of the gross value of the mineral products, up to a maximum of 50 percent of the new profits computed for that year's operations. *Reglamentos del código de minería*.

21. *Ibid.*

22. *Ibid.*

23. DeWind, "Peasants Become Miners," pp. 77-78.

24. *Ibid.*, pp. 84-85.

25. For the intracacies of these claims, counter-claims, and legal decisions see Hamilton, "Factors Influencing Investment and Production," pp. 130 ff.

26. The Southern Peru Copper Corporation is known in Peru as "La Southern," "Southern," and "Southern Peru." I will use these various names when referring to the company.

27. For the details of this contract see Hamilton, "Factors Influencing Investment and Production," pp. 133-136.

28. In 1955 the American Smelting and Refining Company (ASARCO) held 57.7 percent of the stock, the Cerro de Pasco Corporation held 16 percent, the Phelps Dodge Corporation held 16 percent, and the Newmont Mining Corporation held 10.25 percent. In 1960 the Cerro de Pasco Corporation acquired an additional 6.25 percent of the stock from ASARCO, giving the Cerro de Pasco Corporation 22.25 percent and ASARCO 51.50 percent. Hamilton, "Factors Influencing Investment and Production," p. 133.

29. DeWind, "Peasants Become Miners," p. 94.

30. *Ibid.*, p. 112.

31. Sulmont, *El movimiento obrero en el Perú / 1900-1956*, p. 23.

32. *Ibid.*, pp. 30-33.

33. *Ibid.*, p. 32.

34. *Ibid.*, p. 29.

35. For discussions of these movements see William F. Whyte, "Rural Peru: Peasants as Activists"; Giorgio Alberti, "Peasant Movements in the Yanamarca Valley"; and David Chaplin, "La Convención Valley and the 1962-65

Guerilla Uprising," in David Chaplin, ed., *Peruvian Nationalism: A Corporatist Revolution* (New Brunswick: Transaction, 1976); José María Caballero, *Economía agraria de la sierra peruana antes de la reforma agraria de 1969* (Lima: Instituto de Estudios Peruanos, 1981); and Hugo Blanco, *Land or Death: The Peasant Struggle in Peru* (New York: Pathfinder Press, 1972). For an interesting analysis and useful background see David Scott Palmer, *Peru: The Authoritarian Tradition* (New York: Praeger Publishers, 1980).

36. Sulmont, *El movimiento obrero en el Perú / 1900-1956*, p. 33.

37. *Ibid.*, p. 29.

38. *Ibid.*

39. According to Kruijt and Vellinga by 1972, 70 percent of the work force in the Cerro de Pasco Corporation had uninterrupted work records. Another 17 percent had career patterns that included only one major period when they did not work for the corporation. While this suggests a higher degree of labor stablity than formerly existed in the central mining zone, there is also evidence that many of the workers in the Cerro de Pasco Corporation continued to preserve ties to their communities well into the 1970s. Krujit and Vellinga also report that in 1972, 40 percent of the workers of the corporation were fined for taking unauthorized leave from their jobs for periods ranging from several days to several weeks. The company administrators associated these leaves with peak agricultural periods when workers/peasants would cultivate, plant, and harvest their fields. Kruijt and Vellinga, *Labor Relations and Multinational Corporations*, p. 65. Other studies provide additional evidence that in the early 1970s many miners retained active ties to traditional highland communities. See for example, Alberto Flores Galindo, *Los Mineros de la Cerro de Pasco 1900-1930* (Lima: Editorial de la Pontificia Universidad Católica del Perú, 1974), p. 62; and R. José Mejía, "Informe de nuestra visita a la comunidad de Laraos" (Lima: Pontificia Universidad Católica del Perú, 1971), mimeographed, cited in Mallon, *The Defense of Community in Peru's Central Highlands*, Chapter 6.

40. For a similar analysis see John Weeks, *Limits to Capitalist Development: The Industrialization of Peru, 1950-1980* (Boulder: Westview Press, 1985), Chapter 7.

41. An anonomous reviewer of the original manuscript of this book suggested that "it is the relationship of the wage bill in dollars to worker productivity that is of concern to corporate accounting departments. When Dore's wage indices are restated in dollars, most of the observed wage inflation disappears...." To determine whether this critique is correct I analyzed the wage cost to capital using wages converted into dollars at the official exchange rate. This exercise produces results that are very similar to those of the analysis of the wage cost to capital using wages paid in Peruvian *soles*. For the wage cost to capital in U.S. dollars see Appendix K.

Chapter Six

1. For an elaboration of this argument see Elizabeth Dore, "Un ensayo de interpretación del desarrollo del capitalismo en el Perú," *Revista Latinoamericana de Historia Económica y Social* (HISLA), 7 (1986), pp. 131-142.

2. Baltazar Caravedo Molinari, *Burguesía e Industria en el Perú: 1933-1945* (Lima: Instituto de Estudios Peruanos, 1976), pp. 75-165.

3. Víctor Villanueva, "The Petty-Bourgeois Ideology of the Peruvian Aprista Party," *Latin American Perspectives*, 4:3 (Summer 1977).

4. John Weeks, *Limits to Capitalist Development: The Industrialization of Peru, 1950-1980* (Boulder, Colorado: Westview Press, 1985).

5. Banco Central de Reserva del Perú, *Cuentas Nacionales 1950-1957* (Lima: 1968); *Cuentas Nacionales 1960-1973* (Lima: 1974); *Memoria* (1973).

6. Elizabeth Dore and John Weeks, "The Intensification of the Assault Against the Working Class in 'Revolutionary' Peru," *Latin American Perspectives*, 3:2 (Spring 1976), pp. 55-83; Weeks, *Limits to Capitalist Development*; and Thomas Bamat, "From Plan Inca to Plan Tupac Amaru: The Recomposition of the Peruvian Power Bloc, 1968-1977," Ph.D. dissertation, Rutgers University, 1978.

7. For a more detailed analysis of the crisis and its implications see Weeks, *Limits to Capitalist Development*, Chapter 4.

8. Víctor Villanueva, *El CAEM y la Revolución de la Fuerza Armada* (Lima: Instituto de Estudios Peruanos, 1972).

9. Dore and Weeks, "The Intensification of the Assault Against the Working Class in 'Revolutionary' Peru," p. 67.

10. Elena Alvarez, *Política Económica y agricultura en el Perú, 1969-1979* (Lima: Instituto de Estudios Peruanos, 1983); José María Caballero, *Economía Agraria de la Sierra Peruana* (Lima: Instituto de Estudios Peruanos, 1981); Cristóbal Kay, "Agrarian Reform in Peru: An Assessment," in Ajit Kumar Ghose, ed., *Agrarian Reform in Contemporary Developing Countries* (New York: St. Martin's Press, 1983), pp. 185-239; and Cynthia McClintock, *Self-Management and the Peasant: Aspirations and Realities in Peruvian Cooperatives*, 1968-1977 (Princeton: Princeton University Press, 1980).

11. The exception was Aníbal Quijano, the first major critic of the regime to question the anti-capitalist and anti-imperialist nature of the government. See his thought-provoking book, *Nationalism and Capitalism in Peru: A Study in Neo-Imperialism* (New York: Monthly Review, 1971).

12. For analyses of this period see *Latin American Perspectives*, 4:3 (Summer 1977); Abraham F. Lowenthal, ed., *The Peruvian Experiment* (Princeton: Princeton University Press, 1975); Julio Cotler, *Clases, Estado y Nación en el Perú* (Lima: Instituto de Estudios Peruanos, 1978); David Chaplin, ed., *Peruvian Nationalism: A Corporatist Revolution* (New Brunswick, N.J.: Transaction Books, 1976); David Scott Palmer, *Peru: The Authoritarian Tradition* (New York: Praeger, 1980).

13. Again, the first to suggest that the emperor had no clothes, or at the least that the clothes were quite different from the ones we were led to expect,

was Aníbal Quijano. His penetrating analyses were published regularly in the journal *Sociedad y Política* (Lima).

14. Shane Hunt, "Direct Foreign Investment in Peru: New Rules for an Old Game," in Abraham F. Lowenthal, ed., *The Peruvian Experiment*, pp. 314-317.

15. Hunt, "Direct Foreign Investment in Peru: New Rules for an Old Game"; and David G. Becker, *The New Bourgeoisie and the Limits of Dependency* (Princeton: Princeton University Press, 1983), Chapter 6.

16. Weeks, *Limits to Capitalist Development*, pp. 231-232.

17. This argument is elaborated in Dore and Weeks, "The Intensification of the Assault Against the Working Class in 'Revolutionary' Peru."

18. *Ibid.*

19. *Ibid.*

20. Theodore H. Moran, *Multinational Corporations and the Politics of Dependence: Copper in Chile* (Princeton: Princeton University Press, 1974), Chapter 5, pp. 119-152.

21. Moran, *Multinational Corporations*, pp. 119-152.

22. For calculations of the profits of the Cerro de Pasco Corporation see Adrian W. DeWind, Jr., "Peasants Become Miners: The Evolution of Industrial Mining Systems in Peru," Ph.D. dissertation, Columbia University, 1977.

23. "Estructura de la propiedad en la minería" (Lima: Instituto Nacional de Planificación, 1973, mimeo), p.1; and "Diagnóstico de la sub-rama metalurgia no ferrosa" (Lima: Ministerio de la Industria y Comercio, Oficina Sectorial de Planificación, 1971), mimeographed.

24. Kirk Kruijt and Menno Vellinga, "The Political Economy of Mining Enclaves in Peru," presented at the conference, *The State and Multinational Companies in Latin America*, Institute of Latin American Studies, University of Glasgow, January, 1976; and Cerro Corporation *Annual Report* (New York: 1975).

25. Becker, *The New Bourgeoisie and the Limits of Dependency*, pp. 154 ff.

26. For details about corporate strategy and personalities and maneuvers by The Cerro de Pasco Corporation and the Peruvian government see Becker, *The New Bourgeoisie and the Limits of Dependency*, pp. 154 ff.

27. For an elaboration and a slight variation of this argument see Elizabeth Dore, "Accumulation and Crisis in the Peruvian Mining Industry, 1968-1977," *Latin American Perspectives* 4:3 (Summer 1977), pp. 77-102.

28. "Marcona Expropriation," *The Andean Report* (August 1975), pp. 3-5; and *Latin American Economic Report* (October 1, 1976), p. 149.

29. Carlos Alarcón Aliaga, *Privilegios y Capital Transnacional: El Caso de Southern Peru Copper Corporation* (Lima: Instituto José María Arguedas, n.d.), pp. 35-44; and Fernando Sánchez Albavera, *Minería, Capital Transnacional y Poder en el Perú* (Lima: Centro de Estudios y Promoción del Desarrollo [DESCO], 1981), Chapter 4.

30. For details of the contract between Southern Peru and the Government of Peru and revisions of the more infamous provisions of the Mining Code of

1950 see Alarcón Aliaga, *Privilegios y Capital Transnacional*, pp. 35-33; and Sánchez Albavera, *Minería, Capital Transnacional y Poder en el Perú*, Chapter 4.
31. For a very different interpretation of the regime, see E. V. K. Fitzgerald, *The State and Economic Development: Peru Since 1968* (Cambridge: Cambridge University Press, 1976).
32. Sánchez Albavera, *Minera, Capital Transnacional y Poder en el Perú*. For a detailed discussion of the marketing of minerals see Chapters 5 and 6.
33. For an excellent and detailed analysis of Peruvian indebtedness see Oscar Ugarteche, *El Estado Deudor: Economía Política de la Deuda: Perú y Bolivia 1968-1984* (Lima: Instituto de Estudios Peruanos, 1986). For an interpretation of structural adjustment as a means of insuring that debtors pay their creditors rather than as a strategy to restore economic growth see Albert Fishlow, "The Debt Crisis: Round Two Ahead?", in Richard E. Feinberg and Valeriana Kallab, eds., *Adjustment Crisis in the Third World* (New Brunswick, N.J.: Transaction Books, 1984), pp. 31-58.
34. Manuel Cisneros Orna, *Minería: Riqueza y Pobreza del Perú* (Lima: Instituto Cultural José María Arguedas, 1986), p. 127; and Manuel Cisneros Orna and Oswaldo Carpio Villegas, *Realidad Minera* (Lima: September, 1984), mimeographed, p. 25.
35. *Nueva Minera*, 1:1 (June 1987).
36. Despite popular belief that the accumulated debt of the Velasco era was caused by the military's insatiable desire for armaments, it was under the Belande administration, not Velasco's, that defense spending accounted for the highest proportion of new foreign loans. See Ugarteche, *El Estado Deudor*, Chapters 3 and 4.
37. Cisneros Orna, *Minería*, p. 183 and Table 6.6.
38. Since companies' financial reports are notoriously subject to manipulation, there is some question as to whether such data should be used and how the information should be interpreted. I present these data only to suggest major trends.
39. Kenji Takeuchi, et al., *The World Copper Industry: Its Changing Structure and Future Prospects* (Washington, D.C.: The World Bank, World Bank Staff Commodity Working Papers No. 15, 1987), pp. xxiii-xxv.
40. *Latin America Commodities Report* (October 15, 1987), p. 3; and December 10, 1987, p. 1.

Appendix A

1. Copper, lead, silver, and gold have been commercially mined in Peru throughout the period covered in this study. The industrial exploitation of zinc began in 1925, of iron in 1952.
Implied 1963 prices are derived by dividing the current value of production of one metal in 1963 by the weight in 1963.

$$\frac{PQ\ 1963}{weight\ 1963}$$

This gives the constant (1963) price. By adding together the value in constant prices for each metal in each year I derive the value of production in constant prices for that year.

2. It is possible that the price of one or more of the metals might have been extraordinarily high or low in 1963, or the relationship among the prices unusual. This would give a skewed picture of the volume of production for the different years, as measured by the value of production in constant 1963 prices.

3. The "Introductions" to the *Anuario de la Minería* for 1973 and 1974 state that the volume of production declined in these years. *Anuario de la Minería* (1973), p. 11; and (1974), p. 3.

4. Another scholar of the Peruvian mining industry has independently reached similar conclusions regarding the unreliability of official production figures for 1973 to 1975. See Claes Brundenius, "Growth, Stagnation and the Role of Foreign Capital in the Peruvian Mining Industry" (Lund, Sweden: Research Policy Program, University of Lund, March 1978), discussion paper no. 118.

5. A *tarea* is legally constituted as a working day of eight hours. According to Peruvian law, any extension beyond eight hours must be paid for at an overtime rate and is considered to be part of another *tarea*.

6. *Obreros* are considered unskilled or blue-collar workers and are paid an hourly wage. *Empleados* are traditionally considered to be skilled workers. They generally receive a monthly salary.

7. From 1924 to 1945 total wages paid in the metal mining sector can be deduced by subtracting the wages paid in the petroleum sector from the total wage bill of the mining industry as a whole. The average wage then can be calculated by dividing total wages paid in metal mining by the number of people employed in that sector.

STATISTICAL SOURCES

Area de Estadísticas, Archives. Ministerios de Energía y Minas, Lima. Unpublished material.

Anuario de la Industria Minera en el Perú. Lima: Ministerio de Fomento, 1945-1949.

Anuario de la Industria Minera en el Perú. Lima: Ministerio de Fomento y Obras Públicas, 1950-1965.

Anuario Minero del Perú. Lima: Ministerio de Energía y Minas, 1966-1972.

Anuario de la Minería del Perú. Lima: Ministerio de Energía y Minas, 1973-1985.

Anuario Minero Comercial. Lima: 1966-1975.

Banco Central de Reserva del Perú. *Renta Nacional del Perú: 1942-1947,1942-1949, 1941-1954.* Lima: 1948, 1950, 1955.

_____. *Boletín.* Lima: February, 1975.

_____. *Cuentas Nacionales 1950-1957.* Lima: 1968.

_____. *Cuentas Nacionales 1960-1973.* Lima: 1974.

_____. *Memoria.* Lima: 1972.

_____. *Memoria.* Lima: 1973.

Boletín del Cuerpo de Ingenieros de Minas. Lima: 1902-1922.

Boletín Oficial de Minas y Petróleo (1924-1932). Lima: 1924-1932.

Cerro Corporation: Titles Archives. Files 1-133 (1901-1910), Cerro de Pasco, Peru.

Cisneros Orna, Manuel, and Oswaldo Carpio Villegas. *Realidad Minera.* Lima: 1984.

Dávalos y Lisson, Pedro. "Revista Anual Sobre la Industria de Plata y Cobre de Cerro de Pasco, con la Estadística de sus Productos, Gastos y Utilidades." *Boletín de la Sociedad Nacional de Minería* (March 31, 1901).

"Declaraciones Anuales Consolidadas de Concesionarios, Empresas y Empresarios Mineros." Archivos de la División de Estadística, Lima: Ministerio de Energía y Minas, Dirección General de Minería, 1945-1975.

Extracto Estadístico. Lima: 1906-1915; 1934-1935.

Hohagen, Jorge. *La Industria Minera en el Perú* Lima: 1932-1939.

_____. *Anuario de la Industria Minera en el Perú.* Lima: 1940-1945.

Las Huelgas en el Perú. Servicio de Estadísticas de Recursos Humanos (SERH). Lima: Ministerio de Trabajo, 1970.

Industria de la Construcción. Lima: Ministerio de Energía y Minas, Dirrección General de Estadísticas, 1945-1976.

Informe Socio-Económico. Lima: Instituto Nacional de Planificación, 1974-1976.

Latin American Commodities Report. London: various.

Macera, Pablo. *Estadísticas Históricas del Perú: Sector Minero I (precios).* Lima: Centro Peruano de Historia Económica, 1972.

Macera, Pablo, and Honorio Pinto. *Estadísticas Históricas del Perú: Sector Minero II (volumen y valor)*. Lima: Centro Peruano de Historia Económica, 1972.

Metal Statistics: 1965-1975, 63rd ed. Frankfurt Am Main: Metallgesellschaft AG, 1976.

Metal Statistics: 1968-1978, 66th ed. Frankfurt Am Main: Metallgesellschaft AG, 1979.

La Minería en el Perú. Lima: Anuario Minero-Comercial, 1980.

Ridgway, Robert H. *Summarized Data of Gold Production*. Washington, D.C.: U.S. Department of Commerce, Bureau of Mines Economic Paper No.6, 1929.

"Servicio de Empleo y Recursos Humanos." Lima: Ministerio de Trabajo, 1967. Unpublished data.

Sociedad de Minería, Departamento de Estudios Económicos y Estadísticas, Archives.

Statistische Zusammenstellungen Über Aluminíum, Blei, Kupfer, Nickel, Quecksilber, Zink und Zinn. Am Main, Frankfurt: Metallgesellschaft, 1907-1977.

The United Nations. *Statistical Yearbook*, Department of Economic and Social Affairs, Statistical Office. New York: United Nations, 1948-1949, 1952, 1955, 1958-1959, 1965, 1974-1976, 1978.

United States Bureau of the Mines. *Mineral's Yearbook: 1963, 1968*. Washington, D.C.: Bureau of the Mines, U.S. Department of the Interior, 1964, 1970.

_____. *Mineral's Yearbook: 1971: Area Reports: International, III*. Washington, D.C.: Bureau of the Mines, U.S. Department of the Interior, 1973.

_____. Unpublished data.

United States Department of Commerce. *Survey of Current Business*. Washington, D.C.: U.S. Government Printing Office, 1977.

GENERAL BIBLIOGRAPHY

Actualidad Económica. Lima: 1978-1980.

Adams, Richard N. *A Community in the Andes: Problems and Progress in Muquiyauyo*. Seattle: University of Washington Press, 1959.

Alarcón Aliaga, Carlos. *Privilegios y Capital Transnacional: El Caso de Southern Peru Copper Corporation*. Lima: Instituto José María Aruguedas, n.d.

Alberti, Giorgio. "Peasant Movements in the Yanamarca Valley." In *Peruvian Nationalism: A Corporatist Revolution*, ed. David Chaplin. New Brunswick: Transaction, 1976.

Alberti, Giorgio, and Rodrigo Sánchez. *Poder y Conflicto Social en el Valle del Mantaro*. Lima: Instituto de Estudios Peruanos, 1974.

Alvarez, Elena. *Política Económica y Agricultura en el Perú, 1969-1979*. Lima: Instituto de Estudios Peruanos, 1983.

Amin, Samir. "The End of a Debate." Dakar: United Nations, African Institute for Economic Development and Planning, 1973. Reprinted in Samir Amin, *Imperialism and Unequal Development*. New York: Monthly Review Press, 1977.

_____. "Reply to Weeks and Dore." *Latin American Perspectives*, 4:2 (Spring 1979).

Andean Report. London: various.

Annual Report: 1946. Cerro de Pasco Copper Corporation. Reprinted in Ministerio de Fomento y Obras Públicas, *Anuario de la Industria Minera del Perú en 1946*. Lima: 1947.

Annual Report. Cerro de Pasco Copper Corporation. New York: 1975.

Aranda S., Carlos A. "Algunos Aspectos Sobre Relaciones Industriales." Lima: División de Operaciones, Cerro de Pasco Corporation, 1971. Mimeographed.

Arévalo Ramirez, Roger, and Daniel Rodriguez Hoyle. "Economic Analysis of Metal Mining." In *Peruvian Metal Mining 1971*, ed. Daniel Rodriguez Hoyle. Lima: Sociedad Nacional de Minería y Petróleo, 1973.

Assadourian, C. Sempat, Heraclio Bonilla, Antonio Mitre, and Tristan Platt. *Minería y Espacio Económico en los Andes, Siglos XVI-XX*. Lima: Instituto de Estudios Peruanos, 1980.

Assadourian, Carlos Sempat. "Modos de Producción, Capitalismo y Sub-desarrollo en América Latina," chap. in *Modos de Producción en América Latina*. Córdoba, Argentina: Cuadernos de Pasado y Presente/40, 1973.

_____. "La Producción de la Mercancía Dinero en la Formación del Mercado Interno Colonial. El Caso del Espacio Peruano, Siglo XVI." In *Ensayos Sobre el Desarrollo Económico de México y América Latina*, ed. E. Florescano. Mexico: 1979.

Aston, T. H., and C. H. E. Philpin, eds. *The Brenner Debate: Agrarian Class Structure and Economic Development in Pre-Industrial Europe.* Cambridge: Cambridge University Press, 1985.

Bakewell, Peter. "Mining in Colonial Spanish America." In *The Cambridge History of Latin America: Colonial Latin America,* Vol. II, ed. Leslie Bethell. Cambridge: Cambridge University Press, 1984.

Baldwin, Robert E. *Economic Development and Export Growth: A Study of Northern Rhodesia, 1920-1960.* Los Angeles: University of California Press, 1966.

Ballantyne, Janet Campbell. "The Political Economy of Peruvian Gran Minería." Ph.D. diss., Cornell University, 1976.

Bamat, Thomas. "From Plan Inca to Plan Tupac Amaru: The Recomposition of the Peruvian Power Bloc, 1968-1977." Ph.D. diss., Rutgers University, 1978.

Banks, Ferdinand E. *The World Copper Market: An Economic Analysis.* Cambridge, MA: Ballinger Publishing Company, 1974.

Baran, Paul A. *The Political Economy of Growth.* New York: Monthly Review Press, 1968.

Baran, Paul A., and Paul M. Sweezy. *Monopoly Capital.* New York: Monthly Review Press, 1966.

Basadre, Jorge. *Historia de la República del Perú, 1822-1933,* 17 vols. Lima: Ediciones Universitarias, 1965.

Basadre Ayulo, Jorge. *Derecho Minero Peruano.* Lima: P. L. Villanueva, 1975.

Becker, David G. *The New Bourgeoisie and the Limits of Dependency: Mining, Class and Power in "Revolutionary" Peru.* Princeton: Princeton University Press, 1983.

Bergsten, C. Fred. "The Threat from the Third World." *Foreign Policy,* 2 (Summer 1973).

Bernstein, Marvin D. *The Mexican Mining Industry 1890-1950: A Study of the Interaction of Politics, Economics, and Technology.* Albany: The State University of New York, 1965.

Bertram, I. G. "Development Problems in an Export Economy: A Study of Domestic Capitalists, Foreign Firms and Government in Peru, 1919-1930." Ph.D diss., Linacre College, University of Oxford, 1974.

_____. "Entry of the Cerro de Pasco Mining Company to Peru." TS. Lima: 1974.

Bettelheim, Charles. "Theoretical Comments." In Aghiri Immanuel, *Unequal Exchange.* London: New Left Books, 1972.

Blanco, Hugo. *Land Or Death: The Peasant Struggle in Peru.* New York: Pathfinder Press, 1972.

Bleaney, Michael. *Underconsumption Theories: A History and Critical Analysis.* London: Lawrence and Wishart, 1976.

Blostrom, Magnus, and Bjorn Hettne, eds. *Development Theory in Transition: The Dependency Debate and Beyond.* London: Zed Books Ltd.,1984.

Bollinger, William. "The Rise of U.S. Influence in the Peruvian Economy, 1867-1921." M.A. Thesis, University of California at Los Angeles, 1972.
_____. "The Bourgeois Revolution in Peru: A Conception of Peruvian History." *Latin American Perspectives*, 4:3 (Summer 1977).
Bonilla, Heraclio. *Guano y Burguesía en el Perú*. Lima: Instituto de Estudios Peruanos, 1974.
_____. *El Minero de los Andes: Una Aproximación a su Estudio*. Lima: Instituto de Estudios Peruanos, 1974.
Bonilla, Heraclio, and Karen Spalding, eds. *La Independencia en el Perú*. Lima: Instituto de Estudios Peruanos, 1972.
Bosson, Rex, and Bension Varon. *The Mining Industry and the Developing Countries*. New York: Oxford University Press, 1977.
Bostock, Mark, and Charles Harvey, eds. *Economic Independence and Zambian Copper: A Case Study of Foreign Investment*. New York: Praeger Publishers, 1972.
Bradby, Barbara. "The Destruction of Natural Economy." *Economy and Society*, 4 (May 1975).
Braverman, Harry. *Labor and Monopoly Capital: The Degradation of Work in the Twentieth Century*. New York: Monthly Review Press, 1974.
Bravo, José J. "Informe Sobre los Humos de La Oroya." *Boletín del Cuerpo de Ingenieros de Minas del Perú*, 108 (1926).
Brenner, Robert. "Agrarian Class Structure and Economic Development in Pre-Industrial Europe." *Past and Present*, 70 (February 1976).
_____. "The Origins of Capitalist Development: A Critique of Neo-Smithian Marxism." *New Left Review*, 103 (July-August 1977).
Brundenius, Claes. "The Anatomy of Imperialism: The Case of the Multinational Corporation in Peru." *Journal of Peace Research*, 9 (1972).
_____. "Growth, Stagnation and the Role of Foreign Capital in the Peruvian Mining Industry." Discussion paper no. 118, Research Policy Studies, Lund University, March 1978. Lund, Sweden: Lund University, 1978.
Bukharin, Nikolai I. "Imperialism and the Accumulation of Capital." In *The Accumulation of Capital: An Anti-Critique and Imperialism and the Accumulation of Capital*, ed. Rosa Luxemburg and Nikolai Bukharin. New York: Monthly Review Press, 1968.
Burga, Manuel. *De la Encomienda a la Hacienda Capitalista: El Valle del Jequetepeque del Siglo XVI al XX*. Lima: Instituto de Estudios Peruanos, 1976.
Caballero, José María. *Economía Agraria de la Sierra Peruana Antes de la Reforma Agraria de 1969*. Lima: Instituto de Estudios Peruanos, 1981.
Campaña, Pilar, and Rigoberto Rivera. "Highland *Puna* Communities and the Impact of the Mining Economy." In *Miners, Peasants and Entrepreneurs: Regional Development in the Central Highlands of Peru*, eds. Norman Long and Bryan R. Roberts. Cambridge: Cambridge University Press, 1984.

Caravedo, Baltazar Molinari. *Burguesía e Industria en el Perú: 1933-1945.* Lima: Instituto de Estudios Peruanos, 1976.

Caravedo, Baltazar Molinari, P. Saint Pol Maydieu, and D. Tarnawiecki. "Introducción al Estudio de la Historia de la Minería." Lima: Departamento de Economía, CC.SS. Universidad Católica, 1972. Mimeographed.

_____. *Clases, Lucha Política y Gobierno en el Perú 1919-1933.* Lima: Retama Editorial, 1977.

Chaplin, David. "La Convención Valley and the 1962-65 Guerrilla Uprising." In *Peruvian Nationalism: A Corporatist Revolution,* ed. David Chaplin. New Brunswick: Transaction, 1976.

"Cincuenta Años de Minería 1903-1953." *Anuario de la Industria Minera: 1953.* Lima: 1953.

Cisneros Orna, Manuel. *Minería: Riqueza y Pobreza del Perú.* Lima: Instituto Cultural José María Arguedas, 1986.

Cisneros Orna, Manuel, and Oswaldo Carpio Villegas. *Realidad Minera* (Lima), 1 (September 1984).

Clarfield, Kenneth W., et al. *Eight Mineral Cartels: The New Challenge to Industrialized Nations.* New York: McGraw-Hill, 1975.

Cole, Jeffrey A. *The Potosí Mita, 1573-1700.* Stanford: Stanford University Press, 1985.

"La Concentración de la Producción Minera en el Perú, 1967-1971." Lima: Instituto Nacional de Planificación, 1973. Mimeographed.

"Copper as a Factor of Industrial Development." Paper presented at the Second General Conference of UNIDO, March 12-26, 1972. Lima: Intergovernmental Council of Copper Exporting Countries, 1975.

Cornblitt, Oscar. "Society and Mass Rebellion in Eighteenth Century Peru and Bolivia." In *Latin American Affairs,* ed. Raymond Carr. St. Anthony's Papers No. 22. London: 1970.

Cotler, Julio. "Political Crisis and Military Populism in Peru." *Studies in Comparative International Development.* 1970-71.

_____. *Clases, Estado y Nación en el Perú.* Lima: Instituto de Estudios Peruanos, 1978.

Crispi, Jaime. *El Agro Chileno Después de 1973: Expansión Capitalista y Campesinización Pauperizante.* Santiago: Grupo de Investigaciones Agrarias, 1980.

Cuadernos Mineros. Lima: 1975.

Dávalos y Lisson, Pedro. *¿Porque Hice Fortuna?,* 2 vols. Lima: Librería y Imprenta Gil, 1941-1942.

DeWind, Adrian W. "From Peasants to Miners: The Background to Strikes in the Mines of Peru." *Science and Society,* 39:1 (Spring 1975).

DeWind, Adran W., Jr. "Peasants Become Miners: The Evolution of Industrial Mining Systems in Peru." Ph.D. diss., Columbia University, 1977.

Diagnóstico de la Sub-Rama Metalúrgia no Ferrosa. Lima: Ministerio de la Industria y Comercio, Oficina Sectorial de Planificación, 1971. Mimeographed.

Dietz, James L. "Imperialism and Underdevelopment: A Theoretical Perspective and a Case Study of Puerto Rico." *Review of Radical Political Economics*, 11:4 (Winter 1979).

Dore, Elizabeth. "Accumulation and Crisis in the Peruvian Mining Industry, 1968-1977." *Latin American Perspectives*, 4:3 (Summer 1977).

_____. "Social Relations and the Barriers to Economic Growth: The Case of the Peruvian Mining Industry." *Nova Americana*, 1:1 (Fall 1978).

_____. "La Burguesía Nacional en el Perú: 1968-1977." *Estudios Andinos*, 9:16 (1980).

_____. Book review of Long and Roberts, eds., *Miners, Peasants and Entrepreneurs*. *Studies in Comparative International Development*, 20:4 (Winter 1985-86).

_____. "Un Ensayo de Interpretación del Desarrollo del Capitalismo en el Perú." *Revista Latinoamericana de Historia Económica y Social (HISLA)* 7 (1986).

_____. *Acumulación y Crisis en La Minería Peruana: 1900-1977*. Lima: Universidad Nacional Mayor de San Marcos, 1986.

Dore, Elizabeth, and John Weeks. "The Intensification of the Assault Against the Working Class in 'Revolutionary' Peru." *Latin American Perspectives*, 3:2 (Spring 1976).

Drysdall, Alan. "Prospecting and Mining Activity: 1895-1970." In *Economic Independence and Zambian Copper: A Case Study of Foreign Investment*, eds. Mark Bostock and Charles Harvey. New York: Praeger Publishers, 1972.

"El Establecimiento Mineral de Casapalca." *Boletín de la Sociedad Nacional de Minería* (February 28, 1898).

"El Estado Actual de la Industria Minera de Morococha." *Boletín del Cuerpo de Ingenieros de Minas*, 25 (1905).

Emmanuel, Aghiri. *Unequal Exchange*. London: New Left Books, 1972.

Estatutos del Banco Minero del Perú. Lima: Banco Minero del Perú, 1966.

Estructura Ocupacional, Demanda de Personal Calificado y Acciones en el Sector Minero 1974-1980. Lima: Ministerio de Energía y Minas, Dirección General de Minería, November 1974.

"Estructura de la Propiedad en la Minería." Lima: Instituto Nacional de Planificación, 1973. Mimeographed.

Evaluación del Sector Minero, 1968-1973. Lima: Ministerio de Energía y Minas, Oficina Sectorial de Planificación, 1974.

Evolución de la Política Monetaria y Crediticia Peruana. Lima: Instituto de Ciencias Económicas y Sociales de la Universedad Nacional Federico Villareal, 1970.

Fine, Ben. "Landed Property and the British Coal Industry Prior to World War I." London: Birkbeck College, 1982. Discussion Paper No. 120.

_____. "Land, Capital and the British Coal Industry Prior to World War II." In *Land, Rent, Housing and Urban Planning*, ed. Michael Ball. London: Croom Helm, 1985.

Fisher, John. *Minas y Mineros en el Perú Colonial, 1776-1824.* Lima: Instituto de Estudios Peruanos, 1977.

_____. *Silver Mines and Silver Miners in Colonial Peru, 1776-1824.* Monograph Series, 7. Liverpool: Centre for Latin American Studies, University of Liverpool, 1977.

_____. "Silver Production in the Viceroyalty of Peru, 1776-1824." *Hispanic American Historical Review,* 55:1 (February 1985).

Fishlow, Albert. "The Debt Crisis: Round Two Ahead?" In *Adjustment Crisis in the Third World,* eds. Richard E. Feinberg and Valeriana Kallab. New Brunswick, NJ: Transaction Books, 1984.

Fitzgerald, E. V. K. *The State and Economic Development: Peru Since 1968.* Cambridge: Cambridge University Press, 1976.

Fitzgerald, E. V. K. *The Political Economy of Peru, 1956-78: Economic Development and the Restructuring of Capital.* Cambridge: Cambridge University Press, 1979.

Flores Galindo, Alberto. *Los Mineros de la Cerro de Pasco, 1900-1930.* Lima: Pontificia Universidad Católica del Perú, 1974.

Flores Marín, José. *Minería Colonial y Coyuntura Mundial, 1913-1919.* Lima: Centro Peruano de Historia Económica, 1974.

Frank, Andre Gunder. *Capitalism and Underdevelopment in Latin America.* New York: Modern Reader, 1969.

García-Sayan, Diego. *El Caso Marcona: Análisis Histórico-Jurídico de los Contratos.* Lima: Centro de Estudios y Promoción del Desarrollo, 1975.

Garland, Alejandro. "Cerro de Pasco." *Boletín de la Sociedad Nacional de Minería* (Peru), (Summer 1901).

Golte, Jürgen. *Repartos y Rebeliones, Túpac Amarú y las Contradicciones de la Economía Colonial.* Lima: Instituto de Estudios Peruanos, 1980.

Gómez, Walter. *La Minería en el Desarrollo Económico de Bolivia 1900-1970.* La Paz: Editorial Los Amigos del Libro, 1978.

Hamilton, Stanley Kerry. "Factors Influencing Investment and Production in the Peruvian Mining Industry 1940-1965." Ph.D. diss., University of Wisconsin, 1967.

Herfindahl, Orris. *Copper Costs and Prices: 1879-1957.* Baltimore: The Johns Hopkins University Press, 1971.

Himmelweit, Susan. "Mode of Production." *A Dictionary of Marxist Thought,* ed. T. Bottomore, pp. 335-337. Oxford: Basil Blackwell, 1983.

Hilton, Rodney, ed. *The Transition from Feudalism to Capitalism.* London: New Left Books, 1976.

Hobsbawm, Eric J. *Primitive Rebels: Studies in Archaic Forms of Social Movement in the 19th and 20th Centuries.* Manchester: University of Manchester Press, 1971.

Hunt, Shane. "Direct Foreign Investment in Peru: New Rules for an Old Game." In *The Peruvian Experiment,* ed. Abraham F. Lowenthal. Princeton: Princeton University Press, 1975.

Ingeniero Andino. Lima: 1975.

Joo Chang, Jorge, et al. "Estudio Económico Laboral de la Minería." Lima: Ministerio de Energía y Minas, Dirección General de Minería, 1972. Mimeographed.

Kapsoli, Wilfredo. *Los Movimientos Campesinos en Cerro de Pasco: 1880-1963*. Huancayo, Peru: Instituto de Estudios Andinos, 1975.

Kay, Cristóbal. *El Sistema Señorial Europeo y la Hacienda Latinoaméricana*. Mexico: Serie Popular Era, 1980.

_____. "Agrarian Reform in Peru: An Assessment." In *Agrarian Reform in Contemporary Developing Countries*, ed. Ajit Kumar Ghose. New York: St. Martin's Press, 1983.

Kemp, Tom. *Theories of Imperialism*. London: Dennis Dobson, 1967.

Klarén, Peter F. *Modernization, Dislocation and Aprismo: Origins of the Peruvian Aprista Party, 1870-1932*. Austin: University of Texas Press, 1973.

Kruijt, Dirk. "Mining and Miners in Central Peru, 1968-1980." *Boletín de Estudios Latinoamericanos y del Caribe* (1982).

Krujit, Dirk, and Menno Vellinga. "The Political Economy of Mining Enclaves in Peru." Paper presented at the Institute of Latin American Studies. University of Glasgow, conference, "The State and Multinational Companies in Latin America," January 1976. Glasgow: University of Glasgow, 1976.

Krujit, Dirk, and Menno Vellinga. *Labor Relations and Multinatioinal Corporations: The Cerro de Paco Corporation in Peru (1907-1974)*. Assen, The Netherlands: Van Gorcum, 1979.

Kula, Witold. *An Economic Theory of the Feudal System*. London: New Left Books, 1976.

Laclau, E. "Imperialism in Latin America." *New Left Review*, 67 (May-June 1971).

Laite, Julian A. "Industrialization, Migration and Social Stratification at the Periphery." *The Sociological Review* (November 1978).

_____. "Miners and National Politics in Peru, 1900-1974." *Journal of Latin American Studies* (1980).

_____. *Industrial Development and Migrant Labor*. Manchester: Manchester University Press, 1981.

_____. "Migration and Social Differentiation Amongst Mantaro Valley Peasants." In *Miners, Peasants and Entrepreneurs: Regional Development in the Central Highlands of Peru*, eds. Norman Long and Bryan R. Roberts. Cambridge: Cambridge University Press, 1984.

Laite, Julian. "Circulatory Migration and Social Differentiation in the Andes." In *Labour Circulation and the Labour Process*, ed. Guy Standing. London: Croom Helm, 1985.

Latin American Economic Report. London: various.

Latin American Perspectives, 4:3 (Summer 1977).

Lenin, V. I. "On the So-Called Market Question." *Collected Works*. Vol. I. Moscow: Progress Publishers, 1972.

Ley Orgánica del Sector Energía y Minas. Lima: Ministerio de Energía y Minas, Oficina de Asesoria Jurídico, 1975.

"Libro de Registro de las Organizaciones Sindicales Reconocidas." Lima: Ministerio de Trabajo, Archives, n.d.

Long, Norman, and Bryan R. Roberts, eds. *Peasant Cooperation and Capitalist Expansion in Central Peru.* Austin: University of Texas Press, 1978.

_____, eds. *Miners, Peasants and Entrepreneurs: Regional Development in the Central Highlands of Peru.* Cambridge: Cambridge University Press, 1984.

López Soria, José Ignacio. *El Modo de Producción en el Perú.* Lima: Mosca Azul Editores, 1977.

Lowenthal, Abraham F., ed. *The Peruvian Experiment.* Princeton: Princeton University Press, 1975.

Luxemburg, Rosa. *The Accumulation of Capital.* New York: Monthly Review Press, 1968.

_____. "The Accumulation of Capital: An Anti-Critique." In *The Accumulation of Capital: An Anti-Critique and Imperialism and the Accumulation of Capital,* eds. Rosa Luxemburg and Nikolai Bukharin. New York: Monthly Review Press, 1972.

Madero Bracho, Enrique. "La Minería, su Pasado, Presente, y Proyección Futura en el Programa de México." In *La Minería en México: Estudios Sobre su Desarrollo Histórico,* eds. Miguel León-Portilla, et al. Mexico: Universidad Nacional Autónoma de México, 1978.

Mallon, Florencia E. *The Defense of Community in Peru's Central Highlands: Peasant Struggle and Capitalist Transition, 1860-1940.* Princeton: Princeton University Press, 1983.

Mallon, Florencia E. "Gender and Class in the Transition to Capitalism: Household and the Mode of Production in Peru." *Latin American Perspectives,* 48 (Winter 1985).

Malpartida, Elias. "Memoria que Presenta a la Junta General de la Sociedad de Minería el Vice Presidente Sr. Alejandro Garland." *Boletín de la Sociedad Nacional de Minería* (February 28, 1899).

Martínez Alier, Juan. *Los Huacchilleros del Perú.* Lima: Instituto de Estudios Peruanos, 1973.

Martínez de la Torre, Ricardo. *Apuntes Para una Interpretación Marxista de Historia Social del Perú.* 4 vols. Lima: Impresora Peruana S.A., 1949.

Marx, Karl. *Capital.* 3 vols. Moscow: Progress Publishers, 1971.

_____. *Capital.* Vol. I of 3 vols. Harmondsworth, England: Penguin Books, 1976,.

Mauro Marini, Ruy. "Dialéctica de la Dependencia." *Sociedad y Desarrollo* (January-March 1972).

Mayer, Dora. *La Conducta de la Compañía Minera del Cerro de Pasco.* Lima: Asociación Pro-Indígena, 1914.

McArver, Charles H., Jr. "The Role of Private American Economic Interests in the Development of Cerro de Pasco, 1877-1901." Thesis, University of North Carolina, 1970.

McClintock, Cynthia. *Self-Management and the Peasant: Aspirations and Realities in Peruvian Cooperatives, 1968-1977.* Princeton: Princeton University Press, 1980.

Mejía, R. José. "Informe de Nuestra Visita a la Comunidad de Laraos." Lima: Pontificia Universidad Católica del Perú, 1971. Mimeographed.

"Memorandum Sobre La Cerro Corporation." Lima: Instituto Nacional de Planificación, 1972. Mimeograph.

Mezger, Dorothea. *Copper in the World Economy.* New York: Monthly Review Press, 1980.

Mikesell, Raymond F. *Foreign Investment in Copper Mining: Case Studies of Mines in Peru and Papua, New Guinea.* Baltimore: The Johns Hopkins University Press, 1975.

Miller, R., et al. *Social and Economic Change in Modern Peru.* Liverpool: Centre for Latin American Studies, University of Liverpool. Monograph Series 6, n.d.

Minería y Petróleo. Lima: 1972-1975.

Mohun, Simon. "Abstract Labor and its Value Form." *Science and Society,* 48:4 (Winter 1984-85).

Montoya Rojas, Rodrigo. *Al Propósito del Carácter Predominantemente Capitalista de la Economía Peruana Actual.* Lima: Ediciones Teoría y Realidad, 1970.

Moran, Theodore H. *Multinational Corporations and the Politics of Dependence: Copper in Chile.* Princeton: Princeton University Press, 1974.

The Multinational Corporation, Studies on U.S. Foreign Investment. Vol. I. Washington, D.C.: U.S. Government Printing Office, 1972.

Murra, John. "Current Research and Prospects in Andean Ethnohistory." *Latin American Research Review,* 5 (Spring 1970).

Noriega, Alberto. "El Enganche en la Minería del Perú." *Boletín de Minas, Industrias y Construcciones,* 2-3 (1911).

Oroya Metallurgical Operations. Lima: Cerro de Pasco Corporation, February 1971.

Palmer, David Scott. *Peru: The Authoritarian Tradition.* New York: Praeger Publishers, 1980.

Parry, J. H. *The Spanish Seaborne Empire.* New York: Alfred A. Knopf, 1970.

Peruvian General Mining Law. Lima: Banco Minero del Péru, 1972.

Peruvian Times. Lima: 1940-1974.

Pilling, Geoffrey. "Imperialism, Trade and 'Unequal Exchange': the Work of Aghiri Emmanuel." *Economy and Society,* 2 (May 1973).

Pinto Herrera, Honorio. *Un Sector Exportador Dependiente: La Minería Metálica en el Perú 1945-1970.* Lima: Universidad Nacional Mayor de San Marcos, 1973.

Poblete Troncoso, Moisés. *Condiciones de Vida y de Trabajo de la Población Indígena del Perú.* Geneva: Oficina Internacional de Trabajo, 1938.

Purser, W. F. C. *Metal-mining in Peru, Past and Present*. New York: Praeger Publishers, 1971.

Quijano, Aníbal. *Nationalism and Capitalism in Peru: A Study in Neo-Imperialism*. New York: Monthly Review, 1971.

Reglamentos del Código de Minería. Lima: Ministerio de Fomento y Obras Públicas, 1951.

"Reporte Económico No. 22." Lima: Sociedad de Minería, Departamento de Estudios Económicos y Estadísticas, November 1975.

Rodriguez Hoyle, Daniel, ed. *La Minería Metálica en la Economía Peruana*. Lima: Sociedad Nacional de Minería y Petróleo, 1970.

_____. *Perú Minero 1967*. Lima: Sociedad Nacional de Minería y Petróleo, 1967.

_____. *Perú Minero 1974*. Lima: Sociedad Nacional de Minería y Petróleo, 1974.

_____. *Peruvian Metal Mining*. Lima: Sociedad Nacional de Minería y Petróleo, 1977.

Rostow, W. W. *The Stages of Growth: A Non-Communist Manifesto*. Cambridge: Cambridge University Press, 1971.

Samamé Boggio, Mario. *Minería Peruana*. Lima: Privately printed, 1974.

_____. *Minería Peruana - Bibliografía*. Lima: Privately printed, 1974.

Sánchez Albavera, Fernando. "Las Corporaciones del Cobre: Un Ensayo Exploratorio." *Apuntes*, 2 (1975).

_____. *Minería, Capital Transnacional y Poder en el Perú*. Lima: Centro de Estudios y Promocion del Desarrollo (DESCO), 1981.

Santos, Abelardo. "La Estatización de la Cerro de Pasco." *Debate Socialista*, 1 (February-March 1974).

Shaikh, Anwar. "Political Economy and Capitalism: Notes on Dobb's Theory of Crisis." *Cambridge Journal of Economics*, 2 (1978).

_____. "Foreign Trade and the Law of Value: Part I." *Science and Society*, 43 (Fall, 1979).

_____. "On the Laws of International Exchange." *Science and Society*, 43:1 (Fall and Winter 1979).

Spalding, Karen. *De Indio a Campesino: Cambios en la Estructura Social del Perú Colonial*. Lima: Instituto de Estudios Peruanos, 1974.

_____. "Hacienda-Village Relations in Andean Society to 1830." *Latin American Perspectives*, 2 (Spring 1975).

_____. *Huarochirí: An Andean Society Under Inca and Spanish Rule*. Stanford: Stanford University Press, 1984.

Stern, Steve J. *Peru's Indian Peoples and the Challenge of Spanish Conquest*. Madison: University of Wisconsin Press, 1982.

Sulmont, Denis. *El Movimiento Obrero en el Perú 1900-1956*. Lima: Editorial Pontificia Universidad Católica del Perú, 1975.

Sulmont, Denis. *Historia del Movimiento Obrero Peruano (1890-1977)*. Lima: Tarea, Centro de Publicaciones Educativas, 1977.

Sulmont, Denis. *Historia del Movimiento Obrero Minero Metalúrgico.* Lima: Federación Nacional de Trabajadores Mineros y Metalúrgicos del Perú, 1980.

Sweezy, Paul. "The Debate on the Transition to Capitalism." In *The Transition from Feudalism to Capitalism,* ed. Rodney Hilton. London: New Left Books, 1976.

Takeuchi, Kenji, et al. *The World Copper Industry: Its Changing Structure and Future Prospects.* World Bank Staff Commodity Working Papers No. 15. Washington, D.C.: The World Bank 1987.

Tandeter, Enrique. "Forced and Free Labour in Late Colonial Potosí." *Past and Present,* 93 (November 1981).

Taylor, Lewis. "Main Trends in Agrarian Capitalist Development: Cajamarca, Peru, 1880-1976." Ph.D. diss., University of Liverpool, 1979.

Thorp, Rosemary, and Geoffrey Bertram. *Peru 1890-1977: Growth and Policy in an Open Economy.* London: The Macmillan Press, 1978.

U.S. Dept. of Commerce. *Economic Analysis of the Copper Industry.* Charles River Associates, Inc. Washington, D.C.: 1970.

_____. *Survey of Current Business.* Washington, D.C.: U.S. Government Printing Office.

Ugarteche, Oscar. *El Estado Deudor: Economía Política de la Deuda: Perú y Bolivia 1968-1984.* Lima: Instituto de Estudios Peruanos, 1986.

Vargas Fernández, Jorge, and Abel Astete González. *Estudio de la Productividad en la Industria Minera Peruana.* Lima: Ministerio de Energía y Minas, Dirección General de Minería, 1975. Mimeographed.

Varón, Rafael. "Minería Colonial Peruana: Un Ejemplo de Integración al Sistema Económica Mundial, Siglos XVI-XVII." *Revista de Museo Nacional de Historia.* Lima: 1978.

Villanueva, Víctor. *El CAEM y la Revolución de la Fuerza Armada.* Lima: Instituto de Estudios Peruanos, 1972.

_____. *La Sublevación Aprista de 1948: La Tragedia de un Pueblo y un Partido.* Lima: Editorial Milla Batres, 1973.

_____. *El APRA en Busca del Poder.* Lima: Editorial Horizonte, 1975.

_____. "The Petty-Bourgeois Ideology of the Peruvian Aprista Party." *Latin American Perspectives,* 4:3 (Summer 1977).

Wallerstein, Immanuel. "The Rise and Future Demise of the World Capitalist System: Concepts for Comparative Analysis." *Comparative Studies in Society and History,* 16 (January 1974).

_____. "From Feudalism to Capitalism: Transition or Transitions?" *Social Forces,* 55 (December 1976).

Warren, Bill. "Imperialism and Capitalist Industrialization." *New Left Review,* 81 (September-October 1973).

_____. *Imperialism: Pioneer of Capitalism,* ed. John Sender. London: New Left Books, 1980.

Weeks, John. *Capital and Exploitation.* Princeton: Princeton University Press, 1981.

Weeks, John. "A Note on Underconsumption and the Labor Theory of Value." *Science and Society*, 46:1 (Spring 1982).

_____. *Limits to Capitalist Development: The Industrialization of Peru, 1950-1980*. Boulder: Westview Press, 1985.

_____. "Epochs of Capitalism and the Progressiveness of Capital's Expansion." *Science and Society* 49:4 (Winter 1985-86).

_____. "An Interpretation of the Central American Crisis." *Latin American Research Review*, 21:3 (Fall 1986).

_____. "Abstract Labor and its Relation to Commodity Production." TS, 1986.

Weeks, John, and Elizabeth Dore. "International Exchange and the Causes of Backwardness." *Latin American Perspectives*, 4:2 (Spring 1979).

_____. "Reply to Samir Amin." *Latin American Perspectives*, 4:3 (Summer 1979).

The West Coast Leader. Lima: 1912-1940.

Whyte, William F. "Rural Peru: Peasants as Activists." In *Peruvian Nationalism: A Corporatist Revolution*, ed. David Chaplin. New Brunswick: Transaction, 1976.

Yepes del Castillo, Ernesto. *Perú 1820-1920: Un Siglo de Desarrollo Capitalista*. Lima: Instituto de Estudios Peruanos, 1972.

INDEX

Series in Political Economy
in Economic Development in Latin America

Series Editor
Andrew Zimbalist
Smith College

Through country case studies and regional analyses this series will contribute to a deeper understanding of development issues in Latin America. Shifting political environments, increasing economic interdependence, and the difficulties with regard to debt, foreign investment, and trade policy demand novel conceptualizations of development strategies and potentials for the region. Individual volumes in this series will explore the deficiencies in conventional formulations of the Latin American development experience by examining new evidence and material. Topics will include, among others, women and development in Latin America; the impact of IMF interventions; the effects of redemocratization on development; Cubanology and Cuban political economy; Nicaraguan political economy; and individual case studies on development and debt policy in various countries in the region.

Series in Political Economy
and Economic Development in Latin America

Series Editor
Andrew Zimbalist
Smith College